D. H. LAWRENCE:
BODY OF DARKNESS

English Literature

Editor
JOHN LAWLOR
Professor of English Language and Literature
in the University of Keele

D. H. LAWRENCE:
BODY OF DARKNESS

R. E. Pritchard
Lecturer in English Language and Literature
University of Keele

HUTCHINSON UNIVERSITY LIBRARY
LONDON

HUTCHINSON & CO (*Publishers*) LTD
3 Fitzroy Square, London W1

London Melbourne Sydney Auckland
Wellington Johannesburg Cape Town
and agencies throughout the world

First published 1971

*This book has been set in Fournier type, printed in Great Britain
on opaque wove paper by Anchor Press, and
bound by Wm. Brendon, both of Tiptree, Essex*
ISBN 0 09 108130 0 (cased)
0 09 108131 9 (paper)

TO MY WIFE

CONTENTS

PREFACE

There is a considerable quantity of scholarly and critical material concerning Lawrence's work, and it did not seem appropriate to burden a work intended primarily for students with complete annotation and reference. It is hoped that the bibliography makes some small amends. It has not been possible to acknowledge every debt to others—often the source of an observation was lost to memory. I must, however, acknowledge my indebtedness to the work of Colin Clarke, H. M. Daleski, George Ford and Keith Sagar. I read David Cavitch's book too late to benefit from it, but was delighted and reassured by the extent of our agreement. I would particularly like to thank John Lawlor for his help in preparing this book for print.

R.E.P.

ACKNOWLEDGMENTS

Acknowledgments are due to the following for the use of copyright material: Laurence Pollinger Ltd and the Estate of the late Mrs Frieda Lawrence, from the works of D. H. Lawrence; Dover Publications Ltd, from *Language and Myth* by Ernst Cassirer; the Estate of Christopher Caudwell, from *Studies in a Dying Culture* by Christopher Caudwell; Faber and Faber Ltd, from 'East Coker' by T. S. Eliot; Jonathan Cape Ltd, from *Love and Death in the American Novel* by Leslie Fiedler; Sigmund Freud Copyrights Ltd, The Institute of Psycho-Analysis and the Hogarth Press Ltd, from the Standard Edition of the Complete Psychological Works of Sigmund Freud, revised and edited by James Strachey; Northwestern University Press, from *Sense and Non-Sense* by M. Merleau-Ponty; Oxford University Press, from *The Nature of Narrative* by R. Scholes and R. Kellogg; M. B. Yeats and Macmillan and Co. Ltd, from 'Crazy Jane Talks with the Bishop' by W. B. Yeats; and Cambridge University Press for permission to base the chronology in this book on that by Keith Sagar in his *Art of D. H. Lawrence*.

Every effort has been made to trace copyright holders and the publishers apologise for any omission.

ABBREVIATIONS

Most of Lawrence's work being available in various editions and texts, page references are given solely for works such as *Phoenix* and *Apocalypse*, that exist only in one form:

CL   *The Collected Letters of D. H. Lawrence*, Ed. H. T. Moore, Heine-mann, 1962.

CP   *The Complete Poems of D. H. Lawrence*, Ed. V. de Sola Pinto and Warren Roberts, Heinemann, 1964.

LH   *The Letters of D. H. Lawrence*, Ed. Aldous Huxley, Heinemann, 1932.

P   *Phoenix, The Posthumous Papers of D. H. Lawrence,* Ed. E. D. McDonald, Heinemann, 1936.

P2   *Phoenix II, Uncollected, Unpublished and Other Prose Works by D. H. Lawrence,* Ed. Warren Roberts and Harry T. Moore, Heinemann, 1968.

SCAM   *Studies in Classic American Literature*, Seltzer, 1932.

SM   *The Symbolic Meaning*, Ed. Armin Arnold, Centaur Press, 1962.

A man who is well balanced between the male and female, in his own nature, is, as a rule, happy, easy to mate, easy to satisfy, and content to exist. It is only a disproportion, or a dissatisfaction, which makes the man struggle into articulation.

'Study of Thomas Hardy', P 460

I always say, my motto is 'Art for my sake'. The difficulty is to find exactly the form one's passion wants to take.

Letter to Ernest Collings, CL 171

. . . the act of death may itself be a consummation, and life may be a state of negation.

It may be that our state of life is itself a denial of the consummation, a prevention, a negation, that this life is our nullification, our not-being . . .

'The Crown', P2, 383

I

THE BURIED SELF

I

INTRODUCTION

To begin with fact: D. H. Lawrence was born in 1885; his father was a coal-miner and his mother had been a schoolteacher. The consequences for him of his parents' mis-mating are well known: an Oedipal love for his mother that frustrated his development into sexual and artistic maturity, at least until her death and his marriage, which was followed by a reaction in favour of the father-principle of unselfconscious physicality and integrated being.

Lawrence seems to belong so much to our own times, and to speak to us of the crisis in our culture, that it is a shock to realise that he grew up in the late Victorian and Edwardian era. This was the heyday of the belief in individualism, in the right of the individual will to assert itself by exploiting and suppressing what in fact supported and fed it—whether in the sphere of politics, economics, personal relations, or within the individual himself. 'Liberal' individualist rationalism implied the possibility of subjecting and controlling not only the material world and other men but also the world within, of the body and the instincts: the 'heart of darkness', to use Joseph Conrad's phrase.

Conrad's fable of 1899 indicates the reaction against the empire of reason, the reaction in which Lawrence, as child of his times, took part. Belonging to the time of the Romantic Decadence, as a young man he responded to the diabolism and sexual disturbance of Baudelaire and of Beardsley, the voluptuous synaesthesia and erotic mysticism of Wagner; strove, better than Pater, to catch the transient and to burn with 'a hard gem-like flame';[1] dabbled in the occult and sketched

[1] Superior figures refer to end-of-chapter notes.

out his own religion, though less thoroughly than Yeats; explored the primitive roots of man's culture in the mythological and anthropological works of Frazer, Harrison and Tylor; and read Nietzsche and Schopenhauer, and prophesied cultural collapse, apocalypse, and a new life. It is this context to which he belongs, as much as to any tradition of Victorian moral earnestness. All helped to feed his profound yearning for a renewed mode of being in which man was an organic unity, with his intellect and ego in harmony with his desires and feelings, and with the individual in proportional harmony with his community and the natural world.

An interesting link between the socio-political ethos of the time and Lawrence's own psychology (as characteristic of his time) was made by Christopher Caudwell,[2] who, as a Marxist, interprets the cause of modern cultural malaise as 'the cash nexus' and bourgeois economic exploitation: this may reasonably be linked with the rationalist-individualist ethos suggested above. Quotation will best indicate Caudwell's argument:

These defects in bourgeois social relations all arise from the cash nexus which replaces all other social ties, so that society seems held together, not by natural love and tenderness or obligation, but simply by profit. . . . The notion of private property, aggravated by its importance and overwhelming power in bourgeois relations, extends to love itself. . . . Bourgeois defects are implicit in bourgeois civilisation and therefore in bourgeois consciousness. Hence man wants to turn against the intellect, for it seems that the intellect is his enemy . . .

This is because in such a society the instincts and feelings are also exploited or suppressed, so that it seems as if they are

being penalised by the environment, and that, therefore, the instincts and feelings must be "given their due", must be exalted even if it means breaking up and abandoning the civilised environment for a more primitive one. Today this exaltation of the instincts is seen in all demands for a return to deeper "feeling", as with Lawrence. . . . In individuals this mechanism is infantile regression.

Caudwell points out how Lawrence hated the world of competitive individualism,

the selfishness which is the pattern of bourgeois culture and is revealed in pacifism, Protestantism, and all varieties of salvation obtained by individual action. . . . Lawrence wanted us to return to the past, to the "Mother". He sees human discontent as the yearning of the solar plexus for the umbilical connexion, and he demands the substitution for sharp sexual love of the unconscious fleshy identification of foetus with mother.

He acutely perceives the relation between the class organisation and the psychological patterns and complexes of a culture; yet he is also attempting within his neo-Freudian interpretation of Lawrence to invalidate a critique of society in competition with his own, that has different objectives. Certainly Lawrence's aims had more genuine humanity and reverence for community, and more sincerity, than those of the guilty, public-school Marxists of the 'thirties, like Auden, Spender—and Caudwell.

Caudwell's essay, though hostile and somewhat doctrinaire, contains many shrewd insights into both society and Lawrence—who, of course, was aware of the unhealthiness of deliberate primitivism in society and the individual, but felt that the loss of a sense of organic community between man and man, and man and nature, was real and disastrous, and caused by something more than capitalism.

In his reaction against the materialist-rationalist ethos (of which, of course, Caudwell is in his way an exponent) Lawrence would seem to have much in common with other artists of the turn of the century, particularly the Symbolists and Expressionists. A similar subtle analysis of extreme and perverse feeling can be seen in the work of Edvard Munch; in Gauguin is an equivalent interest in symbolism, formalism, and the primitive religious community. Van Gogh in particular seems very like, in the early sympathetic portrayals of the industrial proletariat, the passionate identification with Christ, and the visionary intensity of the gaze directed upon the symbols of fierce (phallic) energy, the flame-like cypresses and blinding sun. Yet the painter with whom Lawrence felt greatest sympathy was Cézanne, whose work he discussed in 'Introduction to these Paintings' (P 551–84), an essay written in 1929, the year before his death, and which will serve excellently as an introduction to his beliefs and practice.

Introducing his own paintings, Lawrence wonders why the English have produced so few painters. The plastic arts are characteristically concerned with the physical appearance of the body of life, and what inhibits the English as painters, particularly of the human body, he asserts, is their fear of life, of organic creation, of the body. This fear of the body, and consequently of physical imagery, he traces to the traumatic shock upon the English consciousness, at the time of the Renaissance, of the realisation of the nature and consequences of syphilis. Renaissance art displays

almost a horror of sexual life. The Elizabethans, grand as we think them, started it. The real "mortal coil" in Hamlet is all sexual, the young man's horror of his mother's incest, sex carrying with it a wild and nameless terror which, it seems to me, it had never carried before. . . . Hamlet is overpowered by horrible revulsion from his physical connexion with his mother, which makes him recoil in similar revulsion from Ophelia, and almost from his father, even as a ghost. He is horrified at the merest suggestion of physical connexion, as if it were an unspeakable taint.

Clearly this syphilis-trauma theory is a rationalisation of Lawrence's own fear of his Oedipally incestuous desires, the fear and suppression of his physical being consequent upon his desires having been directed towards his 'intellectual-spiritual' mother. He himself is aware of the insufficiency of his theory:

This, no doubt, is all in the course of the growth of the "spiritual-mental" consciousness, at the expense of the instinctive-intuitive consciousness. Man came to have his own body in horror, especially in its sexual implications: and so he began to suppress with all his might his instinctive-intuitive consciousness, which is so radical, so physical, so sexual.

In Lawrence's historical myth the Renaissance was analogous to adolescent self-consciousness and sexual discovery, after the simplicity of childhood.

He then provides a brief and lively account of the decline of English poetry (analogous to T. S. Eliot's view of the consequences of the 'dissociation of sensibility' of the seventeenth century[3]) indicating its perverse reaction to the organic (whether sexual or excremental). In so far as people reject the physical and deny the possibility of the fusion of the physical and the psychical, they can neither respond to —nor create—real art or real life. Modern bourgeois man, says Lawrence, denies the validity of the physical and so can only despise or exploit it.

Lawrence indicates the consequences of such an attitude for

the plastic arts, which depend entirely on the representation of substantial bodies, and on the intuitional perception of the *reality* of substantial bodies. The reality of substantial bodies can only be perceived by the imagination, and the imagination is a kindled state of consciousness in which intuitive awareness predominates. The plastic arts are all imagery, and imagery is the body of our imaginative life, and our imaginative life is a great joy and fulfilment to us, for the imagination is a more powerful and more comprehensive flow of consciousness than our ordinary flow. In the flow of true imagination we know in full, mentally and physically at once, in a greater, enkindled awareness. At the maximum of our imagination we are religious. And if we deny our imagination, and have no imaginative life, we are poor worms who have never lived.

The passage is classical, characteristic of Lawrence's repetitive, accretive style, and central to his beliefs. Art, like science, is not merely abstract, but involves the whole consciousness of man,[4] the intuitive apprehension of the complex of reality. To affirm the life and value of the physical world is, for Lawrence, to affirm the life and value of his own physical and psychic being.

The image-making faculty apprehends the essential quality of what is before it, by seeing it as the embodiment (or 'objective correlative' as Eliot would say[5]) of hitherto-unrealised feelings in the observer[6]; so, he says, 'An artist *can* only create what he really religiously *feels* is truth, religious truth really *felt*, in the blood and the bones'. The interaction between artist and object is further explained in the earlier 'Morality and the Novel' (1925; P 527–32):

When van Gogh paints sunflowers, he reveals, or achieves, the vivid relation between himself, as man, and the sunflower, as sunflower, at that quick moment of time. His painting does not represent the sunflower itself. . . . The vision on the canvas is a third thing. . . . the offspring of the sunflower itself and van Gogh himself.

And this perfected relation between man and his circumambient universe is life itself, for mankind. It has the fourth-dimensional quality of eternity and perfection. Yet it is momentaneous.

Man and the sunflower both pass away from the moment, in the process of forming a new relationship. The relation between all things changes from day to day. . . .

Hence art, which reveals or attains to another perfect relationship, will be for ever new.

At the same time, that which exists in the non-dimensional space of pure relationship is deathless, lifeless, and external. [We feel that an art-work] is beyond life, and therefore beyond death [which suggests that] there is something inside us which must also be beyond life and beyond death.

So art, presenting the actuality of man's physical existence, and of his relationship with other existence, provides a sense of identity with something 'other'—lifeless, deathless—immanent in, and transcending the stability of, the phenomenal world. It should be noted that the relation of observer with observed is directly analogous to the sexual relationship, when

each party, inevitably, must "seek its own" in the other, and be denied. When, in the two parties, each of them seeks his own, her own, absolutely, then it is a fight to the death. And this is true of the thing called "passion". On the other hand, when, of the two parties, one yields utterly to the other, this is called sacrifice, and it also means death . . .

If the woman (as mate or mother) is completely subjugated, then the man will be alone; if he is subordinate and possessed, then his independent being will have been smothered. Better, the essay suggests, to abandon 'love', the possessive, sexual impulse, and for each to remain separate, self-possessed, but responsive to the other. The relationship between artist and object should not be one of subjectivity (possessing and obliterating the object), nor of objectivity (denying oneself, in an overpowering world,) but an acceptance of detachment and independence.

In 'Introduction' Lawrence then summarises English post-Renaissance civilisation and art as a 'deliberate denial of intuitive awareness' that is struck down by 'the puritan and the intellectual'; artists were incapable of imaginatively confronting the human body, escaping to the less disturbing genre of landscape. At last, they escaped into Impressionism, dissolving solidity and the human body into colour and 'light and almost ecstasy'.

After this came the reaction, and the presentation of the independent solidity of substance by Cézanne:

The actual fact is that in Cézanne modern French art made its first tiny step back into real substance, to objective substance, if we may call it so. Van Gogh's earth was still subjective earth, himself projected into the earth. But Cézanne's apples are a real attempt to let the apple exist in its own separate identity, without transfusing it with personal emotion. Cézanne's great effort was, at it were, to shove the apple away from him, and let it live of itself. It seems a small thing to do: yet it is the first real sign that man has made for thousands of years that he is willing to admit that matter *actually* exists.

(Apparently since the Fall, the beginning of sexual guilt.)

It is essential to pause to insist that Cézanne was not the objective artist that Lawrence here presents him as (and that Lawrence himself would like to be), but simply less obviously subjective than van Gogh. M. Merleau-Ponty in his essay 'Cézanne's Doubt',[7] which reinforces many of Lawrence's points, insists on the interaction between Cézanne and the objects he painted, quoting various remarks by the artist: "Everything comes to us from nature; we exist through it . . ." (mother-nature, it would seem); "the landscape thinks itself in me, and I am its consciousness". Cézanne explained that he had "replaced reality by imagination and by the abstraction which accompanies it"— the phenomenal world was reshaped to reveal the essence that the artist desired to find there. M. Merleau-Ponty interprets the 'inhuman character' of Cézanne's portraits, and his obsession with landscape as 'a flight from the human world, the alienation of his humanity' (echoing Lawrence's remarks about landscape painting); Cézanne displaced the union with humanity with a union with nature, that he had animated. The final account of Cézanne's art is remarkably like Lawrence's account of van Gogh's painting, quoted above:

Forgetting the viscous, equivocal appearances, we go through them straight, to the things they present. The painter recaptures and converts into visible objects what would, without him, remain walled up in the separate life of each consciousness; the vibration of appearances which is the cradle of things. Only one emotion is possible for this painter—the feeling of strangeness—and only one lyricism—that of the continual rebirth of existence.

This could be a comment upon Lawrence's writing—and confirms the sense of identification that Lawrence felt for Cézanne. Cézanne's attempt at objectivity was also Lawrence's, who feared that he was too much like Van Gogh, that is, subjective, a solipsist, a solitary being in an unreal world that reflected and manifested only himself. In 1914, he wrote to Gordon Campbell,

I think there is the dual way of looking at things: our way, which is to say "*I* am all. All other things are but radiation out from me".—The other way is to try to conceive the whole, to build up a whole by means of symbolism, because symbolism avoids the I and puts aside the egotist; and, in the whole, to take our decent place. That was how man built the cathedrals. He didn't say "out of my breast springs this cathedral!" But "in this vast whole I am a small part, I move and live and have my being." (CL 302)

The great enclosure of the cathedrals echoes the circumambient universe, the cosmic womb that would shelter him from isolation, that by its animate palpableness confirmed his physical being and centrality.

Further illustration may be found in the poem 'New Heaven and Earth' (CP 256–61), where he expresses the horror of solipsism, 'everything was tainted with myself'. There, release from purely mental consciousness and awareness of the body of life came through contact with hitherto-unapprehended matter:

> I put my hand out further, a little further
> and I felt that which was not I . . .

so that

> new-risen, resurrected, starved from the tomb,
> starved from a life of devouring always myself,
> now here was I, new awakened, with my hand stretching out
> and touching the unknown, the real unknown, the unknown unknown.

This realisation of physical being came through touching his wife's body: not her genitals but the dark body behind, at the back of her body—in fact, her anus (this, however, must be discussed later).

In 'Introduction' he uses simpler imagery of the resurrection to indicate Cézanne's attempt to escape from 'mental consciousness, the enclosed ego in its sky-blue heaven self-painted'. Cézanne, he says, 'wanted to *express* what he suddenly, convulsedly *knew*! the existence of matter. . . . He wanted to be himself in his own procreative body'; his intuitive re-presentation of a solid apple 'rolled the stone from the mouth of the tomb'.

Cézanne's painting, then, presents for Lawrence his own discovery of his 'procreative body' and realisation of the surrounding body of creation, achieved by breaking-through the stereotyped responses imposed on feeling by inhibitory mental consciousness. Lawrence correctly interprets Cézanne's 'bad drawing' as the struggle against cliché responses—which parallels his own struggles with conventional poetic techniques. Such a pretended union with a fantasy body of life is masturbation, bad art, says Lawrence, while true art is the genuine creative response to the real body of life. This reality is apprehended by means of abstraction, that suggests the essential nature of objects by ignoring their superficial appearance.

Cézanne's technique was the reduction of objects to their basic forms, and the use of multiple perspective (to imply a shifting viewpoint); so, in his portraits, he treated people as he had treated apples.

When he said to his models: "Be an apple! Be an apple!" he was uttering the foreword . . . to the collapse of our whole way of consciousness, and the substitution of another way. If the human being is going to be primarily an apple, as for Cézanne it was, then you are going to have a new world of men: a world which has very little to say, men that can sit still and just be physically there, and be truly non-moral. . . .

The only part of [his wife as a model] that was not living cliché was her appleyness. Her body, even her very sex, was known nauseously. . . . He knew it all, he hated it all, he refused it all. . . .

It is the appleyness of the portrait of Cézanne's wife that makes it so permanently interesting: the appleyness, which carries with it also the feeling of knowing the other side as well, the side you don't see, the hidden side of the moon. . . . The eye sees only fronts, and the mind, on the whole, is satisfied with fronts. . . . The true imagination is for ever curving round to the other side, to the back of presented appearance.

The artist ignores the woman's appearance, her human personality, and her sex, which are all at the 'front', to apprehend her essential 'non-moral' self at the inside, at 'the back of presented appearance'. This links with the poem quoted above, and that with a slightly earlier letter to Edward Garnett (CL 281–3). There, discussing the Italian Futurists' techniques of abstraction, Lawrence explains how

that which is physic—non-human—in humanity, is more interesting to me than the old-fashioned human element—which causes one to conceive a character in a certain moral scheme. . . . I don't so much care about what the woman *feels*—in the ordinary usage of the word. That presumes an ego to feel with. I only care about what the woman *is*—what she IS—inhumanly, physiologically, materially. . . .

For him, varying moods and personalities are only manifestations of an essential reality, whether in one or more individuals. Different characters are not important to Lawrence as independent individuals, but only as manifestations of the common principle with which he has imbued them, as aspects of his own feelings,

like as diamond and coal are the same pure single element of carbon. The ordinary novel would trace the history of the diamond—but I say, "Diamond, what! this is carbon." And my diamond might be coal or soot, and my theme is carbon.

His illustration is not arbitrary, but very revealing: by burrowing into the underworld, the bowels of the earth, is discovered the black primary material and living body of darkness associated with his father.

So human consciousness is replaced by a primary, organic, non-moral body, a dehumanisation paralleled by the animation of the landscape and non-human world (by the same techniques):

In the best landscapes [of Cézanne] we are fascinated by the mysterious *shiftiness* of the scene under our eyes; it shifts about as we watch it. And we realise, with a sort of transport, how intuitively *true* this is of landscape. It is *not* still. It has its own weird *anima* . . .

The primacy of Cézanne–Lawrence's individual intuitive being is assured when the pressure of other observing consciousnesses is elimi-nated, by dehumanising them into embodiments of the artist's feelings; behind the individual, the conscious and the sexual are what Lawrence elsewhere calls 'the darkest sources' and the 'mystic body of reality', that core of feeling unaffected by problems of personality and sexuality; and all around is the shelter of animate nature.

He concludes by suggesting that when—as now, in contemporary society, and as in his inhibited youth—the intellect and spirit are seen as the essence of being, and the body as the mere container or instru-ment,

when the enclosure in the ego is final, when [men] are hermetically sealed and insulated from all experience, from any *touch*, from anything *solid*

then the sense of being 'man alive' (P 535), the sense of harmony within the individual or with the environment, is lost; but when things cannot get any worse, they can only get better.

The argument may be developed through some of Lawrence's favourite images. The enclosure of the ego is the negative of the enclosing cosmic womb, an enclosure that must be broken out of. If the seed or nut fallen from the (parental) tree does not break open, there can be no life or growth into any fuller, larger organism, but simply an accretion of hard, self-contained shells—like so many beetles, to use another recurrent image of the subhuman, unnatural existence (such as individualist democracy, or homosexuality!). The violence of breaking from enclosure is destructive, but essentially creative, as revolutionary activity must be: 'pure passionate destructive activity and pure passionate constructive activity are the same, religiously.' (*Fantasia*, p. 124)

The organic flood from the darkest sources must be released, to fertilise new life. A dammed life-flow is like constipation(!):

I feel as if I had a child of black fury curled up inside my bowels. I'm sure I can feel exactly what it is like to be pregnant, because of the weary bowel burden of a kind of contained murder which I can't bring forth. (LH 483)

We want to realise the tremendous *non-human* quality of life—it is wonderful. It is not the emotions, nor the personal feelings and attachments, that matter. . . . Behind in all are the tremendous unknown forces of life, coming unseen and unperceived as out of the desert to the Egyptians,[8] and driving us, forcing us, destroying us if we do not submit to be swept away. (CL 291)

Some of the implications for Lawrence of such a phrase as 'living body of darkness' (*Women in Love* XXIII), possibly already apparent, may be clarified by considering his psychological make-up through interpretation of recurrent images. While, as a good Symbolist, Lawrence distinguished between indefinitely suggestive Symbol, and the 'use of images to express certain definite qualities' as mechanical Allegory (P 295–6) it is clear that in extended narrative (or sequence of narratives) the multiplicity of contexts for recurring images serves to define their meanings, often quite precisely.[9] The following summary treatment may well seem crude and reductive, but confirmation of these interpretations should be found in the more elaborate discussion in the rest of the book, to which this early exposition is designed as a useful guide.

As a child, Lawrence's love (both the 'tender' and the sexual) was directed towards his mother, as is normal; however she reciprocated these loves abnormally. Partly because her values were intellectual-spiritual, but chiefly, of course, because of his filial status, his physical being had to be suppressed. Normally such desires would be displaced on to other women, but in so far as these women were only surrogate mothers, he still felt guilt in his sexual relations, which inhibited him from achieving full satisfaction. It seemed to Lawrence that women possessed him, exploiting him for their own satisfaction (emotional or sexual); this produced the image of the winged, beaked harpy gnawing on his body. The passions he had fearfully suppressed were imaged as dark flood-waters; the tension of his unnatural restraint produced an intense, exaggerated sexuality, appearing like lightning, flashes of (yellow) light, and an iridescent or phosphorescent glow on the surface of deep water. Conversely, inhibition and sublimation of libidinal energy into abstract, inhuman activity aroused associations of whiteness and cold. The contemplation of such inhibition (as in frozen mountains) frequently evoked a reaction into hot, dark, corrupt sensuality (in the valley of the flesh) that savagely sacrificed the spirit for the flesh. The final reaction would then be an exhausted or frightened desire for unimpassioned solitariness (like a star) or uninvolved relationship ('polarity of stars').

Lawrence had initially feared his father's passionate nature, confusing violence with sexuality (that seemed to threaten both his mother and himself). His inability to achieve the necessary relationship and identification with his father led—as is common in such cases—to a homosexual desire to submit to and be possessed by father-figures of male potency. Partly because of his confusion of violence with sexuality, partly because of his fear of expressing his sexual being with his mother, he saw masculine, phallic energy as loveless, cruel and savage —this last term to be taken literally. To obtain such power was, he felt, to revert to a pre-civilised condition (associating civilisation with his mother, sublimation, and tender self-sacrificing love), a condition he feared as degenerate; furthermore society not only appeared to condemn physical passion, but certainly condemned homosexuality. So, in Lawrence, savagery usually implied a fierce, dehumanising passion or mindless sensuality, often with guilty homosexual overtones; something he desired as a release for his sexual energies, but feared as a separation from the social body and the love of woman.

Phallic power in its subhuman aspect may appear in reptilian form, such as the lizard, salamander or fish; more sympathetic manifestations of the phallic include the horse, the swan, the lily and the lotus (images with a wide range of connotation, including the religious). The lily is pre-eminently the pure phallic flower: finer than intellectual Solomon's external materialist glory, it has no care, that is no guilt or anxiety, but is insouciant. There are also *fleurs du mal*, the male flower in its perverse-seeming aspect, when it roots itself in the mud of the human body and psyche. Sublimated homosexual passion evokes cruel eagles, frozen mountains, and mechanical activity.

The 'feminine' principle of self-possession and egoistic self-assertion is imaged in the white light of the moon, that may be sterile, but may also, by wilfulness or excited selfish passion, prevent submergence in the dark flesh; the sun emanates the heat of passion and life-energy, the source of life that might burn one up. These opposing elements could not be reconciled, so that it seemed that the condition of life was eternal painful conflict, while 'true' life was harmonious and restful in the womb or tomb. The sexual conflict within himself was an agony, a crucifixion of the spirit by the flesh—and *vice versa*—and he saw himself as Christ, Dionysus and Osiris, all fertility gods torn apart, wept over by women, and in the last case, restored by an adoring woman.

Woman as the 'Magna Mater' (to use the term he borrowed from Jung) seemed to dominate and dispossess his masculinity; the resentful reaction produced a furtive subversive quality, jeering grotesqueness and perverse sexual self-assertion, associated with images of rat, seal, weasel and the bat that is 'reversed', with a gargoyle human-devil face. As women seemed to devour him emotionally and sexually, one reaction was to sacrifice them and their values to brutal male power. Yet when his feminine self, or anima, identified him with the woman, he again saw subjection to phallicism as a terrifying sacrifice of his own civilised self. Another impulse was to gain power by frustratingly withdrawing from sexual engagement. In so far as the erect phallus embodied a potency that was exhausted by sexual activity, non-involvement ensured the retention of potency: so man was most himself, most powerful, when not in any way subjected to woman's demands. The sexuality produced by the egoistic forcing and exploiting of the body and instincts evoked associations of dry friction (linked also with the accumulation of separate egos like beetles or shells); against this, positive sexuality was a unitive-destructive flux. Sometimes, passivity was best of all: not to prove oneself, or *do*, but simply *be*.

His mother-possessed, mother-inhibited youth made him fear the competition of other apparently self-confident men, and he yearned for maternal security in the womb, where he had not been tortured by self-consciousness and sexual conflict; such he found within an animate cosmos, while to be bathed by a woman was not only to be like his father, but repeated an infantile and foetal comfort. As his mother had seemed to deny his physical being, he desired to be possessed and sheltered by paternal and male strength, and even, as in the important little essay 'David' (P 60–4), to return to a paternal womb.

In reaction against the demands and frustrations of sexuality, he returned to another aspect—and the most denied and guilt-ridden—of the physical being: the anal and excremental. In infant psychology, excretion is pleasurable and a form of creation; furthermore, it does not require—as does sexual intercourse—another person for its satisfaction. Awareness of the anal-excremental emphasises the physical reality of the body, as suppressed by consciousness, and the independence of the individual. Lawrence frequently asserts that the true self is located in the regions of the lower back, at the base of the spine.

These 'shameful' dark regions like the other 'lower' organs, the genitals, are the Underworld of the consciousness and the body,

Hades, the world of the preconscious, amoral fertilisers of life, the origin of 'daemons', which are not mere devils (though conventionally regarded as such) but spirits of great power animating and controlling life. The underworld is also associated with the epitome of male potency, his coal-miner father, who is 'in' Dis, the god of the dead who stole Persephone. The flow of dark water may (as in Ursula's embrace of Birkin, *Women in Love* XXIII) imply the excremental flow: its full meaning is more complex, suggesting the powerful natural forces in man's nature precedent to his conscious, morally approved, self that would deny them. It is only, Lawrence insists, through the recognition and complete acceptance of one's physical organic condition in its totality (that includes the physical, corrupt and 'shameful' as well as the mental, spiritual and conventionally moral) that freedom and energy in the body and spirit can be achieved. Out of the mud rise the lotus and the swan.

Possession of the anal principle may be not only imaginative but physical, by means of touch, or through intercourse. The 'negative' form of this, in homosexual intercourse, is regarded by Lawrence with fascinated, fearful horror—imaged as the copulation of black-beetles or, in *The Plumed Serpent*, the disembowelling of a horse by a bull (the destruction of the primary self by the embodiment of phallic power). Anal possession of a woman provides the man's sexual satisfaction while denying the woman's, but is also regarded as liberation from shame of the body and basic childish pleasures. So, anal intercourse may be imaged as the harrowing of hell (as in *Lady Chatterley's Lover*), preceding the resurrection of the fully living body, or as the entry into the forbidden Paradise (two regressive impulses here coalescing), which will re-establish Eden on earth.

Another favourite image is of the dolphin (sometimes the flying-fish) leaping in the dark blue water (the importance of the blue—as in water or flowers—may be traced back to his mother's blue eyes); this is the self-sufficient 'phallic' being, free from emotional demands, delighting in its own energy for its own sake, and uniting itself only with its mother element, the womb-water of the sea. Lawrence's most famous symbol is, of course, the Phoenix, the unique motherless bird that knows no mate, but recurrently re-enters its nest, dies, and is reborn out of flame. The Phoenix anciently symbolises the death and rebirth of the libido; it is, of course, traditionally a type of Christ ('Woman, what have I to do with thee?'—as Lawrence was fond of quoting), and its life-cycles are equated with the cycles of human existence: the next reincarnation will be the last, heralding apocalypse and new heaven and earth.[10]

The implication for Lawrence of the 'living body of darkness', the

buried self or 'dark sun' could include, then: the unconscious primary
being beneath and suppressed by self-conscious existence; the 'non-
human' life in the dark security of the womb, that is akin to death,
of which ordinary living is the negation; the primary, preconscious
forces in nature, of which the sexual forces were the most obvious, but
even more suppressed and 'therefore' more fundamental and real was
the anal-excretory complex—the 'primal loam' and excremental flow
that, though unliving, fertilise new life and assert the essential validity
of the organic body; the reality of the material and physical; the
(anal) core of the individual self-sufficient being; and subsuming all
these, 'the ground of all being', that which, while not itself individual
or living, is yet the primary reality, the source and essence of the living
phenomenal world that serves to manifest it. It may be interpreted as
the unconscious, or as the immanent God in man.

Such a 'Freudian' analysis is open to the charge of being reductive,
dissipating and 'explaining away' the complex fullness of life and art.
No critical work can hope to render the totality of work of such quality,
but what seems central, the essential motivations and their effects, can
be indicated. It seems clear that Lawrence was indeed grappling with
such almost unconscious impulses, impulses that, in varying degrees,
are present and—perhaps unfortunately—unrecognised in many
people. Another charge may be of writing disguised biography, or of
transgressing the shibboleth of the 'intentional fallacy'. Surely 'inten-
tions' at such a level are not separable from meaning and form. Certainly Lawrence himself rejected any distinction between 'the life'
and 'the work': all were events in the great 'thought-adventure', the
'savage pilgrimage'.

II

INEXORABLE LOVE

The chief interest of Lawrence's first novel, *The White Peacock* (1911),
lies not in its inherent quality—for it is overwritten and uncertain
in its grasp on structure and theme—but in the use of situations,
images and themes more fully developed later. The narrator Cyril
serves chiefly to report scenes (a technique abandoned in mid-career,
as too limiting); in so far as he exists at all, he is characterised by effete
melancholy and ineffectuality—a mother's boy incapable of independent existence. He fails in his love for Emily (based on Lawrence's
first love, Jessie Chambers), his true love being for the sturdy George
(who combines Jessie's brother Alan and Lawrence's father) whom
he sees as the protection he needs from the cold world.

The main interest is in the triangle of George, Lettie and Leslie.

For all George's masculinity (of which the narrator is remarkably aware), a lack of essential self-confidence saps his sexual drive, so that Lettie, the most vividly created character, makes the 'wrong' choice, marrying the higher-class industrialist Leslie, despite some unexplained sexual distaste for him, and her strong sexual attraction to George. Lawrence indicates how the Leslie–Lettie bourgeois world is based upon exploitation of the working class: while two boys work down the mine at Christmas-time, Lettie has her party, distorting her humanity behind egoistic posturing and the social mask. George throws himself into marriage with buxom Meg of the Ram Inn (significantly named!), whose chief fulfilment proves to be in motherhood; excluded from her maternal love, and lacking Lettie's stimulation, George 'turns into' Lawrence's father, degenerating through drink, 'a man condemned'. Lettie becomes Lawrence's mother, aloof from her husband, filling her time with social-intellectual activity, and living for her children.

Perhaps most intriguing, as an embodiment of the suppressed natural violence in the world of the novel, is the gamekeeper Annable, who has qualities in common with George and with Cyril's father (all sensual males diminished by feminine superiority), and is a precursor of Mellors in *Lady Chatterley's Lover*. His first wife (the defiling white peacock of the title) having despised—while perversely enjoying—his physical being, he rejects 'feminine' civilisation, recommending Cyril to "Be a good animal, true to your animal instinct" (2, II). He himself is more than that, appearing 'like some malicious Pan' (2, I), associated with ancient savage religious mystery. It is clear at this stage Lawrence saw no hope of fulfilment of the sexual-religious self in civilised society and its values, but only in such a cruel embodiment of male power, the demonic 'malicious Pan'.

So masculinity is at present unattainable: Leslie gets his woman by pitiably falling ill; the bull—or minotaur—George goes meekly to his end; Cyril remains meekly and sadly with his mother. Woman, whether as frigid, inaccessible love-object or as smothering mother, reigns supreme.

In December 1910 Lawrence's mother died:

In that year, for me everything collapsed, save the mystery of death, and the haunting of death in life. I was twenty-five, and from the death of my mother the world began to dissolve around me, beautiful, iridescent, but passing away substanceless. Till I almost dissolved away myself, and was very ill: when I was twenty-six. (P 253)

The sense of the failure of life, and the greater reality behind life, are the keynotes of the novel from this period, *The Trespasser* (1912).

On occasion almost as flowery as its predecessor, it is superior in its organisation and intensity of focus, though the theme is still the impossibility of sexual fulfilment.

In weary middle age, the protagonist Siegmund (the novel almost sinks under the pretentious Wagnerian allusions) attempts to break from his frustrating existence with his unsympathetic wife through an affair with Helena that culminates in a brief holiday on the Isle of Wight and ends with his suicide. Helena—based on Helen Corke, whose story it is—seems a more intellectual and perverse Miriam, one of 'that class of "dreaming women" with whom passion exhausts itself at the mouth' (IV), arousing unreciprocated sexual desire. Contemplating his 'rediscovered' body after swimming (and the bloody scratch on his thigh made by some rocks—a sexual wound, as of some latter-day Adonis) Siegmund thinks,

"She ought to be rejoiced at me, but she is not; she rejects me as if I were a baboon under my clothing." (VI)

More satisfying than this tortured relationship is union with the earth. He swims into a small 'virgin' bay and lies on the warm sand:

"Surely," he said to himself, "it is like Helena;" and laid his hands again on the warm body of the shore ... then shrinking from the deep weight of cold his hand encountered as he burrowed under the surface wrist-deep. In the end he found the cold mystery of the deep sand also thrilling ... the sun and the white flower of the bay were breathing and kissing him dry, were holding him in their warm conclave ... lovingly; yet, under all, was this deep mass of cold, that the softness and warmth merely floated upon. (VIII)

After this quasi-sexual union with the body of darkness he feels puri-fied and reborn. Chiefly important here is Lawrence's sense of the great dark nonhuman reality beneath the surface of life, such as Helena had earlier sensed in the man's body:

deep in the world a great God thudding out waves of life, like a great heart, unconscious. (VI)

Because of Siegmund's inability to believe in his 'life', to escape from his wife, or conquer Helena's inhibition, he feels doomed and unreal. He meets his 'double', who analyses his condition:

... the great mass of life that washes unidentified, and that we call death, creeps through the blue envelope of the day, and through our white tissue, and we can't stop it, once we've begun to leak. (XIII)

Siegmund–Lawrence's desire for intense feeling[11] will destroy him:

A craving for intense life is nearly as deadly as any other craving. You become a *concentré*; you feed your normal flame with oxygen, and it devours your tissue . . . you . . . are one whose flame nearly goes out, when the stimulant is lacking. . . . You're like a tree that'll flower till it kills itself . . . (XIII)

This acute and prophetic self-analysis provides a clue to the phosphorescence and flaring lights of *Sons and Lovers* and *Women in Love*, that evoke an unnatural self-consuming intensity. The 'double' interprets the cause of this condition as the perverse suppression of the 'animal' and excitation of the 'spiritual', by such women as Helena.

The lovers' affair is dominated by three images: the sea, akin to the underground cold, the great 'brute force' that is the unliving source and destroyer of life; the moon that embodies the primacy of the individual self; and the ambivalent sun, life-giver and life-consumer, that burns up Siegmund with its passion and even marks Helena. The deadly effect of sexual passion is indicated by an incident, anticipating Aaron's dream in *Aaron's Rod* XXI, when on Siegmund's last swim in the sea-cave inhabited by imaginary mermaids of fearful attractiveness, his elbow, symbolising his phallic body, is again wounded by rocks.

He has found no sexual liberation, cannot reconcile himself to a life of frustration (the portrayal of his family's hostility shows Lawrence's increasing sympathy for his father), and commits suicide. Helena has no further interest in passion, and with her next lover, the feebly tender Cyril, relapses into a desire for mere 'rest and warmth'.

However, in March 1912, the month after the novel was completed, Lawrence met Frieda Weekley (*née* von Richthofen), five years older than him, an aristocrat, his professor's wife, and mother of three children. She was everything his mother was not—youthful and beautiful, proudly unconventional and sensual—and yet also a mother-figure who was accessible, who would leave her husband for him; to her Lawrence transferred his emotional security, and entrusted his sensual self, and in May 1912 'these lovers fled away' into a new life.

Sons and Lovers was the first work completed in the new life with Frieda, the work that marked the conclusion of his apprenticeship and the diminution of his mother's debilitating influence: after this he moved with a new energy. Before considering that work, some attention should be given to another aspect of his first phase, the early poems. Though hampered by the influence of other poetry, both good and bad, and by some technical clumsiness, many lyrics show Lawrence moving towards his characteristic concerns and freer verse forms, achieving considerable sensitivity and penetration in the presentation and analysis of feeling.

The famous early poem 'Piano' (CP 148) is one of the best, employing a regular rhyme scheme though—as often in Lawrence—not all
the rhymes are pleasing, while the lines waver between five and six
stresses. The poem is not so much nostalgic as about nostalgia. The
poet recognises his inability to respond properly to the woman now
singing to him—for all the 'appassionato' quality of the music, her
singing seems mere 'clamour'—and can contemplate, though not in
completely numbing 'aesthetic' aloofness, how his 'manhood is cast
down' by the power of his mother's more tender ('piano') appeal.
Though he may 'weep like a child for the past' he is well aware of 'the
insidious mastery' of the regressive impulse so sensitively realised here.

'End of Another Home Holiday' (CP 62) is probably the most
successful poem from these years, where the varied rhythms and formal devices embody and define the shifting moods of the young man's
guilty struggle against mother-love. The moon sinking behind the
black sycamore implies the absorption of the individual self into
deathly imprisonment, the funeral tolling bell suggests endless
meaningless repetition, the little houses choke with self-abnegation.
In this claustrophobic half-light his crisp question, the clip of the
pony's feet and the hoot of the distant train create vigour and energy
to confront the problem directly. His personal situation is presented
explicitly, related to the wider perspective of natural life. He sums it
up: 'Love is the great Asker'—not a liberator or energiser, but
demanding and consuming. As he remembers other poets' visions of
the moon's solitariness, he yearns for loveless isolation; but

> . . . ever at my side,
> Frail and sad, with grey, bowed head,
> The beggar-woman, the yearning-eyed
> Inexorable love goes lagging.

There is no escape from pity and guilt; the moon submits and dies,
and the voice ends, brokenly, with love still insatiably

> Asking something more of me,
>   Yet more of me.

There is none of the detached, essentially defensive irony and sophisti-
cation of, say, Eliot's earlier poetry; the speaker, moving between the
conventionally poetic and the speaking voice as easily as Prufrock,
is intent only on expressing the inner voice of feeling as accurately
as possible.[12]

Several poems express the sexuality produced by Lawrence's
frustration. 'Virgin Youth' (CP 38–40) is an artless celebration of the
underworld divinity that is denied:

> ... flame of the living ground
> He stands, the column of fire by night.
> And he knows from the depths; he quite
> Alone understands.
>
>   .   .   .
>
> Dark, ruddy pillar, forgive me! I
> Am helpless bound
> To the rock of virginity. Thy
> Strange voice has no sound.

Frustrated sexuality is harshened and strengthened into savagery, becomes fatal. In 'Love on the Farm' (CP 42–3), speaking through a woman, he identifies passion with killing, that demands submission and self-obliteration. After the man has killed a rabbit, she thinks

> I know not what fine wire is round my throat;
> I only know I let him finger there
> My pulse of life, and let him nose like a stoat
> Who snuffs with joy before he drinks the blood.
>
>   .   .   .
>
>   ... I drown
> Against him, die, and find death good.

Similarly in 'Snap-Dragon' (CP 122–6); again regular stanzas operate intermittently with other rhythms to catch different levels of feeling. In a scene anticipating 'Rabbit' (*Women in Love* XVIII) the squeezing of the flower is like a strangulation, exciting a blood-lust, a passion that is both self-destructive and completely satisfying. He feels that this sensationalist sexuality is 'wrong' and doomed—'the large hands of revenge Shall get my throat at last'—but the end, though somewhat obscured by an unconscious attempt at self-censorship, still presents the identification of sex, death, and fulfilment: 'And death, I know, is better than not to be.'

Two other poems, not in themselves altogether successful, particularly in their rhymes, are yet of interest, showing in their anticipation of Lawrence's very last poems, notably 'The Ship of Death' and 'Bavarian Gentians', the continuity of his attitudes and imagery. In the first, 'The Shadow of Death' (CP 132–3), he sails from dark death into day, moving towards darkness again. He feels insecure in the world of light and normality.

> I who am substance of shadow, I all compact
> Of the stuff of night, finding myself all wrongly
> Among crowds of things in the sunshine jostled and racked.

(That last line is as bad as it could be.) The clouds also are only shrouds containing darkness; preponderantly the darkness of death, it is also the dark preconscious, the dark existence behind mere life. That this is so is borne out by 'Blueness' (CP 136), a poem that is useful in suggesting some of this colour's implications for him. At the source of life is a blue-darkness that is the unmoving centre of movement,[13] the unliving origin of varied individual life.

> Out of the darkness, fretted sometimes in its sleeping
> Jets of sparks in fountains of blue come leaping
> To sight, revealing a secret, numberless secret keeping.
>
> Sometimes the darkness trapped within a wheel
> Runs into speed like a dream, the blue of the steel
> Showing the rocking darkness now a-reel . . .
>
> . . . All these pure things come foam and spray of the sea
> Of Darkness abundant, which shaken mysteriously
> Breaks into dazzle of living, as dolphins leap from the sea
> Of midnight and shake it to fire, till the flame of the shadow
>   we see.

The leaping dolphin is developed more in Lawrence's later years as the embodiment of the released 'phallic' energy and self-confidence; in *Sons and Lovers*, however, there is little sense of such leaping, or of 'Darkness abundant', but rather of the smothering mists, as he struggles hopelessly to release himself.

'Never trust the artist. Trust the tale', wrote Lawrence (SCAM 9), and if ever there were a work that demonstrated how essential and how difficult is such a discrimination, it is *Sons and Lovers* (1913). Closely autobiographical, an attempt to present and master the agonies and sexual disorientation consequent upon his 'Oedipal' feelings for his mother, the novel betrays the involvement in—or lack of detachment from—the experience presented by its author (or one might even say authors, for Jessie Chambers, the original of Miriam, and Frieda Lawrence, one of the sources of Clara, both influenced the writing of the book). One result of this involvement is that the continual slight falsification of the character's originals causes the falsification of the characters themselves, so that they are not seen and presented in their full complexity: not the father, nor Miriam, nor even the mother gets full due.

In Lawrence's best-known account of the novel he describes how

a woman of character and refinement goes into the lower class,[14] and has no satisfaction in her life . . . as her sons grow up she selects them as lovers —first the eldest, then the second. These sons are *urged* into life by their reciprocal love for their mother—urged on and on. But when they come to manhood, they can't love, because their mother is the strongest power in their lives, and holds them . . .

The second son, Paul, finds Miriam, 'who fights for his soul—fights his mother'; eventually the mother 'realises what is the matter' and dies (the ultimate self-sacrifice), and

the son is left in the end naked of everything with the drift towards death.
It is a great tragedy[15] ... It's the tragedy of thousands of young men in England ... (CL 160)

A letter written while his mother lay dying indicates the intensity of their relationship:

We have loved each other, almost with a husband and wife love, as well as filial and maternal. .... We have been like one, so sensitive to each other that we never needed words. It has been rather terrible, and has made me, in some respects, abnormal.
I think this peculiar fusion of soul (don't think me high-falutin) never comes twice in a life-time—it doesn't seem natural. When it comes it seems to distribute one's consciousness far abroad from oneself, and one understands! ... Nobody can have the soul of me. My mother has had it, and nobody can have it again. (CL 69)

After completing the novel Lawrence wrote, 'One sheds one's sickness in books—repeats and presents again one's emotions, to be master of them' (CL 234); but it is clear that, however obsessively repetitive is some of the writing, he had not shed or mastered his 'sicknesses', which were to remain with him to his death.

His belief in the generality of his tragedy is confirmed by another paper of the same year, Freud's essay 'The Most Prevalent Form of Degradation in Erotic Life',[16] an important piece of work, worth attention here. In it Freud discusses what he terms 'psychical impotence', the inability to achieve satisfaction in normal heterosexual relations, which he claims is caused by the son's early fixation of desire on the mother. As only tender filial love is acceptable here, sexual desire is displaced on to other women, but if they remain only mother-substitutes, the man will still feel guilt at subjecting them to his sexuality. Freud writes,

To ensure a fully normal attitude in love, two currents of feeling have to unite—we may describe them as the tender, affectionate feelings and the sensual feelings—and this confluence of the two currents has not been achieved. .... The sensual feeling that has remained active seeks only objects evoking no reminder of the incestuous persons forbidden to it; the impression made by someone who seems deserving of high estimation leads, not to a sensual excitation, but to feelings of tenderness which remain erotically ineffectual. .... Where such men love they have no desire and where they desire they cannot love ...
I shall put forward the proposition that psychical impotence is far more
B

widespread than is generally supposed, and that some degree of this condition does characterise the erotic lives of civilised peoples . . .

. . . the man almost always feels his sexual activity hampered by his respect for the woman, and only develops full sexual potency when he finds himself in the presence of a lower type of sexual object; and this again is partly conditioned by the circumstance that his sexual aims include those of perverse sexual components, which he does not like to gratify with a woman he respects.

Lawrence himself provides an attempt at explicit analysis of Paul's situation, when in Chapter XI Paul thinks of other young men like himself:

Being the sons of mothers whose husbands had blundered rather brutally through their feminine sanctities, they were themselves too diffident and shy . . . for a woman was like their mother . . .

This analysis does not go far enough, and Lawrence's lack of full comprehension weakens the novel. It was naturally some years until he achieved such a mature understanding, which found expression in the autobiographical 'Prologue to *Women in Love*' (P2 92–108). Here Birkin–Lawrence reflects upon his relationship with Hermione (at this stage based much more on Jessie Chambers than on Lady Ottoline Morell):

To be spiritual, he must have a Hermione, completely without desire: to be sensual, he must have a slightly bestial woman. . . . His fundamental desire was, to be able to love completely, in one and the same act: both body and soul at once, struck into a complete oneness in contact with a complete woman.
And he failed in this desire. (P2 102–3)

The 'perverse sexual components' of which Freud wrote, now appear in a homosexual attraction to men:

It was the man's physique which held the passion and the mystery to him. The woman he seemed to be kin to, he looked for the soul in them. (P2 104)

This remained largely true throughout Lawrence's life. This element in Paul–Lawrence receives insufficient treatment in *Sons and Lovers*, appearing only partly in his attachment to Baxter Dawes; his love for Miriam's brother Edgar, which in any case really needs fuller presentation, is notably underplayed—presumably what is omitted here is in *The White Peacock*, in the relationship between Cyril and George (who combines both Jessie's brother and Lawrence's father).
Years later, in 1922, Lawrence apparently said

that he had not done justice to his father in *Sons and Lovers*, and felt like rewriting it. When children they had accepted the dictum of their mother that their father was a drunkard, therefore was contemptible, but as Lawrence had grown older he had come to see him in a different light; to see his unquenchable fire and relish for living. Now he blamed his mother for her self-righteousness, her invulnerable Christian virtue in which she was entrenched.[17]

In his later years he found it difficult to recognise what he owed his mother, and probably would have achieved less than the very rough justice that he managed in 1912.

The first part of the novel, presenting the early years of the marriage and Paul's youth, is closer to fact than the second, and its greater success is largely due to this, and its 'playing off' of vivid scenes, drawn from life and essentially 'true', against Lawrence's interpretations and didactic purpose.[18] So, in the first scene between husband and wife, when Morel returns home late and 'merry', with the present of a coconut, we see not only how her irritation is provoked by his waste of money, but also how his instinctive courtesy prevented him testing his friend's gift, whereas Mrs Morel does this—as a concession! Her chilly self-righteousness cuts him short, while he is presented as warm and lively, if feckless. His vitality and male glamour (a word usually evoking sensual appeal for Lawrence) are well suggested in the scene of their first meeting, as well as the (unfortunately) romantic appeal he has for her, on the rebound from a feeble man.

She was a puritan, like her father, high-minded and really stern. Therefore the dusky, golden softness of this man's sensuous flame of life, that flowed off his flesh like the flame from a candle, not baffled and gripped into incandescence by thought and spirit as her life was, seemed to her something wonderful, beyond her. . . . She realised the life of the miners, hundreds of them toiling below the earth and coming up at evening. He seemed to her noble. He risked his life daily, and with gaiety. (I)

In a letter of January 1913, Lawrence wrote,

I conceive a man's body as a kind of flame, like a candle flame, forever upright and yet flowing: and the intellect is just the light that is shed on to the things around . . . we only *think* we know such a lot. A flame isn't a flame because it lights up two, or twenty objects on a table. It's a flame because it is itself. And we have forgotten ourselves. (CL 180)

This flame of unselfconscious integrated life is contrasted with her 'incandescence', a metaphor that implies something unnatural, as in the 'phosphorescence' of the city at the end. Lawrence's synoptic letter spoke of the mother's 'passion for her husband' but apart from this and possibly one other scene, there is no indication that he

could yet realise it; only six months of happiness are indicated, before
she discovers that he has not told her the truth about their financial
situation:

She said very little to her husband, but her manner had changed towards
him. Something in her proud, honourable soul had crystallised out hard as
rock. (I)

Lawrence's desire to reduce as much as possible the period of his
mother's sexual subjection to his father has made her seem more
unsympathetic than she probably was; here it seems that her pride
very easily overcame her love, while the phrase 'crystallised out hard
as rock' has unpleasant connotations that the mature Lawrence would
have developed. (Coming to *Sons and Lovers* from Lawrence's later
work makes it seem curiously muffled in impact: images and themes
appear that are to be important later, but here seem hardly realised.) It
is no surprise that Morel begins to drink, and within half a dozen pages
of their first meeting there has begun the 'fearful, bloody battle that
ended only with the death of one', that, as Lawrence says, caused
Morel 'knowingly or unknowingly, grossly to offend her where he
would not have done', while 'she wielded the lash unmercifully'.
Lawrence attempts a detached analysis:

The pity was, she was too much his opposite. She could not be content with
the little he might be; she would have him the much he ought to be. So,
in seeking to make him nobler than he could be, she destroyed him. She
injured and hurt and scarred herself, but she lost none of her worth. She also
had the children. (I)

The rhythms are balanced, but the judgment is not: it is from her
point of view, with her values.

The father's physical gusto, simplicity and humanity are brought
out in many scenes: the descriptions of his noisy washing, his soldering,
his account of life down the mine; his loneliness is also apparent, in
his solitary happiness in the early morning before the others get up.
In all such scenes of record, Lawrence's sympathy, conscious or
otherwise, comes out clearly, and usually more convincingly than the
later disparaging comments. While Morel's coarsening is revealed, it
is clear that this is partly caused by his family's hostility. His childlike
attempt to run away is an unconscious plea for sympathy, but Mrs
Morel has little sympathy for his agonies, mental or physical; when
he is seriously injured, the main concern of his wife and son is for
each other; when Paul is ill, Morel is tender and anxious for him,
but the child only wants the mother; when the elder son William
dies, Paul manages not to 'see' his father's silent grief; and when Paul

wins a prize, the father's memory of William's potential is ignored by the others. Even in the fierce fights between him and his wife, where he appears at his worst, he is obviously goaded beyond self-control—and in the scene when, in unthinking reaction to pain, he throws a drawer at her, cutting her head, she is not above using her baby to win the quarrel.[19] He frequently feels guilty after their quarrels; she never does, but returns in renewed strength and self-assertion.

The occasion when he locks her out in the garden at night is one of the finest symbolic scenes in the book. The image of the moon presents withdrawal from the heat of human passion into solitary self-assertion:

She hurried out of the side garden to the front, where she could stand as if in an immense gulf of white light, the moon streaming high in face of her, the moonlight standing up from the hills in front, and filling the valley where the Bottoms crouched, almost blindingly. (I)

In Lawrence's usual pattern a withdrawal from a crisis in human relationships is followed by solitary, quasi-sexual union with nature, that can recharge the individual with power:

The tall white lilies were reeling in the moonlight, and the air was charged with their perfume, as with a presence. Mrs Morel gasped slightly in fear. She touched the big, pallid flowers on the petals, then shivered. They seemed to be stretching in the moonlight. She put her hand into one white bin: the gold scarcely showed on her fingers by moonlight . . . she rested with the hills and lilies and houses, all swum together in a kind of swoon. (I)

After this intensely sensual experience comes the sense of the night-world, beyond the human world and larger—another element more fully developed later.

The following chapters in the first part trace Mrs Morel's withdrawal from her husband, dispossessing him of authority or influence in the family, and possessing the eldest son William, who is to be 'her knight who wore *her* favour in the battle' (IV). She so hinders William's interest in girls that it is only when away in London that he can develop any relationship. His response to 'Gypsy' Western (worrying about her lack of warm clothing) repeats the only sexual situation he understands, the parental one; chiefly his response is merely passionate, for nothing more is possible with such an empty-head (who contrasts with, but does not compete with his mother). Pushed into 'success' and an impossible sexual situation, he dies; Mrs Morel also despairs of life, until Paul's nearly fatal illness, that 'saves' them both.

Paul's childhood development is presented with considerable sensitivity and truth, tracing his ambivalent feelings about his father,

and increasing intimacy with his mother. The account of her visit
to the market sympathetically displays her energetic response to life,
winning small victories (for her, life is a battle at every level); her
and Paul's delight over her trophy, a small dish, seems like the delight
of a newly wed couple over their first furnishings. A significant
incident is Paul's burning of his sister's doll: the 'sacrifice', releasing
him from guilt, anticipates his later self-liberation from unconscious
feelings of guilt and resentment directed against his mother, when he
releases her from painful death ('caused' he feels by his 'betrayal' with
other women).

Associated with the family's new house on the hill is a cluster of
images that later become very important. The father's violent passions
are linked with the 'demoniacal noise' made in the night wind by the
tree outside:

Having such a great space in front of the house gave the children a feeling
of night, of vastness, and of terror. This terror came in from the shrieking
of the tree and the anguish of the home discord. . . . There was a feeling of
horror, a kind of bristling in the darkness, and a sense of blood. (IV)

The bristling darkness, the sense of blood and of the demonic later
aroused more openly ambivalent responses in Lawrence, associated
with intense passion, masculine energy, and even his sense of his true
self. Here the more positive element appears in the children's

wild intense games . . . under the lamp-post, surrounded by so much darkness. . . . They sounded so perfectly absorbed in the game as their voices
came out of the night, that they had the feeling of wild creatures singing . . .
(IV)

This singing and dancing in the dark, in a 'pre-civilised' community,
reappear in the rituals of *The Plumed Serpent*. In the meantime young
Paul is his mother's creature, pushed into clerking at Jordan's Appli-
ance Factory, whence he returns daily to render his account:

His life-story, like an Arabian Nights, was told night after night to his
mother. It was almost as if it were her own life. (V)

Yet Paul must lead his own life—which is when the struggle against
the mother, and the mother-principle, begins. His relations with his
other women, Miriam Leivers and Clara Dawes, are crippled by his
mother's possession of him—and by their close identity with her.

The similarity between Mrs Morel and Miriam is remarkable: the
piety, intellectual aspirations, the sense of unrecognised superiority
and of having been 'done out of her rights', the romantic dream of a
Walter Scott knight to wear '*her*' favours in the battle'. Paul encourages
Miriam also in resistance to male domination. He attempts to give her

confidence, but her inhibition (exhibited in her inflexible body—
passed on to Hermione in *Women in Love*) is too strong; her fear of
his thrusts, pushing her on the swing, foreshadow her fears when he
at last makes sexual demands on her. His impatience echoes his exas-
peration with his mother's continued self-imprisonment. We may
compare the following:

It hurt the boy keenly, this feeling about [his mother], that she had never
had her life's fulfilment: and his own incapability to make up to her hurt
him with a sense of impotence ... (IV)
  ... when he saw [Miriam's] hand trembling and her mouth parted with
suffering, his heart was scalded with pain for her. (VII)

Her responses are always reacted to (and presented) unsympathetically.
We may contrast his cry,

"What do you tremble your *soul* before it for?" he cried. "You don't learn
algebra with your blessed soul. Can't you look at it with your clear simple
wits?" (VII)

with the sympathetic account of Ursula in *The Rainbow*:

She trembled like a postulant when she wrote the Greek alphabet for the
first time. (X)

Her open affection for her little brother (with whose frailty and elfin
quality he identifies) alarms him:

This fearful, naked contact of her on small occasions shocked him. He was
used to his mother's reserve. (VII)

One evening Miriam shows him a beautiful rose bush that is the
physical, feminine equivalent of the male pine trees in the red sunset-
glare[20] that he had painted as 'God's burning bush ... that burned
not away':

The dusk came like smoke around, and still did not put out the roses.
  Paul looked into Miriam's eyes. She was pale and expectant with wonder,
her lips were parted, and her dark eyes lay open to him ...
  Something made him feel anxious and imprisoned ...
  And soon as he [had left her, and] was out of the wood, in the free open
meadow, where he could breathe, he started to run as fast as he could. It
was like a delirium in his veins. (VII)

Inhibited in the encounter, his passion is released in flight.
His mother counter-attacks immediately, and repossesses him.
Though he and Miriam on a country walk manage, on a romantic
wind-rocked tower, a moment 'in the purest manner of chivalry', he
is now too inhibited for normal feeling—'if she put her arm in his,

it caused him almost torture'. At the seaside with her one night, he is possessed by a vision of the moon, in all the stimulating, passionate power that it had for Lawrence.[21]

His blood was concentrated like a flame in his chest. But he could not get across to her. There were flashes in his blood. . . . She was expecting some religious state in him [so we are told—without evidence; it is not clear whether the statement is authorial, or Paul's supposition]. . . . He was afraid of her. The fact that he might want her as a man wants a woman had in him been suppressed into a shame. When she shrank in her convulsed, coiled torture from the thought of such a thing, he had winced to the depths of his soul. (VII)

When? No such incident between them has appeared in the novel, and Paul does not know of Miriam's prayer. It is another example of the authorial misrepresentation to which Miriam is subjected, either by unsubstantiated assertions or by the blurring of the supposedly impartial narrative voice with the thoughts and comments of the characters.

With his brother Arthur's departure, Paul has one fewer rival for his mother, and the sexual crisis becomes more acute. He attempts to spiritualise and domesticate passion by taking Miriam to chapel.

Mrs Morel, like a little champion, sat at the head of the pew, Paul at the other end; and at first Miriam sat next to him. Then the chapel was like home. (VIII)

It is worth noting that the chapel religion of Lawrence's mother and his own youth is underplayed in the novel, rarely presented as anything more than bland, so that to describe Mrs Morel as 'a little champion' seems odd. Had he presented the chapel faith as he was to later, in 'Hymns in a Man's Life' (1928; P2 597–601) and the opening pages of *Apocalypse*, then Mrs Morel's religious life and the life of the 'spirit' would have had more weight and significance; but this would not have fitted the over-simple scheme of bloodless 'virtue' versus flesh and passion. As it is, Paul's sadistic torturing of Miriam's faith (displaced from his mother) seems almost acceptable.

His passion is sublimated into perverse intellectuality:[22]

fingering the very quivering tissue, the very protoplasm of life. . . . There he lay in the white intensity of his search, and his voice gradually filled her with fear, so level it was, almost inhuman . . . (VIII)

Paul's frustrated passion, aroused by the sight of his father's body (translated into a sense of his mother's former passion for it), and by an excited flirtation with another young woman, results in a sadism towards Miriam's tenderness, as in his reading of Baudelaire to her, 'soft and caressing, but growing almost brutal. . . .' Mrs Morel's later reproaches for his 'betrayal' of her produce his denial of any love for Miriam, and an over-intense embrace when she claims not to have had a husband "—not really—", culminating in 'a long, fervent kiss'. Paul's dispossession of his father is completed, even to telling his mother not to sleep with her husband. Hamlet's mother was also, we remember, named Gertrude. Not surprisingly, the next chapter is entitled 'Defeat of Miriam'.

His rejection of Miriam is not simply because he is possessed by his mother, but because, having come so close to incest, he feels that Miriam, as his mother's representative, must be purged of sexuality. His 'farewell' note echoes that of Lawrence to Jessie Chambers (see CL 4):

You see, I can give you a spirit love, I have given it you this long, long time, but not embodied passion. See, you are a nun. (XI)

Yet no fulfilled life is possible with his mother, as the 'lovers' outing' to Lincoln makes clear. Even Mrs Morel now realises his need for sexual release, and welcomes his interest in Clara Dawes (originally introduced by Miriam, as an object of guilt-free sexuality for Paul).

Ironically, Clara's first function is to serve as another mother-surrogate. Her husband Baxter Dawes, from whom she is separated, is a degenerate version of Paul's father; she herself is older than Paul, critical of men, aloof and superior, and seems to him 'denied and deprived of so much'. (X) Having in effect transferred his filial response to her, the pressure is taken off Miriam, and he can accept what Clara tells him, that Miriam does desire him sexually.

He returns to make 'The Test on Miriam', but both of them feel that he is sacrificing her. Though he feels that she only desires his conscious self, calling him back from 'the impersonality of passion' to 'the littleness, the personal relationship' he is clearly ignoring her as a person, to satisfy his physical needs:

He had always, almost wilfully, to put her out of count, and act from the brute strength of his own feelings. (XI)

The 'consummation' begins one evening when Paul is high on the cherry-tree (high positions are throughout the novel associated with power and self-assertion) that is reminiscent of his childhood's ash-tree:

The wind, moaning steadily, made the whole tree rock with a subtle, thrilling motion that stirred the blood . . .

He looks down on her:

Beside her, on the rhubarb leaves, were four dead birds, thieves that had been shot. Paul saw some cherry-stones hanging quite bleached, like skeletons, picked clean of flesh. (XI)

Miriam hangs some cherries over her ears; and Paul comes down to take her and devour her,[23] in the darkness of the fir trees and pines: pine trees, savagery, and sacrifice in the cause of phallic assertion remain associated throughout Lawrence's writing. Afterwards Paul feels that

life seemed a shadow, day a white shadow; night, and death, and stillness, and inaction, this seemed like *being*. To be alive, to be urgent and insistent —that was *not-to-be*. The highest of all was to melt out into the darkness and sway there, identified with the great Being. (XI)

While this feeling here seems post-coital lassitude, Lawrence elsewhere presents it as existence in fulfilled sensuality, beyond the strain of frustrating, conscious life, in the 'living body of darkness'. However, Paul cannot overcome his guilt feelings towards Miriam, and turns to Clara, Freud's 'lower type of sexual object'.

Clara's personality is less successfully presented than Miriam's, perhaps because she had no single counterpart in reality; her body, and its sensual power over Paul, are nevertheless extremely palpable and vivid (perhaps recording Lawrence's initial delight with Frieda). Their sexual union takes place not in the sacrificial aura of the pine forest but by the dark, swirling waters of the river, that suggest the deep power of pre-conscious 'inhuman' nature; the blood-red petals spattering her body present the encounter as deeply carnal, and even as a sort of defloration. Yet Clara comes to seem to him like what Lawrence was later to call the 'Magna Mater', the woman who overwhelms the man who serves her:[24]

There was no himself. The grey and black eyes of Clara, her bosom coming down on his, her arm that he held gripped between his hands, were all that existed. Then he felt himself small and helpless, her towering in her force above him. (XII)

She is a mother-figure who gives her body to him to satisfy his physical needs. Lawrence asserts that their intercourse in the open one night had 'included in their meeting the thrust of the manifold grass-stems, the cry of peewit, the wheel of the stars' (XIII), but the claim of mutual fulfilment in cosmic union is not borne out by the narrative; we have been told 'She did this for him in his need, even if he left her, for she loved him', like a mother who must feed her child and let him go. There is no mutuality in their relationship, and the movement apart now begins. Their sexual activity acquires a new 'muddy'

sensuality and perversity, stimulating itself by danger; Clara realises
that he has never given himself to her, and he finds her insignificant
compared with the great sea of life. His sense of guilt at having taken
another man's wife, exactly analogous to his dispossession of his
father, is assuaged when Baxter Dawes beats him, as he unconsciously
feels his father should have done before.

Now both surrogate father and real mother fall desperately ill; Paul
feels responsible, and becomes again the dutiful son. The agony of his
mother's long-drawn-out death—or refusal to let go of life, and of
him—and her slow degeneration is too much for him, and he mixes
a fatal dose of morphia in her milk. The motives here are complex.
Familial roles have been reversed: she is like a child to him, and he
releases her into the true being of death. While he releases himself
from the old woman's grip, at the same time his killing of her makes
her seem a young maiden again, and provides his ultimate possession
of her.

Her substitute Clara, no longer needed, is now returned to her
husband, with whom Paul has developed the incipiently homosexual,
submissive relationship repeated later in Lawrence's work. The other
mother-figure, Miriam, also 'dies':

Her comfort and her life seemed in the after world. . . . Her bloom of youth
had quickly gone. A sort of stiffness, almost of woodenness, had come
upon her. (XV)

His mother—though living in him—is dead in her, and she cannot
'take him and relieve him of the responsibility of himself': and why
should she, especially as he obviously does not want her? The favourite
child has lost his mother's protection:

Whatever spot he stood in, there he stood alone. From his breast, from his
mouth, sprang the endless space, and it was there behind him, everywhere.
(XV)

Yet he has achieved sufficient sense of his own identity not to submit
to the impulse of suicide; but the move 'towards the city's gold
phosphorescence' does not promise a movement towards healthy life
—such light is associated in the novel, and even more later, with the
forced and unnatural, the complex subtleties and perversities of feeling
explored in *Women in Love* especially.

The novel relates the death of Lawrence's mother, but not of her
spirit, that seemed to live on in him for many years, to be partially
exorcised by the savage glamour of *The Plumed Serpent*. The phosphorescent city in a motherless world had no home for him. Instead he
dreamed of other communities: Rananim, 'the heaven beneath the

wave', 'Mexico', a womb-like cosmos assuring foetal centrality and security, the tombs of the ancient Etruscans, and the dark underworld of 'Bavarian Gentians', where at last he came home to the lord of the underworld and his bride, and was at peace in the dark body of life, reconciled with his mother and his father.

1. Walter Pater, 'Conclusion', *The Renaissance* (London, 1873).

2. C. Caudwell, *Studies in a Dying Culture* (London, 1938), pp. 44–72.

3. T. S. Eliot, 'The Metaphysical Poets', *Selected Essays* (London, 1951), p. 288.

4. cf. the poem 'Thought' (CP 673); 'Thought is a man in his wholeness wholly attending'. Lawrence's thinking belongs with the Gestalt psychology and, Symbolist philosophy of the time. Ernst Cassirer saw all modes of understanding as essentially symbolic, knowledge not as absolute but relative and conditioned by the psyche of the observer: 'Myth, art, Language and science appear as symbols . . . in the sense of forces each of which produces and posits a world of its own . . . the special symbolic forms are not imitations, but *organs* of reality, since it is solely by their agency that anything real becomes an object for intellectual apprehension, and as such is made visible to us. The question as to what reality is apart from these forms . . . becomes irrelevant.' E. Cassirer, *Language and Myth* (1924) trans. S. K. Langer (N.Y., 1946), p. 8.

5. T. S. Eliot, 'Hamlet', op. cit., p. 145.

6. cf. *The Trespasser* X, where Siegmund, contemplating the view, tells Helena, "It is a moment to me, not a piece of scenery, I should say the picture was in me, not out there."

7. M. Merleau-Ponty, 'Cézanne's Doubt', *Sense and Non-Sense* (Northwestern U.P., 1964), pp. 9–25. Since writing this I have read John Remsbury, 'Real Thinking: Lawrence and Cézanne', *The Cambridge Quarterly*, spring 1967, vol. II, no. 2.

8. cf. 'Not I, not I but the wind that blows through me . . .' (CP 250).

9. 'In narrative any recurring symbol . . . becomes defined and limited by its contexts. Narrative requires an irreducible minimum of rationality which inevitably tames and limits the meaning of the vaguest of images. The kind of non-intellectual and anti-rational evocation practised by the symbolist poet is incompatible with the laws of narrative.' R. Scholes and R. Kellogg, *The Nature of Narrative* (N.Y., 1966), p. 107.

10. Lawrence's Typical figures are essentially solitary—the Phoenix, Osiris, Dionysus, David, Christ—while Yeats, by contrast, initiates his cycles of human existence with sexual encounters, such as Jupiter and Semele or, most notably, Leda and the Swan.

11. 'More life! More *vivid* life!' (P2 483).

12. 'I think, don't you know, that my rhythms fit my mood pretty well, in my verse. And if the mood is out of joint, the rhythm often is. I have always tried to get an emotion out on its own course, without altering it. It needs the finest instinct imaginable, much finer than the skill of the craftsmen' (1913; CL 221).

13. 'The still centre of the turning world.' T. S. Eliot, 'Burnt Norton', *Four Quartets* (London, 1944).

14. The class origins of Lawrence's parents were not so different as is here implied. See H. T. Moore, *The Intelligent Heart* (Penguin, 1960), p. 27.

15. 'The old son-lover was Oedipus. The name of the new one is legion' (LH 102).

16. S. Freud, *Collected Papers*, vol. IV (London, 1949), pp. 203–16.

17. E. and A. Brewster, *D. H. Lawrence: Reminiscences and Correspondence* (London, 1934), p. 254.

18. 'It is such a bore that nearly all the great novelists have a didactic purpose, otherwise a philosophy, directly opposite to their passional inspiration. In their passional inspiration, they are all phallic worshippers . . . when it comes to their philosophy, or what they think-they-are, they are all crucified Jesuses' (P2 417).

19. 'A woman who has her child in her arms is a tower of strength, a beautiful, unassailable tower of strength that may in its turn stand quietly dealing death' (*The White Peacock* 3, VI).

20. cf. Kate's vision of Cipriano's body in the red dawn, *The Plumed Serpent* XXVI.

21. cf. note 11, Chapter 2, p. 78.

22. cf. 'Prologue to *Women in Love*', describing Birkin's moonlit conversation with Hermione: '. . . their two disembodied voices distilled in the silvery air, two voices moving and ceasing like ghosts . . . they penetrated further and further into the regions of death, and soon the connection with life would be broken' (P2 97).

23. 'Cherry-Robbers' confirms Paul's cruelty: 'Against the haystack a girl stands laughing at me,/Cherries hung round her ears./Offers me her scarlet fruit: I will see/If she has any tears' (CP 36–7).

24. '. . . women . . . have got each an internal *form*, an internal self which remains firm and individual whatever love they may be subject to . . . there is in women such a big sufficiency unto themselves, more than in men' (CL 157).

2

MY GREAT RELIGION

I

'HOW BARBARIC ONE GETS WITH LOVE'[1]

The first letters from Europe, after the elopement, indicate clearly Lawrence's feelings of exuberance and new energy—

Here, in this tiny savage little place, F. and I have got awfully wild. I loathe the idea of England, and its enervation and misty miserable modernness. I *don't* want to go back to town and civilisation. I want to rough it and scramble through free, free. I *don't* want to be tied down. And I can live on a tiny bit. I shan't let F. leave me, if I can help it. I feel I've got a mate and I'll fight tooth and claw to keep her. She says I'm reverting, but I'm not—I'm only coming out wholesome and myself. (LH 46)

My great religion is a belief in the blood, the flesh, as being wiser than the intellect. We can go wrong in our minds. But what our blood feels and believes and says, is always true. The intellect is only a bit and a bridle. What do I care about knowledge. All I want is to answer to my blood, direct, without fribbling intervention of mind, or moral, or what-not. I conceive a man's body as a kind of flame . . . (CL 180)

This new sexual relation, and rediscovery of passion, fed directly into his work; what he had discovered was what the world needed:

I can only write what I feel pretty strongly about: and that, at present, is the relation between men and women. After all, it is the problem of today, the establishment of a new relation, or the readjustment of the old one, between men and women. (CL 200)

I think the only re-sourcing of art, revivifying it, is to make it more the joint work of man and woman . . .

(as *Sons and Lovers* had been—though he is probably not thinking of Jessie's contribution.)

. . . Because the source of all life and knowledge is in man and woman, and the source of all living is in the interchange and the meeting and mingling of these two: man-life and woman-life, man-knowledge and woman-knowledge, man-being and woman-being. (CL 280)

Here is Lawrence's sense of life as being conditioned by the inter-action of opposed forces—woman and man, conscious and unconscious, civilised and savage. Yet this is not an equal balance—one element of the 'polarity' is stronger, and more real. In the letter about the Italian Futurists (CL 279–81) quoted in Chapter 1 (p. 20), he indicated his interest in the subhuman and impersonal; that letter put it in formalist, aesthetic terms, but others reveal further implications. *A propos* of his new work, he writes,

There is something in the Greek sculpture that my soul is hungry for—something of the eternal stillness that lies under all movement, under all life, incorruptible and inexhaustible. It is deeper than change, and struggling. So long I have acknowledged only the struggle, the stream, the change. And now I begin to feel something of the source, the great impersonal which never changes and out of which all change comes. I begin to feel it in myself. . . . And there is a glimpse of it everywhere, in somebody, at some moment—a glimpse of the eternal and unchangeable that they are. (CL 241–2)

In another letter (also quoted in Chapter 1) he writes,

I believe there is no getting of a vision, as you call it, before we get our sex right: before we get our souls fertilised by the *female*. . . . Then the vision we're after, I don't know what it is—but it is something that contains awe and dread and submission, not pride or sensuous egotism and assertion. . . . We want to realise the tremendous *non-human* quality of life . . . driving us, forcing us, destroying us if we do not submit to be swept away. (CL 291)

Life must submit to the still source of nonhuman power within and beneath individual life, to be wholly changed, or destroyed. The nature of Lawrence's insight, which is fundamental to *The Rainbow* and *Women in Love*, and the process by which it was attained, are indicated in the sequence of poems entitled *Look! We Have Come Through!* (1917); beginning with 'Ballad of a Wilful Woman' (CP 200), to 'Craving for Spring' (CP 270), it traces the progress of Lawrence's relationship with Frieda, from summer 1912 to early 1916, and his progress from uncertainty and insecurity to an unusual self-confidence.

Few of these poems are successful as individual poems, the loose Whitmanesque lines having no 'life', while rhyme and enjambement are often clumsily handled; however, as Lawrence himself said, 'These poems should not be considered separately as so many single pieces. They are intended as an essential story, or history, or confession, unfolding one from the other in organic development' (CP 191), and simply the main line of the sequence will be considered here. 'First Morning' reports some initial sexual failure by Lawrence. 'And oh—that the man I am might cease to be' indicates his desire to escape from self-consciousness into 'sealing darkness' (the Macbeth allusion proves not inappropriate). In 'She Looks Back', Frieda's regret for her abandoned children identifies her as the Mother-Woman, the Magna Mater who resists man's sexual powers; her cold separation and indifference make her 'the pillar of salt' that will corrode the phallic pillar of dark fire (cf. the description of Ursula as such a corroding pillar in *The Rainbow* XI). 'In the Dark' (anticipating Anna and Will's struggle in ch. VI) presents her fear of being overcome by his 'darkness upright' that obliterates her conscious daylight ego; he insists that his sexual darkness has the power to unite them with the suprahuman forces in nature:

> In the darkness we all are gone, we are gone with the trees
> And the restless river;—we are lost and gone with all these. (CP 211)

Soon, in 'A Young Wife', she comes to respond to this hitherto unrealised darkness within existence—

> Ah never before did I see
> The shadows that live in the sun! (CP 215)—

that evokes the life-animating 'death' that is true existence:

> It is death still seething where
> The wild-flower shakes its bell
> And the skylark twinkles blue— (CP 216)

They are achieving a liberation from self-conscious, civilised inhibition into non-human sexual energy, as in 'River Roses';

> We whispered: "No one knows us.
> Let it be as the snake disposes
> Here in this simmering marsh." (CP 217)

They both hesitate: in 'Song of a Man Who is Not Loved', he fears his isolation in the world, and frailty before the great power of 'non-human' organic existence that he has discovered. Like Gerald Crich on Willey Water,

> I am terrified, feeling space surround me;
> Like a man in a boat on very clear, deep water, space frightens
> and confounds me. (CP 222)

In 'Why Does She Weep?' he reassures her guilt at her moral trans-
gressions, and at the sexual activity in which she is fearfully participa-
ting:

> Why should you cry then?
> Are you afraid of God
> in the dark?
>
> .   .   .
>
> Weep then, yea
> For the abomination of our old righteousness.
>
> We have done wrong
> many times;
> but this time we begin to do right. (CP 231–2)

His mother and her values are dead and far away, while he has found
a new life, a new self. In 'Lady Wife' he claims that Frieda, believing
essentially in the supremacy of the Magna Mater (as much as did his
mother), despises this new self, and only cynically and perversely
'condescend[s] to be vile' with him. She must cease to view his sexual
demands as merely perverse, 'a common devil's Requisite', to help him
bring about 'the imminent Mystery'. Her old values, identified with
her children (past or future) must be put 'Into the fire Of Sodom that
covers the earth', for normal sexuality is only service of the Magna
Mater and established values, and must be eradicated:

> You woman most holy, you mother, you being beyond
> Question or diminution,
> Add yourself up, and your seed, to the nought
> Of your last solution. (CP 235)

Her 'seed' is denied normal fulfilment; as the mother-principle is
subjected, he acquires a new paternity, when she is reborn from him,
on 'Birth Night'; her new self calls submissively and masochistically
to the sadistic in him, as 'Rabbit Snared in the Night' develops the
theme of the early 'Love on the Farm'.

Now 'Paradise Re-entered' starts to clarify what has been going
on. Here Lawrence suggests that conventional sexual intercourse,
serving the mother to conceive children, is not essentially for sensual
delight, and so is unsatisfactory; but in 'forbidden' anal intercourse,
the lovers

> . . . storm the angel-guarded
> Gates of the long-discarded
> Garden . . .
> . . . as victors we travel
> To Eden home.

> Back beyond good and evil
> Return we. Even dishevel
> Your hair for the bliss-drenched revel
> On our primal loam. (CP 243)

In anal intercourse, 'fundamental' reality is discovered; the depths of
physical and moral corruption are plumbed; the extremes of man's
whole nature are explored and in this complete self-acceptance is an
amoral innocence and liberty.

Though the beautiful 'Song of a Man Who is Loved' expresses the
love that finds security between maternal breasts, 'The Song of a Man
Who has Come Through' expresses the confidence brought by the
new sexuality. He is more than himself, 'not I, but the wind that blows
through me', and, possessed of this more than personal power,

> ... keen and hard, like the sheer tip of a wedge
> Driven by invisible blows,
> The rock will split, we shall come at the wonder, we shall find
> the Hesperides. (CP 250)

His knocking at the door is the annunciation of the new underworld
god of the dark body.

'New Heaven and Earth' traces the course of the 'savage pilgrimage'
from the solipsist world produced by incestuous feelings; with his
mother's death, he also 'died', the war paralleling his annihilation.
After such death, came the resurrection produced by his realisation
of what was 'other' to his mere consciousness—physical matter. This
came through his anal exploration of his wife, discovering that which
is behind the sexual body. Normal heterosexual intercourse is still
associated for Lawrence with incest; though Frieda had already been
a wife and mother, Lawrence found a new virginity to possess:

> Cortes, Pisarro, Columbus, Cabot, they are nothing, nothing!
> I am the first comer!
> I am the discoverer!
> I have found the other world! (CP 259)

'Manifesto' sums up all the needs that have been satisfied: intellectual
life, sexual release, security in a woman's love; now he only wants
her to return this anal caress as best as a woman can, so that they may
both realise essential independent being.

> I want her to touch me at last, ah, on the root and quick of my
> darkness
> and perish on me as I have perished on her.

> Then, we shall be two and distinct, we shall have each our separate
> being.
> And that will be pure existence, real liberty ...

When she knows the fearful *other flesh*, ah, darkness unfathomable and
fearful, contiguous and concrete . . .
Then I shall be glad, I shall not be confused with her . . .
Then we shall be free, freer than angels, ah, perfect. (CP 266–7)

When all men have achieved such self-acceptance and realisation of
bodily integrity, it will be a rebirth into a new existence:

> We shall not look before and after.
> We shall *be, now*.
> We shall know in full.
> We, the mystic NOW. (CP 268)

In this knowledge of what lies beneath, in this relation between
'spirit' and matter, absolute reality, the immanent god, is sensed. In
his introduction to the American edition of *New Poems*, 1918, Lawrence describes the poetry of

. . . the immediate present. In the immediate present there is no perfection,
no consummation, nothing finished. The strands are all flying, quivering,
intermingling into the web, the waters are shaking the moon. There is no
round, consummate moon on the face of the running water, nor on the face
of the unfinished tide. There are no gems of the living plasm. The living
plasm vibrates unspeakably, it inhales the future, it exhales the past, it is the
quick of both, and yet it is neither . . .
The quivering nimble hour of the present, this is the quick of Time.
This is the immanence. The quick of the universe is the *pulsating, carnal self*,
mysterious and palpable. (CP 182–3; P 218–20)

The relevance of this both to this poem, and to 'Moony' (*Women in
Love* XIX) does not require labouring.
Understanding of the true nature of the experience and achievement
recorded in this sequence may be aided by turning again to the essay
by Freud quoted above. In its conclusion, Freud fears that sexual
fulfilment is impossible for civilised man, largely because of the
suppression of various 'unacceptable' elements of the sexual instinct.

Above all, the coprophilic elements in the instinct have proved incompatible
with our aesthetic ideas . . . further, a considerable proportion of the sadistic
elements belonging to the erotic instinct have had to be abandoned. All such
developmental processes, however, relate only to the upper layers of the
complicated structure. The fundamental processes which promote erotic
excitation remain always the same. Excremental things are all too intimately
and inseparably bound up with sexual things. . . . What culture tries to make
out of [the erotic instincts] seems attainable only at the cost of a sensible
loss of pleasure; the persistence of the impulses that are not enrolled in adult
sexual activity makes itself felt in an absence of satisfaction. (op. cit., p. 215)

For Freud, frustration and sublimation were the inevitable, necessary conditions of civilisation, so that he could only foresee 'renunciation and suffering as well as the danger of [man's] extinction at some far future time'; he could not imagine Lawrence's break back through the primitive to almost complete sexual liberty. 'Almost', because the effort of Lawrence's rejection of 'civilisation' meant that the pre-civilised and natural that he had discovered became associated for him with the 'savage' and 'unnatural'. He had not overcome his psychical impotence, and turned increasingly for fulfilment to relationships with father-figure men, that he could never wholly accept.

Four considerable bodies of work grow immediately from this experience: the 'Study of Thomas Hardy', the travel-essays, *Twilight In Italy*, the revised short-story collection, *The Prussian Officer*, and the culmination of all these, *The Rainbow*.

'The Study of Thomas Hardy' (P 398–516), though containing some extremely penetrating and stimulating criticism of Hardy's fiction is, as Lawrence admitted, almost only incidentally about Hardy, and is chiefly concerned with Lawrence's own 'philosophy' as applied to Hardy's novels. He analyses the characters' sexual motives, that manifest their true selves, and distinguishes between the pseudo-tragedy of the individual's conflict with convention, and the true tragedy of the conflict with nature, that is, primary being, the living body of preconscious impulse:

What is the great tragic, power in the book? It is Egdon Heath. . . . It is the primitive, primal earth, where the instinctive life heaves up. There, in the deep, rude stirrings of the instincts, there was the reality that worked the tragedy. Close to the body of things, there can be heard the stir that makes us and destroys us. . . . Here is the sombre, latent power that will go on producing, no matter what happens to the produce. Here is the deep, black source from whence all these little contents of lives are drawn. And the contents of the small lives are spilled and wasted. There is savage satisfaction in it: for so much more remains to come, such a black powerful fecundity is working there that what does it matter? (P 415)

Out of the great mother comes the individual being, that will eventually be swallowed up again by primary nature; out of the dark unconscious mass springs, in the characteristic Lawrentian pattern, bright single being, that each individual must fulfil and that 'civilisation' and mental consciousness would hinder.

Man has a purpose which he has divorced from the passionate purpose that issued him out of the earth into being. (P 415) The final aim is the flower . . . the final aim of every living thing, creature or being is the full achievement of itself. This accomplished, it will produce what it will produce, it will bear the fruit of its nature. Not the fruit, however, but the flower is the culmination and the climax ... (P 403)

Life consists in the interaction between the forces of change and the underlying forces of stability and inertia. In this essay Lawrence produces a pattern that would strike most people as normal, but is totally uncharacteristic of Lawrence, and almost the only instance in his writings:[2]

the Will-to-Motion and the Will-to-Inertia ... cause the whole of life. ... And the Will-to-Motion we call the male will or spirit, the Will-to-Inertia the female. This will to inertia is not negative, and the other positive. Rather, according to some conception, is Motion negative and Inertia, the static, geometric idea, positive. (P 348)

Normally for Lawrence the male body contains the unknown, while woman is intellectually active. The change at this time is probably due to his recent discovery in Frieda. The stillness is central, activity is peripheral—'The rapid motion of the rim of the wheel is the same as the perfect rest at the centre of the wheel' (P 448) (cf. 'Blueness' CP 136)—and this still centre underlies the duality of the male and female principles, appearing only in their perfect relation:

When the two are working in combination as they must in life, there is, as it were, a dual motion, centrifugal for the male, fleeing abroad, away from the centre, outward to infinite vibration, and centripetal for the female, fleeing in to the eternal centre of rest. A combination of the two movements produces a sum of motion and stability at once, satisfying. (P 514)

Comparison of this passage with that from the 'Introduction to *New Poems*' and 'Moony' (quoted above) reveals the sexual reverse. In this essay, however, the male principle is associated with the principle of 'Love'—that is, spirit, intellect, transcendence and sublimation (all originally and more profoundly associated with his mother)—while the female is associated with the principle of 'the Law' —the body, instinct, incarnation and immanence (qualities of his father).

Lawrence applies the relationship of these two principles to his historical myth. The Old Testament era he describes as the rule of the Law, with a Monistic father-God as 'the God of the body, the rudimentary God of physical laws and physical functions' (P 450), while the New Testament and Christian era is the rule of Love, the acknowledgment of separation and separate identity. Lawrence repeats this contrast within the Christian era, with the post-Renaissance Church

embodying organic unification. The description of the Cathedrals
links with 'The Cathedral' (*The Rainbow* VII):

It was the profound, sensuous desire and gratitude which produced an art of
architecture, whose essence is in utter stability, of movement resolved and
centralised, of absolute movement, that has no relationship with any other
form, that admits the existence of no other form, but is conclusive, pro-
pounding in its sum the One Being of All. (P 454)

Here the gargoyles are presented as the onset of Renaissance multiplicity and individuality, while in the novel they are partly a feminine
rationalism and criticism, and partly the element of the grotesque and
perverse, that would degrade any absolute principle. The thought in
the fiction is always more profound and complex (though often less
complicated) than in the discursive essays.

Lawrence emphasises the need for acceptance of active inter–relationship between both principles in a culture and in an individual:

A man who is well balanced between male and female, in his own nature, is,
as a rule, happy, easy to mate, easy to satisfy, and content to exist . . .

True balance sounds much like the principle of inertia.

It is only a disproportion or a dissatisfaction, which makes the man struggle
into articulation. And the articulation is of two sorts, the cry of desire or
the cry of realisation, the cry of satisfaction, the effort to prolong the sense
of satisfaction to prolong the moment of consummation. (P 460)

The self-consciousness of life and even art are the products of sexual
struggle, whether between individuals, or within an individual over
his sexual identification; from this ecstatic pain, both life and art strive
to return to calm and silence (so that in Lawrence's last novel, *Lady
Chatterley's Lover*, there appear the motifs of restful chastity, and
the rejection of elaborated speech in favour of basic speech, and even
silence). At this stage, Lawrence felt the problem of his sexual imbalance very keenly—as is suggested by a letter of 1913:

I should like to know why nearly every man that approaches greatness
tends to homosexuality, whether he admits it or not: so that he loves the
body of a man better than the body of a woman . . . it is the hardest thing
in life to get one's soul and body satisfied from a woman, so that one is free
from oneself. And one is kept by all tradition and instinct from loving men
or a man—for it means just extinction of all the purposive influences.
(CL 251)

This love seemed to him to wear a gargoyle face, until he was able to
sublimate it into 'impersonal activity'. Here, only the balance and
union between male and female is seen as purposive, creating Truth,
as Lawrence suggests in his account of a Raphael painting:

This column must always stand for the male aspiration, the arch or ellipse for the female completeness containing this aspiration. And the whole picture is a geometric symbol of the consummation of life . . .

And by the symbol by which Raphael expresses this moment of consummation is by a dark, strong shaft or column leaping up into, and almost transgressing a faint, radiant inclusive ellipse. (P 460)

The second description is less 'balanced' between the two principles; while he concludes with the vision of arched harmony towards which *The Rainbow* strives, the dark shaft has more power; the word 'transgressing' also invites speculation. The essay elaborates a theory of the 'male-female duality' as the condition of life, but the rule of the 'Holy Ghost' that the coming age will produce, the nonhuman quality pent up beneath such painful struggle, seems closer to one element of the proposed duality, that is, unconscious male power in the amoral dark body.

The struggle with dualism, and the attempt at resolution, are the concerns (almost respectively) of *Twilight In Italy*, and the collection, *The Prussian Officer*. *Twilight In Italy* (1916) is more than a series of travel sketches—though the quality of life in various places and people is brilliantly evoked—but embodies Lawrence's main concerns of the time; while what he sees remains intensely real and vivid, it also provides a focus for the exploration of various dualisms, particularly that between sublimation and savage sensuality.

The first and last chapters, set in the Alpine country, frame the rest of the work. In the first, the carved 'folk-art' crucifixes set up in the mountains are the centre of a dualistic scheme. On the one hand are the terrifying cold white mountains, 'the radiant negation of eternity', absolute death in life, that offer 'immunity from the flux and warmth of life', and embody 'the radiant cold which waits to receive back again all that which has passed for the moment into being'. On the other is the hot valley of sensuality:

. . . endless heat and rousedness of physical sensation which keeps the body full and potent, and flushes the mind with a blood heat, a blood sleep. And this sleep, this heat of physical experience becomes at length a bondage, at last a crucifixion. (I)

This is the crucifixion that Lawrence is imaginatively undergoing: the assault by a terrifying and unacceptable (even if only imaginary) sensuality. Two of the crucifixes are of particular power and importance. The first presents the consequences of conquest by brutal, savage passion:

The eyes look at one, yet have no seeing in them, they seem to see only their own blood . . . the heavy body defiled by torture and death. . . . The shrine . . . was a centre of worship, of a sort of almost obscene worship . . . an unclean spirit . . . and the white gleam on the mountain-tops was a glisten of supreme, cynical horror. (I)

The second, broken, with arms dangling upside down, blown through by the icy wind, presents the desolation of denied feeling in an emaciated and unused body. The experience the chapter is concerned with is clearly not even an excess of normal sexuality, but something abnormal and even perverse. The extremes for Lawrence are complete withdrawal from life into sterile isolation, and indulgence and self-destruction in the most degenerate sensuality, which for him was homosexuality.

The next 'chapter' is in seven parts; the first provides a further exploration and attempted solution of the conflict, through repeated metaphors and images of high and low, light and dark, sun and moon. Thus there are two kinds of church architecture: the Churches of the Eagle, the spirit of arrogance and self-assertion, and the Churches of the Dove, the spirit of self-abnegation. With the latter he is not concerned, but with the duality within the church of San Tommaso, 'the world of the eagle, the world of fierce abstraction'. High above the world, like the icy mountains of the first chapter, it produces, like them, its opposite equivalent, an overheated, unnatural sensuality: inside, it is dark, 'like the lair of some enormous creature', evoking 'the contiguity of the physical world . . . the heavy, suggestive substance of the enclosure . . . a thick, fierce darkness of the senses'. This vocabulary is particularly associated, elsewhere in Lawrence's writings, with the anal-excremental, and with homosexuality.

Escaping from this perversity, Lawrence sees outside a clear allegory: the high snowy mountains above, the earth between, and the blue lake below, imaging the sky. Also blue, between the two extremes, is a cloth hung on a wall by an old woman, who is somewhat reminiscent of Wordsworth's leech-gatherer in 'Resolution and Independence', being 'clean and sustained like an old stone upon the hillside . . . slightly more animated than the sunshine and the stone and the motionless caper-bush above her'. She is untroubled by any equivalent of his agony between dualities, being completely unselfconscious; as such, she is in her innocent serenity a sun that obliterates Lawrence, who is now imaged as a night-creature of self conscious perversity.

Leaving her, he scrambles down a Coleridgean water-gorge into a little underworld, 'a complete shadowless world of shadow' where the sunshine of normality seems far away; afraid that he will be benighted here, 'groping about like an otter in the damp and darkness' (a favourite image of subhuman psycho-sexual activity) he struggles up to contemplate the sun-world again. Here allegorical intent so perverts realism that he states that, at four in the afternoon, there are no shadows, but only 'pure sun-substance travelling on the surface of the sun-made world'.

From the dark depths, to the sunny height; between, is the world of the neuter, that escapes 'crucifixion' by being unaware of the tempting extremes, like the two monks he sees pacing with mechanical regularity in the half-light below; 'the flesh neutralising the spirit, the spirit neutralising the flesh, the law of the average asserted.' This will not do for Lawrence, who is all too aware of the extremes of light and dark that he believes may fuse in ecstasy and blossom like a flower: he gathers an allegorical posy—primroses from the gorge, a daisy of the sun, and periwinkles blue as the old woman's eyes, which were like the sky-reflecting lake—that provides a mundane parallel, and emblem of his art. The old woman's limited perception of potentiality is left behind in another (unfortunately somewhat narcissistic) vision of reconciliation, a superb moon looking sensuously at her vivid reflection in the lake. The essay concludes with a series of rhetorical questions as to the possibility of such ecstatic fusion:

Where in mankind is the ecstasy of light and dark together . . . like two angels embracing in the heavens, like Eurydice in the arms of Orpheus, or Persephone embraced by Pluto? . . . Where is the transcendent knowledge in our hearts, uniting sun and darkness, day and night, spirit and senses? Why do we not know that the two in consummation are one; that each is only a part; partial and alone for ever; but that the two in consummation are perfect, beyond the range of loneliness and solitude? (II, 1)

The essay is a successful, if possibly over-schematised, example of Lawrence's allegorical method, though the resolution of his spirit-sense conflict is only asserted.

The next essay is ostensibly concerned with a withered childless old husband whose old-fashioned lemon-farm is collapsing before the industrial efficiency of the north; this provides the occasion for Lawrence's historico-sexual myth, and a glimpse of his underworld. The darkness of the old man's house initiates thoughts on the darkness of the Italian Catholic soul, that is a consequence of the Renaissance dissociation of sensibility. Apparently the 'primitive, animal nature' of medieval Europe was balanced by its yearning for Christlike spirituality and abstraction. Eventually this attempted 'elimination of the flesh' was too successful, the mind becoming the Light, wholly separate from the Dark body that has been 'eliminated'. The body is possessed by an extreme, perverse and destructive sensuality, such as possesses the modern Italian male. The imagery is directly relevant to *Women in Love*:

Aphrodite, the queen of the senses, she, born of the sea-foam, is the luminousness of the gleaming senses, the phosphorescence of the sea, the senses
become a conscious aim unto themselves. . . . The senses are self-conscious.
. . . They seek the maximum of sensation. . . . The reduction of the flesh,
the flesh reacting upon itself, to a crisis, an ecstasy, a phosphorescent
transfiguration in ecstasy. (II, 2)

This is the mode of Blake's 'Tyger, tyger burning bright In the
forests of the night', whose head is flattened as if mindless, or as if the
consciousness were purely physical: 'at the base of the spinal column,
there is the living will, the living mind of the tiger, there in the
slender loins'. Opposed to this dark dehumanised sensuality is the
equally awful northern mode of self-denial, that replaces the 'pagan'
affirmation, "God is that which is Me", with the 'Christian', "God is
that which is not me". In England, the beheading of Charles I symbolised the destruction of the image of God in man, of the sense of the
complete human being as the microcosm; after this, the self-denying
love principle modulated into deliberate benevolence, and that into
mechanical rationalism and the kind of science that evades human
problems in favour of 'the analysis of the outer self . . . the outer world.
And the machine is the great reconstructed selfless power.' Now, for
modern man, especially Lawrence, neither mindless sensuality nor
disembodied mental activity will suffice, but instead something vaguely
called the Holy Ghost, the Third that converts Duality into the
One.

The essay returns to its setting, in a beautiful description of the old
dark lemon-house, the Italian sensual darkness; at first seeming
coffin-like, it turns into an underworld, a Hades lit by 'burning'
oranges and lemons[3] 'like being under the sea'. This is the primitive
regressive mode of unconscious physical existence, whose daemonic
amoral spirit is more powerful than the world of 'light'. Yet Lawrence
recognises that such sensuality is regressive—the old man seems
monkey-like (disgusting in body, subhuman in spirit). Lawrence
knows that, inhuman as the world of competitive individualism seems,
he must not revert to savagery or primitivism, but struggle with it,
to help change it to the new Jerusalem where he might live.

The debate continues in the next essay, a lively account of a visit to
an Italian theatre to see *Amleto*, that is *Hamlet* (the discussion of which
well stands comparison with that by T. S. Eliot). The play is the
sexual-spiritual tragedy of the adolescence of European civilisation
and of the individual, 'the convulsed reaction of the mind from the
flesh, of the spirit from the self, and reaction from the great aristocratic
to the great democratic principle'. For Lawrence, in the 'pagan'
middle ages the individual's sense of integrated being, of containing

god-head in the flesh, found embodiment in the supreme man, the king. With the Renaissance denial of the flesh for the spiritual-intellectual,

The King, the Father, the representative of the Consummate Self, the maximum of all life . . . he must perish. . . . But Shakespeare was also the thing itself. Hence his horror, his frenzy, his self-loathing.
　　The King, the Emperor is killed in the soul of man, the old order of life is over, the old tree is dead at the root. So said Shakespeare. It was finally enacted in Cromwell. (II, 3)

The tragedy, for Lawrence, displays the effect upon him of his mother's possession, developing his intellectual-spiritual self and frustrating his physical sexual being, so that he cannot identify with nor assume his father's masculine power; without this he cannot fulfil his own identity, so that he has to 'unman' himself, in self-denial or perversity:

The supreme representative, King and Father, is murdered, by the Wife. . . . Yet the women-murderers only represent some ultimate judgment in [Hamlet's] own soul. At the bottom of his own soul Hamlet has decided that the self in its supremacy, Father and King, must die. It is a suicidal decision. . . . To be or not to be King, Father, in the Self supreme? And the decision is, not to be. (II, 3)

In a contemporary letter (that about his 'great religion' of the 'blood, the flesh, as being wiser than the intellect') he wrote,

We cannot *be*. "To be or not to be"—it is the question with us now, by Jove. And nearly every Englishman says "Not to be". So he goes in for Humanitarianism and such-like forms of not-being. The real way of living is to answer to one's wants. (CL 180)

So the Italian actor, no longer the integrated being, cannot grasp his part, but only mouths his words insincerely; he exists only in compromise, 'as equivocal as the monks'. Lawrence concludes by insisting on the need to experience the extremes of feeling, so realising the Holy Ghost that unites the two. The essay then breaks up with a survey of the theatre audience. There is a real father, an aristocratic, hawk-like, mountain-spirit, 'the fierce spirit of the Ego come out of the primal infinite'; in contrast is the dark mass of unconscious male force and physicality, essentially homosexual in feeling, in the group of soldiers. Then there is the outsider, 'with a cat-like lightness and grace, and a certain repulsive, *gamin* evil in his face'. He is a forerunner of a frequent figure in Lawrence's fiction, the embodiment of what he feared to become: the parasitic outsider, perverse, bisexual, selfishly sensual and indifferent. Beyond all these are the sterile clerisy and bourgeoisie; and that is all that Lawrence can see in contemporary society.

The next essays show the interaction between the new mechanical-perverse world, and the old physical peasant life; the old withers, dies, and becomes constrictive, the new uproots and unsettles, both are equally negative. Throughout is the theme of frustration, and the brutalising of the spirit. Two essays are of more than intrinsic interest. 'San Gaudenzio' provides a particular example of the life presented at the beginning of *The Rainbow*, while 'The Dance' illuminates the Dionysiac dancing in 'Continental' (*Women in Love* XXIX).

The last chapter, set in the mountains, sums up the elemental conflict that is destroying man:

The valley beds were like deep graves, the sides of the mountains like the collapsing walls of a grave. The very mountain-tops above, bright with transcendent snow, seemed like death, eternal death . . .

The people under the mountains, they seemed to live in the flux of death, the last strange, overshadowed units of life. Big shadows wave over them, there is the eternal noise of water falling icily downwards from the source of death overhead. . . . There is no flowering or coming to flower, only this persistence, in the ice-touched air, of reproductive life. (IV)

This is the very tone of *Women in Love*, the horror of a doomed culture, the failure to reconcile the spirit with the flesh, the heterosexual with the homosexual, the civilised with the natural, the natural with the savage: 'throes of wonder and vivid feeling throbbing over death' (*Etruscan Places*).

The Prussian Officer (1914) goes further; for a first collection, it contains a remarkable number of successes, but only four can be discussed here—the title story, its companion 'The Thorn in the Flesh', 'Daughters of the Vicar' and 'Odour of Chrysanthemums'. It should be noted that the stories were revised for this collection, so that essentially they belong to Lawrence's second phase, usually seen as initiated by *The Rainbow* (published ten months later).

'Daughters of the Vicar' has been praised for its commentary upon the effects of class upon individuals and their relationships, though the handling of the middle class is somewhat uncertain. While the encounter between the Vicar and Mrs Durant is pungent and humorous, the attack on the Vicar and the monstrous little curate is savage, straining at realism. It is incredible that at this time a Vicar's wife (especially this) should think of the curate as 'a little abortion' (the following words are more realistic: 'She was profoundly thankful to God that all her children were decent specimens.'), while, considering her parents, Miss Louisa has an improbable freedom of thought and action.

Realistic social commentary is transcended in the story of two sisters' choice of husbands. One, Mary, chooses security in submission to an abstract, passionless 'virtue', that in fact fulfils her masochistic-idealistic nature, while the younger, Louisa, demands for herself a passional relationship, real love and self-fulfilment, even at the cost of social exclusion. (The elder makes Frieda's first choice, the younger her second.) For this love Louisa turns to Alfred Durant, a miner's son. The Durants' life parallels that of the Lawrences (whom their name echoes) in the feckless father, the socially aspirant mother, and in Alfred who is sensitive and artistic (his piccolo anticipating *Aaron's Rod*). He suffers from the Oedipal conflict, masturbatorily 'debauching' himself with 'the idea of women', while fearing real women, so that he feels himself 'spiritually impotent' (exactly equivalent to Freud's term). Unable to achieve re-integration through submission to external authority (the Navy), 'he would have given anything for this spontaneity and this blind stupidity [that he imagines in the colliers] which went to its own satisfaction direct'. In the male camaraderie and 'glamour of mystery and adventure' of the coal-mine[4] he reattains physical confidence. The mine-world is described as a 'low black, very dark temple', but it is not diabolic, but amoral, daemonic, a force for integrative life as much as his home, that 'crouched darkly and quietly . . . in a quiet little underworld of its own'.

Mrs Durant, on her death, transfers responsibility for him to Louisa; Louisa's washing of the coal-dust from his back is a crucial scene. In the first version Lawrence merely described sensuousness and embarrassment ('His skin was beautifully white and unblemished, of an opaque, solid whiteness. Miss Louisa flushed to the roots of her hair as she sponged him and saw that his neck and ears had grown flaming red. He was proud, however, because he knew he was so perfectly developed, and in such good condition.'[5]) The more mature, later version goes further, to evoke in the reader Louisa's wondering discovery of impersonal maleness, the mystery of unknowable 'otherness'. Also important is the magnificent scene where Louisa breaks through convention and their inhibitions:

Then suddenly, a sharp pang, like lightning, seared her from head to foot, and she was beyond herself.

"Do you want me to go?" she asked, controlled, yet speaking out of a fiery anguish, as if the words were spoken from her without her intervention. . . . The expression of his face was strange and inhuman. She stood utterly motionless. Then clumsily he put his arms round her, and took her, cruelly, blindly . . . he seemed eternal to her. And all the echo of pain came back into the rarity of bliss, and all her tears came up.

The breaking of inhibition is creative destruction that releases them into a new simple truth and unselfconsciousness, the spark that leaps between the two poles to produce the timeless moment, the Holy Ghost. After this, they are totally committed to each other. The story briefly returns to social commentary, indicating her parents' inhumanity: Louisa and Alfred decide to marry—in a registry office—and to emigrate to Canada (at this stage Lawrence's 'Newfoundland' or dream-land) leaving behind family, society, and some at least of the associated moral conventions.

Even finer in its insight and sensitivity is 'Odour of Chrysanthemums', that reveals, in a comparison of its earlier and later versions, how much Lawrence had developed. The story itself uses the family situation of *Sons and Lovers*, but with a more mature and full sense of the relationship between Lawrence's parents, and of his mother's limitations and loss. The play based on this story-material, *The Widowing of Mrs Holroyd*,[6] shows, despite its memory of Synge's *Riders to the Sea*, Lawrence's originality, and power to create scenes of dramatic conflict, of social comedy, and of ritualistic intensity, and suggests how his drama might have revived the theatre of his time. In the play, the father has a rival who fights him but is also tender towards him— clearly the son-lover who continues his perverse career as late as, say, 'Jimmy and the Desperate Woman'. In this fantasy, and the imbalance of sympathies between mother and father, the play seems less 'mature' than the story.

The story begins with the woman like Mrs Morel in a negative aspect, overwhelmed and 'insignificantly trapped' by a harsh life, and herself 'set', disillusioned, and determined to do her sour duty. When her little boy pulls at the chrysanthemum bush, scattering its petals, she reproves him before breaking off a piece for an adornment. The late essay 'Nottingham and the Mining Country' illuminates this. There Lawrence asserts that mining work developed for the men the 'physical, instinctive and intuitional being' of which one manifestation was a genuine, rather contemplative love of flowers. By contrast, the materialistic egotistic women

love flowers, as possessions, and as trimmings. . . . If they see a flower that arrests their attention, they must at once pick it, pluck it. Possession! A possession! Something added on to me! . . . possession and egoism. (P 137)

In that essay the two modes of being are suggested, that operate in this story: male and female, dark and light, reverence and possession, intuition and reason, living death and dead life.

Later, when the mother and the children have been waiting impatiently for the husband's return from the mine, her grumbles are overlaid with an unconscious, portentous irony. 'He'll come home when they carry him. . . . He can lie on the floor . . . I know he'll not go to work tomorrow after that'—these are prophecies fulfilled not by drunkenness, but by death. Her daughter admires her flower adornment, but the mother rejects romanticism:

". . . not to me. It was chrysanthemums when I married him, and chrysanthemums when you were born, and the first time they brought him home drunk he'd got brown chrysanthemums in his button-hole."

Chrysanthemums are involved in her whole life, and now with death also; but Lawrence is concerned to show that 'life' and 'death' are not what she had thought, nor as different as they might seem.

When his body is brought home, it is stripped and washed (for the last time), in the ritual that brings confrontation with the 'other', with reality. The late work, 'A Propos of *Lady Chatterley's Lover*' (1930) is relevant:

The tragic consciousness has taught us, even, that one of the greater needs of man is a knowledge and experience of death . . . the greatest need of man is the renewal forever of the complete rhythm of life and death. . . . We *must* get back into relation, vivid and nourishing relation, to the cosmos and the universe. The way is through daily ritual, and the re-awakening. (P2 510)

Washing the pit-dirt off the unmarked body, she relives her married life, and discovers the reality beneath the superficial. In the early version, she only remembers the youth he had betrayed and lost:

The beauty of his youth, of his eighteen years, of the time when life had settled on him, as in adolescence it settles on youth, bringing a mission to fulfil and equipment therefor, this beauty shone almost unstained again. It was this adolescent "he", the young man looking round to see which way, that Elizabeth had loved. . . . He betrayed himself. . . . He sought the public-house, where, by paying the price of his own integrity, he found amusement . . . little by little the recreant maimed and destroyed himself.

Here still is Mummy's little prig; in the later version the insight has changed, as the woman realises how she had denied her man, through thinking that consciousness was the only reality, and how he had been in life, as now in death, unknown and unknowable:

. . . the wife felt the utter isolation of the human soul . . . was this what it had all meant—utter, intact separateness, obscured by heat of living? . . . she knew she had never seen him, he had never seen her, they had met in the dark and fought in the dark, not knowing whom they met nor whom they fought. And now she saw. . . . She had said he was something he was not; she had felt familiar with him. Whereas he was apart all the while, living as she never lived, feeling as she never felt.

Beneath the surface of living individuality and action is the dark body of life, the impersonal true being, the non-human unliving source of life, where 'death' and 'life' are not opposites but are one. The letter of autumn 1913, quoted above, is relevant here. Discussing 'the eternal stillness that lies under all movement', Lawrence says he has found it in himself:

So much one has fought and struggled, and shed so much blood and made so many scars and disfigured oneself. But all the time there is the unscarred and beautiful in me, even an unscarred and beautiful body. And there is a glimpse of it everywhere, in somebody, at some moment—a glimpse of the eternal and unchangeable that they are. (CL 242)

Yet it can be seen that the woman's insight and acceptance are still limited, incomplete:

. . . she fastened the door of the little parlour, lest the children should see what was lying there. Then, with peace sunk heavy on her breast, she went about making tidy the kitchen. She knew she submitted to life, which was her immediate master. But from death, her ultimate master, she winced with fear and shame.

The reality and power of what is suppressed by conscious living appear in the other two stories, that cannot be dismissed briefly as immature, 'in an early Lawrence vein that he soon outgrew, sultrily overcharged. . . .' Their 'disturbing sensuous intensity' and 'psychological insight'[7] are part of Lawrence at his most penetrating.

'The Prussian Officer' is about more than militarism and homosexuality, though the officer displays a perversity that includes the homosexual.[8] His hostility is directed against the unselfconsciousness and 'natural completeness' in his young orderly, who as a result is thrown into 'a chaos of sensations', feeling that he and the officer are the 'only two people in the world'. The officer's physical assault (a displaced sexual assault) is less important than the psychological one, when he attempts to force the young man to expose and articulate his feelings (for his girl), in an attempt to 'possess' the young man. The later essay on Poe is relevant here:

The lust of hate is the inordinate desire to consume and unspeakably possess the soul of the hated one, just as the lust of love is the desire to possess, or be possessed by, the beloved, utterly. . . . Inquisition and torture are akin to murder: the same lust. It is a combat between inquisitor and victim as to whether the inquisitor shall get at the quick of life itself, and pierce it. (SCAM 82–3)

The young orderly's murderous counterattack on the man who has destroyed his unselfconsciousness serves only to complete his isolation in a new and frightful world. In his delirium (a simple device for handling intense awareness and symbolism) he feels outside the familiar world of normality: 'nothing . . . could give him back his living place in the hot bright morning'; the forest he wanders through deliquesces into the supernatural: 'golden-green glitterings and tall, purple-grey shafts'. He feels he has broken through into a hidden reality:

It was peace. . . . Was it life, or not life? He was by himself. They were on a big, bright place, those others, and he was outside . . . here, in the darkened open beyond, where each thing existed alone. But they would have to come out there sometime. . . . He was conscious of a sense of arrival. He was amid the reality, on the real, dark bottom. . . . The world was a ghastly shadow, thrown for a moment upon the pure darkness, which returned over whole and complete.

The young man has been destroyed by the clash of mighty opposites that was the theme of *Twilight in Italy*, becoming like the crucifix of 'the strong, virile life overcome by physical violence', where 'forbidden' passion brings awareness of nonhuman reality.

Less powerful and successful is 'The Thorn in the Flesh'. Like Arthur Durant, young Bachman has attempted to resolve his inner shame and conflict by submission to military discipline, and as in 'The Prussian Officer', the young man's 'dark enclosure' of anxiety is contrasted with the vivid natural world (and the icy mountains of impossible perfection). Forced to climb a high siege ladder, he is terrified; his will cannot control his body—specifically his bladder. Hauled up and abused, he 'involuntarily' strikes the officer, knocking him into the moat below, and runs away, 'free': 'He couldn't bear his shamed flesh to be put again between the hands of authority.' The will cannot suppress the spirit and the flesh into conformity: the climb up the ladder and the failure of control provide an obvious sexual metaphor.

The second part of the story shows the young man as the guilty outsider, fragmented in his being:

Within his own flesh burned and smouldered the restless shame. He could not gather himself together. There was a gap in his soul. The shame within him seemed to displace his strength and his manhood.

In the early version of the story ('Vin Ordinaire') his love-making with his girl is also a failure, confirming the impossibility of sexual fulfilment and integration. The difference is partly due to Lawrence having learnt, like Tom Brangwen in *The Rainbow*, that there is someone there beside himself: a whole section of the story is now devoted to 'creating' the girl, defining her sincerity and sexually

c

subdued nature against the other, sexually aggressive girls, especially the governess.

In her quiet room, with its crucifix creating a 'religious' atmosphere, he is restored into 'another world'. When she comes into the room, making no demands upon him, he can relax his conscious will:

As if in a spell she waited . . . he sat rather crouching on the side of the bed. A second will in him was powerful and dominating. She drew gradually nearer . . .

Physical self-consciousness is lost in a

furious flame of passion. . . . He buried his face into . . . the terrible softness of her belly . . . his hands spread over her loins, warm as flame on her loveliness. It was intense anguish of bliss.

This is not just 'passion'. Here he partly seeks a maternal comfort, and also, in his grasp on what Lawrence calls her 'loins', he lays hands on what lies behind her sexuality and personality, to achieve awareness of human physical being, and can accept what had seemed to him shameful. Acceptance of the inseparability of the sexual and excremental, of the wholeness of physical being, produces a new strength and self-confidence; the young man can now accept himself: "What I am, I am; and let it be enough." After this, the military authorities can only possess 'the shell of his body', while 'a curious silence, a blankness, like something eternal, possessed him. He remained true to himself,' to the core of physical being discovered in that embrace.

In these stories which, in their revised form, mark the beginning of the 'true', unmuffled Lawrence, conventional understanding of morality, personality and even life are transcended in search of the dark reality buried in the body, where consciousness, individuality and sexuality are absorbed in the nonhuman source of life. In his essay 'Love' he wrote:

There is that which we cannot love, because it surpasses love or hate. There is the unknown and unknowable, which propounds all creation. This we cannot love, we can only accept it as a term of our own limitations and ratification. (P 136)

II

THE RAINBOW

Completing *The Rainbow* (1915) in Cornwall, in the early years of the war, Lawrence was caught up in revolutionary dreams of a renewed England; these visions and the contrast with the reality of a war-fevered people both influenced the nature of the novel. One could imagine how the saga of a Midland family, through three generations, from inarticulate farmer to rootless schoolteachers, might have been treated by Galsworthy or Bennett. Though Lawrence presents a view of the development of English society in the period approximately 1840–1905, from a dream of pastoral community where industrialism is literally only on the horizon to a nightmare of industrialism, capitalism and competitive individualism, his concern is with three couples' engagement in what he sees as the essential struggle for a satisfactory relationship, both between the man and the woman, and between the male principle (physical-intuitive-unitive) and the female principle (idealistic-rational-individualistic). The story-method is one of repetition with variation, as is the style. What he wrote of the sequel *Women in Love* is relevant here:

In point of style, fault is often found with the continual, slightly modified repetition. The only answer is that it is natural to the author: and that every natural crisis in emotion or passion or understanding comes from this pulsing frictional to-and-fro, which works up to culmination. (P2 276)

The sexual implications of this account are apparent: style and content are closely identifiable. It is largely through the style that 'the old, stable *ego* of the character' is broken down, so that individual characters and experiences are dissipated in the analytic presentation of the central, recurrent experience, following that of Lawrence himself. The sense of the unconscious, impersonal forces directing the characters is produced by a variety of devices: the use of recurrent symbols and images; the rainbow-arch, the doorway, sun and moon light and dark, animals and birds, and phrases such as 'seething', 'fragmented', 'chaotic', 'shadowy', etc. Another related technique is the unspecificity of time and place, so that developing relationships are presented through a few fragmentary dramatised scenes with little or no time-place context, set in longer passages that present the feelings of the characters (often impersonalised into 'he' or 'she') through figurative language. Objective, external reality is submerged into the subjective.

Rhetorical repetition is affective rather than informative. The use of apparently redundant connectives, such as 'And', 'But', 'For', 'So', serves to imply significant relationship between events and experiences of different kinds, where none has been made explicit. Verbs like 'must' and 'would' are used ambiguously, so that it is not easy to distinguish between conscious volition and unconscious, impersonal compulsions. The use of Biblical (chiefly Old Testament) parallels is also important, as in the rainbow itself, the suggestion that Tom and Lydia are like Adam and Eve, or that Tom is like Noah; the Biblical parallel suggests that *The Rainbow* covers a movement from a quasi-Edenic, pastoral world, to the end of a world, and the vision of a new world to come.

The book begins with a beautiful sensuous lyricism, establishing Lawrence's male and female duality. It is the men who have the physical intuitive blood-intimacy with nature, that leaves their intellect 'inert', while it is the women, looking up to the church and city beyond, who aspire to the development of the mind and individualism. The first Brangwen couple are in a harmonious relationship with each other —'two separate beings, vitally connected, knowing nothing of each other, yet living in their separate ways from one root' (I)—but already the unsettling effect of the mechanical spirit is apparent: the winding engines' noise is 'a narcotic to the brain', and the train's whistle is responded to with 'fearsome pleasure'.

The story proper begins with Tom Brangwen, who has much in common with Lawrence, being the fourth son (Lawrence was the fourth child), whose mother-love has inhibited his emotional and sexual development; the opportunity for sensuous and imaginative fulfilment comes through meeting a foreign woman, Lydia Lensky, a widowed mother six years older than himself (he is twenty-eight— Lawrence's age when he met Frieda; Lawrence's mother's name was Lydia). Lawrence well conveys the attraction between Tom and his 'Persephone', instinctive and unreasonable, a 'fearsome pleasure'. Particularly fine is the account of his visit to propose to her, when he stands outside in the passionate stormy darkness contemplating the image of Mother and Child, before entering like an inhuman force, an 'invasion from the night . . . a man come for her'. Her acceptance, and their embrace, is a death and rebirth: 'their new life came to pass, it was beyond all conceiving good, it was so good that it was almost like a passing-away' (I) into unconsciousness and 'death' again.

In their early married life she seems to dominate him, as the Magna Mater, withdrawn into her own mental life or preoccupied with a child. Thus displaced, Tom turns to the little girl Anna: the scenes between them have great freshness and charm. On the birth-night of the second child, Anna, distraught without her mother, is comforted by Tom taking her out into the warm, womb-like barn to see the cattle feeding; in this scene is revealed the deep reassurance and renewal provided by the unconscious, protective body of nature, here associ-ated (as, of course, throughout Lawrence's work) with the father. A more frightening aspect of natural energy appears in the almost inhuman, indifferent and self-absorbed expression of the woman in the extremity of childbirth, and in the great downpour of rain in the night: 'There was the infinite world, eternal, unchanging, as well as the world of life' (III).

Now Tom comes to feel frustrated by his inability to come to terms with his wife, until she challenges his self-centred and straying spirit, demanding that he relate with her and with actuality: "I want you to know there is somebody there besides yourself." She calls him to her, 'the awful unknown', for an embrace directly anticipating Ursula's embrace of Birkin (*Women in Love* XXIII): kneeling before him,

> her eyes . . . shining again like terrible laughter . . . she put her arms around him as he stood before her, round his thighs, pressing him against her breast. And her hands on him seemed to reveal to him the mould of his own naked-ness, he was passionately lovely to himself . . . (III)

This is the anal caress, discussed before, initiating acceptance of the body and of physical reality, followed by entry into the core of the living body of darkness—that is, the new world and new life:

> She put her fingers upon him. And it was torture to him, that he must give himself to her actively, participate in her, that he must meet the embrace and know her, who was other than himself. . . . But he let go his hold on himself, he relinquished himself. . . . The reality of her who just beyond him absorbed him. Blind and destroyed, he pressed forward, nearer, nearer, to receive the consummation of himself, he received within the darkness which should swallow him and yield him up himself. If he could come really within the blazing kernel of darkness, if he could be destroyed, burnt away till he lit with her in one consummation, that were supreme, supreme . . . it was the baptism to another life. . . . The new world was discovered, it remained only to be explored. (III)

The anus provides almost a new womb, from which his new self, or sense of it, can emerge. After this acceptance of the wholeness and independence of each other's flesh, Tom and Lydia can relate to each other, forming a protective arch over Anna who is now released from their emotional demands to fulfil herself.

In the next couple, or stage of development, the polarities are more extreme, the relationship more intense and distorted. As a young girl, Anna dreams of glamorous self-assertion; like Tom, she is excited by a foreigner, Count Skrebensky, but her chance of fulfilment lies in her cousin Will Brangwen, whose intuitive-instinctive being has been somewhat suppressed, making him like 'some mysterious animal that lived in the darkness . . . lived vividly, swift and intense'. A prophetic scene occurs when she laughs at his loud singing in church, partly from sexual excitement and partly in reaction against his unselfconsciousness and mystic sense, which she contrasts with the natural sexuality of 'the lilacs towering in the vivid sunshine outside'. The growth of their passion is evoked in images of intense darkness, with images of hawks for moments of sexual tension and excitement.

When Tom Brangwen sees them kissing in the barn one evening he feels jealous, feeling that his life had amounted to no more than 'the long, marital embrace with his wife', and had lacked 'the further, the creative life' that he imagines Will might achieve.

While young Will possesses some capacity for creative self-fulfilment, as evidenced by his sensual carving of Eve, he is not to achieve real fulfilment with Anna, as is suggested in the great ritualistic scene of the moonlight gathering of the sheaves. The alternate carrying of the sheaves seems like a ritual, mythic pursuit of the bride, with the couple at last united amidst the corn; but it does not work out like that. There is a complete fusion between the characters and their setting, which makes the young people's encounter more than individual, but the confrontation of elemental principles. The actual landscape melts into that created by the images used to evoke their feelings. Anna is possessed by the spirit of the moonlight; in the *Fantasia of the Unconscious* Lawrence writes:

The moon is the centre of our terrestrial individuality in the cosmos. . . . She is the fierce centre of retraction of frictional withdrawal into separateness . . . that cold, proud white fire of furious, almost malignant apartness. . . .

The moon, the planet of women, sways us back from our day-self, sways us back from our real social unison, sways us back, like a retreating tide, in a friction of criticism and separateness and social disintegration. That is woman's inevitable mode, let her words be what they will . . . (*Fantasia*, pp. 147 and 174)

Will's dark impulse towards instinctual union cannot, because of his own insufficiency, overcome this spirit in her, and this failure is crucial. After this, he can never possess her, and indeed his own self-belief is destroyed.

After the beautifully bucolic wedding-scene comes the account of the honeymoon, that superbly evokes how, in Donne's words, 'love . . . makes one little room an everywhere'. Further, it reveals, in the image of the chestnut broken open in the fertilising earth, Will's rebirth as a sensuous being in a new-discovered world. Afterwards comes the reaction, occasioned both by Anna's withdrawal into self-satisfaction and by his possessive hunger for her, that drives her to frenzy; his frustrated passion manifests itself in rages like overwhelming black flood-water (anticipatory of Gerald Crich). Her wish is merely to possessively enjoy his sensuality without submitting to him, so that he feels that 'she jeered at his soul'. Will has a belief in male supremacy that neither his character nor his society permit him to assert. Lawrence indicates perceptively the parallel between his couples' sexual relationship, and social changes: as women achieve greater social liberation, it becomes more difficult for men to fulfil their traditional roles.

The young couple's battle, paralleling that in the early part of *Look! We Have Come Through!*, is between 'feminine' egoistic will and selfconsciousness, and 'male' intuition and unconscious—even subhuman—sensuality. 'They were opposites, not complements', as Anna comes to realise:

> She believed in the omnipotence of the human mind.
>
> He, on the other hand, blind as a subterranean thing, just ignored the human mind and ran after his own dark-souled desires, following his own tunnelling nose. She felt often she must suffocate. And she fought him off. (VI)

Her being belongs in the conventional 'human' world, that asserts the primacy of reason and society, and subordinates the male sensual self to woman. She is, in effect, the Magna Mater again, self-satisfied and concerned with herself as child-bearer, in which he is merely instrumental.

> The rage and storm of unsatisfaction tormented him ceaselessly. Why had she not satisfied him? He had satisfied her. . . . It was for her to satisfy him: then let her do it. Let her not come with flowery handfuls of innocent love. He would throw these aside and trample the flowers to nothing. He would destroy her flowery, innocent bliss. Was he not entitled to satisfaction from her, and was not his heart all raging desire, his soul a black torment of unfulfilment. (VI)

His desire for sensual satisfaction makes him seem to her subhuman, unnatural.

> She wanted to desert him, to leave him a prey to the open, with the unclean dogs of darkness setting on to devour him. He must beat her, and make her stay with him. Whereas she fought to keep herself free from him. (VI)

Here, the rapid shift of viewpoint from one sentence to the next is an example of Lawrence's technique of dissolving mere 'event', to present the submerged conflict. Will's sensuality, when controlled and subservient, is to her merely 'a thrill, crisp as pain, for she felt the darkness and the other-world still in his soft, sheathed hands'. All she wants is 'the joy and the vagueness and the innocence of her pregnancy. She did not want his bitter-corrosive love, she did not want it poured into her, to burn her. Why must she have it? Why, oh why was he not content, contained?' He seems to her like a tiger, waiting to pull her down and devour her body, her 'carcass'. Eventually she defeats him, first in a ritual dance to herself as the principle of maternity, that denies him and his sensual being; his 'kingship' is dispossessed, his daemonic power as an embodiment of male sexuality is overthrown, he is reduced to his mere relative, individual self—'But it was a very dumb, weak, helpless self, a crawling nursling'. The Great Mother reigns supreme in her limited power—limited, because she has denied the sensual fulfilment, 'the adventure to the unknown'. Her spiritual journey seems concluded, and it will be her children, and not Anna, who must pass through the purging fires of passion to the new world.

Her second and conclusive victory is over his faith, his sense of the suprahuman power and integrity of existence, when they visit his 'beloved' Lincoln Cathedral. Just before going to the Cathedral they visit a relative of her mother, Baron Skrebensky, and his new wife, a smooth, perverse creature (imaged—within only two pages!—as a kitten, a ferret, a weasel and a stoat, all associated with degraded sexuality). The atmosphere there of perversity and malignant disintegration of being reinforces Anna's resistance to the organic integrity of the Cathedral's ethos.

The Cathedral expresses the Monistic spirit of the cathedrals described in 'The Study of Thomas Hardy', the dark static fecund unity beneath creation, that is womb and tomb in one. Here Will attains an ecstatic[9] quasi-sexual consummation, in an apprehension of absolute, undifferentiating, consuming being. Anna fearfully clings to rationality and individualism:

she caught at little things, which saved her from being swept forward headlong in the tide of passion that leaps on into the Infinite. (VII)

She responds to the grotesque, leering, gargoyles, that mock and degrade the absolute, and proclaim individual self-assertion in a kind of perversity. In the ensuing quarrel with Will, she is victorious, and his last grasp on his faith in the larger being is destroyed: 'somewhere in him he responded more deeply to the sly little face that knew better, than he had done before to the perfect surge of his cathedral.'

Now, like Tom Brangwen before him, he turns to his daughter for satisfaction, becoming intensely involved with her, awakening her emotional responses too early in her life (as Lawrence's mother did to him). The accounts of his jumping with her into the water, and swinging with her at the fair, both occasions when he pushes as near to death as he dare, reveal how his original desire for union has now become perverted into a desire for possession, the pursuit of extreme sensation even to the point of destruction. He then indulges in the thrills of illicit sexuality with a young girl in Nottingham before transferring this to Anna.

They indulge in pure voluptuousness and sensuality: 'it was all the lust and the infinite, maddening intoxication of the senses, a passion of death'. The passion is purely destructive, denying any integrity of the physical and the 'spiritual' or human in them. They repeat the anal intercourse of the first couple, but in a perverse spirit, relishing their degradation and self-reduction:

It was pure darkness also. All the shameful things of the body revealed themselves now to him with a sort of sinister, tropical beauty. All the shameful natural and unnatural acts of sensual voluptuousness which he and the woman partook of together, created together, they had their heavy beauty and delight. Shame, what was it? It was part of extreme delight. It was that part of delight of which man is usually afraid. Why afraid? The secret, shameful things are [the shift of tense implies authorial approval] most terribly beautiful.

They accepted shame, and were one with it in their most unlicensed pleasures. It was incorporated. It was a bud that blossomed into beauty and heavy, fundamental gratification. (VIII)

'Sensational' sexuality, that does not enhance human dignity, produces only mechanical activity: Will becomes more active socially, in 'public life', but Lawrence does not make this seem significant, or genuinely 'life-enhancing'.

The great flood that follows in the next chapter marks the end of a world; drunken Tom Brangwen does not escape like Noah, but is overwhelmed in 'the black swirling darkness', the 'hoarse, brutal roar of a mass of water rushing downwards', that anticipates the black booming water rushing from the lake after the drowning of Diana Crich in *Women in Love*, that makes Birkin yearn for a love like death, beyond humanity.

Lawrence now turns to Ursula, in whom the spirit of 'woman becoming individual, self-responsible, taking her own initiative' (CL 273) is most apparent. At first her intense romanticism and desire for fulfilment is satisfied by the Christian faith, but eventually she cannot accept the self-abnegation and idealistic sublimation that seemed asked of her. For her, religious and sexual, spiritual and physical fulfilment and salvation must be one. Her text is "The Sons of God saw the daughters of men that they were fair: and they took them wives of all which they chose".[10]

It seems to her that this salvation is offered by young Anton Skrebensky, who appears to have a stimulating 'aristocratic' spirit (associated with separatist self-assertion). Though attracted by the masculine world he represents, she rejects it in so far as it is the amorphous 'social' world. His first caress indicates the disintegration of body and spirit that mars their relationship, when he holds her hand furtively:

And the close-working, instinctive subtlety of his fingers upon her hand sent the girl mad with voluptuous delight. His hand was so wonderful, intent, as a living creature skilfully pushing and manipulating in the dark underworld. . . . In outward attention they were entirely separate. (XI)

Their flirtation repeats the sexually self-assertive struggle of Will and Anna:

And after all, what could either of them get from such a passion but a sense of his or her own maximum self, in contradistinction to all the rest of life? Wherein was something finite and sad, for the human soul at its maximum wants a sense of the infinite. (XI)

So they define themselves in separation; while Ursula seems content with this, Skrebensky's frustrated desire for union makes him oscillate between impulses towards domination and self-annihilation. He is shown to be weaker than she, as in their argument when walking along the canal, with the 'grim seethe of the town' (the perverse appeal of mechanical sensation) on one side, the natural harmony of the country on the other, and 'the blue strip of water-way, the ribbon of sky between'. Under Ursula's relentless questioning it is revealed that Skrebensky has no purpose in life, other than his social function. He is inferior to the coal-dusty moustached bargeman they meet, who has a physical confidence and dignity (the strong father-male, envied by Bachman, Durant and Lawrence, and by Skrebensky who anticipates Birkin in the 'Prologue': 'Why could he not desire a woman so? Why did he never really want a woman, not with the whole of him . . . ?)'.

The next crucial encounter is at a wedding party presided over by her uncle Tom Brangwen, a man with a sensual 'bestial' quality to which Ursula had responded before, at her grandfather's funeral. He embodies a perverse, selfish, disintegrative sensuality, seen when talking to a girl 'chill and burning as the sea . . . making her glint . . . like phosphorescence' (imagery that is further developed later, in this and the next novel).

The couples dance at night in the open before 'two great red, flameless fires' in a scene of hellish glamour, that stimulates the senses and obliterates the consciousness. Dancing, their two individual wills are

locked in one motion, yet never fusing, never yielding one to the other. It was a glaucous, intertwining, delicious flux and contest in flux. . . . It was a vision of the depths of the underworld, under the great flood.

There was a wonderful rocking of the darkness, slowly a great, slow swinging of the whole night, with the music rippling on the surface of the dance, but underneath only one great flood heaving slowly backwards to the verge of oblivion. (XI)

The scene is a direct anticipation of 'Water-party' (*Women in Love* XIV) in its revelation of the inhuman reality beneath consciousness (that here is not integrated with the dark unconscious, but is alternately excited and annihilated). Ursula is awakened by becoming aware of the moon, that calls her out to selfish separation and self-assertion;[11] people seem 'impure', 'dross', her hands like 'metal blades of destruction'. Skrebensky seeks her for his sensual prey, to 'enclose her in a net of shadow, of darkness', but her body seems 'cold, salt-burning', a pillar of salt like Lot's wife, in its destructive-resistant power. The experience is extreme, 'burning and corroding' him until his weaker force is subdued, and, in a metaphor of physically sexual as well as psychological import, the woman absorbs and overpowers the man's body and spirit,

fierce, corrosive, seething with his destruction, seething like some cruel, corrosive salt around the last substance of his being, destroying him. (XI)

After this, both feel a loss of significance in life and in their relationship. Skrebensky goes off to the Boer War, and Ursula forms a Lesbian relationship with her schoolmistress, Winifred Inger, a rationalist feminist: 'It was a strange world the girl was swept into, like a chaos, like the end of the world.' The darkness that Ursula enters with Winifred, in the rainy night at her cottage, is an inversion of natural warm bodily darkness, a negation: 'It made her cold, and a deep, bottomless silence welled up in her, as if bottomless darkness were returning upon her.' Such sensuality is seen as in every way sterile, and Ursula eventually wants to return to normality, and decides to marry Winifred to Tom Brangwen, who is equally perverse. The sprawling, ugly town of Wiggiston, where he lives, presents the 'hard, horny shell' and scabby skin of the lifeless rind of civilisation where human beings are disintegrated into urban copulatives and elements of the industrial machine.

Ursula's reaction is to decide that 'her soul's action should be the smashing of the great machine', and gets her chance when she begins to teach in a school in Wiggiston. This section, based on Lawrence's experience in Croydon, is written in a more naturalistic, less symbolic and closely woven style than the rest of the book. Ursula's attempt fails, and she too becomes a machine operative: 'in school, she was nothing but Standard Five teacher'. Some of the account of her university career is written at equally low pressure; important however is her reaction away from the conscious life, that presumes it has all life pinned down and pressed. It seems to her, in a simile based on the children's games under the lamp in *Sons and Lovers* IV,

like the area under an arc-lamp, wherein the moths and children played in
the security of blinding light, not even knowing there was any darkness,
because they stayed in the light.

But she could see the glimmer of dark movement just out of range, she
saw the eyes of the wild beast gleaming from the darkness, watching the
vanity of the camp fire and the sleepers . . . (XV)

She however is aware of the greater reality of the sensual underworld,
and sees

the gleam in the eyes of the wolf and the hyena, that it was the flash of the
sword of angels, flashing at the door to come in, that the angels in the
darkness were lordly and terrible and not to be denied, like the flash of
fangs. (XV)

Skrebensky, whose return from Africa is announced, seems such a
liberating angel to her, who will release her from the reductive mode
of consciousness, and enable her to be like the 'plant-animal' she is
studying under the microscope, that 'intended to be itself . . . it was a
consummation, a being infinite. Self was a oneness with the infinite.
To be oneself was a supreme, gleaming triumph of infinity.'

The sensuality that Skrebensky now possesses is the product of
his disintegration into a corrupt, subhuman, potent darkness (like
Will's—of which she had been aware):

He talked to her all the while, in low tones, about Africa, conveying something strange and sensual to her: the negro, with his loose, soft passion that
could envelop one like a bath. Gradually he transferred to her the hot,
fecund darkness that possessed his own blood. The whole world must be
abolished . . . there came a silence, whilst they walked the darkness beside
the massive river . . . (XV)

When he possesses her in a kiss, the light of conscious mind is extinguished:

the darkness reigned, and the unutterable satisfaction . . . dark and soft and
incontestable, their bodies walked untouched by the lights, darkness supreme
and arrogant.

"The stupid lights," Ursula said to herself, in her dark sensual arrogance.
"The stupid, artificial, exaggerated town, fuming its lights. It does not exist
really. It rests upon the unlimited darkness, like a gleam of coloured oil
on dark water, but what is it?—nothing, just nothing." (XV)

They have lost their human, social, selves, acquiring a leopard-like
sensual vitality. When he at last takes her, under a great oak tree
roaring and vibrating in the passionate night wind, she is possessed
not by his human self, but by 'the indifferentiated man he was', a 'dark
powerful vibration that encompassed her'; 'She entered the dark fields

of immortality.' Yet, for all this sensual rebirth, there is still no unity between 'spirit' and 'flesh' in him or in their relationship, and she begins to reject him again, returning to moon-separateness.

Their final, crucial encounter—one of the most powerful scenes in the book—takes place by 'the salt, bitter indifference of the sea', under a blaze of moonlight that blasts them like an icy furnace. She becomes a 'beaked harpy' using and devouring the male body, in the feminine sexual self-assertion that Mellors was to complain of in *Lady Chatterley's Lover*.[13] While she is temporarily dehumanised in her destruction of the insufficient representative of male darkness, yet this horrific encounter exhausts her involvement in disintegrative sexuality. She has been to the extreme limit, there is no farther to go, and so she is prepared to some extent for her eventual consummation with Birkin in *Women in Love*.[14]

After Armageddon comes death and rebirth. This comes after a period of exhaustion and apathy, when she is chased by a herd of horses. Relevant here is a passage from *Fantasia of the Unconscious* (pp. 154–5) where Lawrence discusses a man dreaming of such an attack by horses. There, the physical being and passion embodied in the horses is feared by the conscious, 'social', self, but is fundamentally desired on the deepest levels of being. In so far as this is a male sexual power, it is not surprising that Lawrence should fear a quasi-homosexual submission to it. For Ursula, the meaning has to be extended to include a subhuman sensuality, to which she had been exposed by Skrebensky's corrupt power. Climbing the hedge with hands 'hard as steel' (slightly more positive, perhaps, than her earlier 'blades' and 'talons') she escapes destruction, and proceeds exhaustedly along the high-road, protected by the hedges, but almost nullified.

After these extreme experiences she has acquired a fuller self-understanding and awareness of her potentialities; she has broken out of the constricting shell of separation and half-being, and the new plant is ready to seek 'Eternity in the flux of Time'. She has a vision of new life, like that expressed in the essay 'The Crown':

. . . new-born on the knees of darkness, new issued from the womb of creation, I open my eyes and know the goal, the end, the light which stands over the end of the journey, the everlasting day, the oneness of the spirit . . .
My source and issue is in two eternities, I am founded in the two infinities. But absolute is the rainbow that goes between; the iris of my being. (P2 378)

The world of men she sees around her seems dead, still enclosed in a 'horny cover of disintegration'. This is not mere nullity, but the crust over corrupt existence, out of which—and if not from there, from nowhere—new life must grow:

Corruption will at last break down for us the deadened forms, and release us into the infinity. ('The Crown', P2 403)

This is the paradox towards which *The Rainbow* moves, and which *Women in Love* will explore more fully. The later book has a white-hot intensity that purges away the 'dross' of realistic writing and (comparative) inhibition that occasionally clogs *The Rainbow*, to focus on the essential paradox of the life-potentiality in corruption. *The Rainbow* seems closer to the original, probably less complex, intention of *The Sisters*; as it is, the concluding vision of the rainbow rooted upon earth remains a fine, but not wholly convincing, rhetorical flourish.

1. '. . . I am often frightened at the thing I find myself' (1912; LH 43).

2. Except in the letter where he insists that we must 'get our souls fertilised by the *female*' (by which he means the physical-intuitive) to enable the 'getting of a vision' of 'the *non-human* quality of life' (CL 291).

3. cf. Andrew Marvell's 'orange bright, Like a golden lamp in a green night', in 'Bermudas', also concerned with an impossible dream of rediscovered sensual innocence.

4. cf. 'Nottingham and the Mining Country', (P 133–40, esp. pp. 135–6).

5. For this, and the passage from 'Odour of Chrysanthemums' quoted below, see the stimulating article by J. F. C. Littlewood, 'D. H. Lawrence's Early Tales', *The Cambridge Quarterly*, spring 1966, vol. 1, no. 2.

6. *The Complete Plays of D. H. Lawrence* (London, 1965), pp. 9–62.

7. F. R. Leavis, *D. H. Lawrence: Novelist*, chs 2 and 7 (Peregrine ed., 1964), pp. 75 and 257.

8. 'Inquisitions [are] all sexual in origin. And soldiers, being herded together, men without women, never being *satisfied* by a woman, as a man never is from a street affair, get their surplus sex and their frustration and dissatisfaction into the blood, and *love* cruelty. It is sex hurt fermented makes atrocity' (CL 156).

9. '. . . there is no real truth in ecstasy. All vital truth contains the memory of all that for which it is not true. Ecstasy achieves itself by virtue of exclusion; and in making any passionate exclusion, one has already put one's right hand in the hand of the lie' (CL 300).

10. Discussing how the horse is mankind's symbol of 'godhead in the flesh', Lawrence points out, 'The sons of men who came down and knew the daughters of men and begot the great Titans, they had "the members of horses"', says Enoch' (*Apocalypse* 110).

11. cf. Jessie Chambers' account of the effect upon Lawrence of the combination of moonlight and sea: 'I was really frightened then—not physically, but deep in my soul. He created an atmosphere not of death which after all is part of mortality, but of an utter negation of life, as though he had become dehumanised.' E. T., *D. H. Lawrence, A Personal Record* (1935), pp. 127–8.

12. cf. 'The Crown', where Lawrence discusses the inter-relationship of sensationalism and social disintegration, where the angels of perversity 'cleave

asunder, terrible and invincible. With cold, irresistible hands they put us apart, they send like unto like, darkness unto darkness. They thrust the seas backward from embrace, backward from the locked strife. They set the cold phosphorescent flame of light flowing back to the light, and cold heavy darkness flowing back to the darkness' (P2, 389).

13. cf. H. M. Daleski, *The Forked Flame*, ch. V, pp. 291–2 (London, 1965).

14. 'I *must* have Ella [Ursula's original name] get some experience before she meets her Mr Birkin' (CL 263).

3

DIES IRAE

I

'THE SPIRIT OF DESTRUCTION IS DIVINE'[1]

In a letter of 1917 Lawrence wrote that *The Rainbow* was not materially affected by the war, but that he knew as he

revised the book, that it was a kind of working up to the dark sensual or Dionysic or Aphrodisic ecstasy, which does actually burst the world, burst the world-consciousness in every individual. . . . But alas, in the world of Europe I see no Rainbow. I believe the deluge of iron will destroy the world here, utterly: no Ararat will rise above the subsiding iron waters. There is a great *consummation* in death, or sensual ecstasy, as in *The Rainbow*. But there is also death which is the rushing of the Gadarene swine down the slope of extinction. . . .

Women in Love . . . actually does contain the results in one's soul of the war: it is purely destructive, not like *The Rainbow*, destructive-consummating. (CL 519)

He interpreted what he observed in the spirit of Apocalypse; in a well-known letter of 1915 he described a Zeppelin raid[2] as like

war in heaven. But it was not angels. It was that small golden Zeppelin, like a long oval world, high up. It seemed as if the cosmic order were gone, as if there had come a new order, a new heaven above us. . . . So it is the end— our world is gone, and we are like dust in the air. . . . But there must be a new heaven and a new earth . . . there remains only to take on a new being. (CL 336)

The world was decomposing, and the organic implications of this metaphor suggest that this death and corruption were the natural condition for new life. In 1915, he wrote to Bertrand Russell:

After this we shall know the change, we shall really move back in one movement to the sun. Except a seed die, it bringeth not forth. . . . Our death must
be accomplished first, then we will rise up. (CL 346)

So Lawrence saw death as ambivalent, like corruption and disintegration; all three were essential for rebirth. The paradoxes implicit
in this were acted out in *Women in Love* and treated discursively in the
essays of the time, notably 'The Crown' and 'The Reality of Peace'.
These show a development from the 'Study of Thomas Hardy' in
an increasing concern with what is fundamental to, or transcends,
duality—that is, the third element or 'Holy Ghost', where positive
and negative, light and dark, life and death are indistinguishable.

While 'The Crown' (1915; P2 365–415) is obscurer than the later
essay, it is the more exploratory and vivid. Beginning with the nursery-
rhyme Lion and Unicorn, Lawrence rapidly modulates 'the king of
beasts' and 'the defender of virgins' into the familiar male-female,
flesh-spirit duality, whose struggle serves to uphold the crown of life.
Struggle is the condition of life, but true being transcends this dualistic
conflict, is absolute, timeless, and the opposite of life:

The act of death may itself be a consummation, and life may be a state of
negation. It may be that our state of life is our nullification, our not-being.
. . . This I, which I am, has no being save in timelessness. In my consummation, when that which came from the Beginning and that which came from
the End are transfused into oneness, then I come into being, I have existence.
Till then, I am only a part of nature; I am not. (P2 383–4)

Lawrence depends on the paradox that he who would save his life
must lose it. Those who let themselves go into 'the flux of creation'
lose their individuality in a larger being. Those who hold on to egoistic
self-consciousness, contained in a hard shell of separateness, are caught
instead in the 'flux of corruption'. Then life-fulfilling energy becomes
redirected into material and social activity; no real union with others
is possible, merely a frictional sensationalism or a conglomeration into
an amorphous mass, a larger unit.

We are a wincing mass of self-consciousness and corruption, within our
plausible rind. The most unselfish, the most humanitarian of us all, he is
the hollowest and fullest of rottenness. The more rotten we become, the
more insistent and insane becomes our desire to ameliorate the conditions
of our poorer, and maybe healthier neighbours. (P2 387)

This is the spirit of the elder Mr Crich. The cult of individuality and
personality seems to Lawrence to be socially disintegrative, productive
only of competitiveness, self-consciousness, and perversity of feeling,[3]
whether sexual or mental, as in sentimentalism or aestheticism.

Within the glassy, mill envelope of the enclosure . . . ego reacts upon ego only in friction. . . . And then, when a man seeks a woman, he seeks not a consummation in union, but a frictional reduction . . . in supreme sensual experience. . . . There remains only the reduction of the contact with death. So that as the sex is exhausted, gradually a keener desire, the desire for the touch of death follows. (P2 398)

However, if the pursuit of absolute experience is taken to the extreme, beyond the conventional restraints imposed by self-consciousness and society, a new ecstasy and inhuman vitality is attained; opposite extremes meet:

The spirit of destruction is divine, when it breaks the ego and opens the soul. . . . In the soft and shiny voluptuous of decay, in the marshy chill heat of reptiles, there is the sign of the Godhead. It is the activity of departure. And departure is the opposite equivalent of coming-together; decay, corruption, destruction is the opposite equivalent of creation. In infinite going-apart there is revealed again the pure absolute, the absolute relation. (P2 402)

The ambiguities in such words as 'dissolution, corruption, reduction' are central to Lawrence's thought here and in *Women in Love*. 'Reduction' may mean simply simplification, or diminution of quantity, but it can also mean (as in cookery) an intensification in quality brought about by the diminution of quantity; 'corruption' can mean a breaking-down into union—co-ruption; 'dissolution' can also imply a melting into union.

The 'divinity' of extreme sensation and sensuality is evoked in images central to *Women in Love*, and to Birkin's philosophy in particular:

The swan is one of the symbols of divine corruption with its reptile feet buried in the ooze and mud, its voluptuous form yielding and embracing the ooze of water, its beauty white and cold and terrifying, like the dead beauty of the moon, like the water lily, the sacred lotus, its neck and head like the snake, it is for us a flame of the cold white fire of flux, the phosphorescence of corruption, the salt, cold burning of the sea which corrodes all it touches, coldly reduces every sun-built form to ash, to the original elements . . . and there was some suggestion of this in the Christ of the early Christians, the Christ who was the Fish. . . . Corruption will at last break down for us the deadened forms, and release us into infinity. (P2 403)

As with Christ, or Yeats's 'Leda and the Swan', the incarnate deity makes the flesh divine: all the body is to be resurrected. Swan, lotus, lily, snake, and fish are all religious symbols, symbols of the libido, the primary life-energy that precedes consciousness. It was man's egoistic consciousness that caused the Fall, and continues to suppress and mould his natural being, here firmly identified with man's bodily roots, the sexual and excremental. To assert the validity of these, to assert one's individual sensual being, breaks the constrictions of self-consciousness and established convention, and so creates the possibility of a new and revitalising completeness and integrity of being.

It is only when man has experienced both extremes, the 'pagan, aristocratic, lordly, sensuous' and the 'Christian, humble, unselfish, democratic', that he is complete, and realises God in himself:

We cannot know God, in terms of the permanent, temporal world; we cannot. We can only know the *revelation* of God in the physical world. And the revelation of God is God. But it vanishes as the rainbow . . . and then God is gone. (P2 414)

'The Reality of Peace' (1917; P 669–694) is a more lyrical work, less extreme in its images and arguments, more concerned with the dark stillness beneath the bright activity of life, the oneness underlying duality. Its opening sentences state the theme: 'Peace is the state of fulfilling the deepest desire of the soul. It is the condition of flying within the greatest impulse that enters us from the unknown.' (P 669). This is achieved by submitting to the great tide coming from the suppressed, real self, and by having the courage to accept one's fundamental nature in its entirety:

We must know that we, ourselves, are the living stream of seething corruption, this also, all the while, as well as the bright river of life. We must recover our balance to be free. From our bodies comes the issue of corruption as well as the issue of creation. We must have our being in both, our knowledge must consist of both. (P 676)

This passage repeats Birkin's words to Ursula (*Women in Love* XIV) about the two rivers of creation and corruption (semen and excrement, spirit and flesh); though where this essay insists on their equality, he insists on the greater reality of the latter. To continue:

If there is a serpent of secret and shameful desire in my soul, let me not beat it out of my consciousness with sticks. It will lie beyond, in the marsh of the so-called subconsciousness. . . . Let me bring it to the fire to see what it is. For a serpent is a thing created. It has its own *raison d'être*. In its own being it has beauty and reality. (P 677)

To attempt to deny one's nature is to prevent self-fulfilment:

There is in me the desire of creation and the desire of dissolution. Shall I deny either? Then neither is fulfilled. If there is no autumn and winter of corruption, there is no spring and summer. All the time I must be dissolved from my old being. . . . How shall it be a shame that from my blood exudes the bitter sweat of corruption . . . that in my consciousness appear the

heavy marsh-flowers of the flux of putrescence which have their natural
roots in the slow stream of decomposition that flows for ever down my
bowels? There is a natural marsh in my belly, and there the snake is naturally
at home. (P 679)

The sexual and excremental are one, both necessary conditions of life.
One may compare with this the lines by Yeats:[4]

> Love has pitched his mansion in
> The place of excrement,
> For nothing can be sole or whole
> That has not been rent.

When serpent and marsh are accepted (as Coleridge's Ancient
Mariner blessed the monstrously beautiful sea-serpents) in 'just
proportion' with the conventionally creative element in life,

then we are free in a world of the absolute. The lark sings in a heaven of pure
understanding, she drops back into a world of duality and change. (P 680)

When all the conditions of mortality are accepted and included, peace
is attained; or so Lawrence hopes. Those who deny their true natures,
insist on the sole reality of consciousness and the ego, remain imprisoned in self-enclosure,

like some tough bugs, and therein remain active and secure from life and
death. So they swarm in insulated completeness obscene like bugs. (P 685)

The obscene swarming suggests a repulsive copulation[5] and also
a vast number of 'multiple identical units'. In reaction Lawrence,
remembering perhaps Whitman's 'Calamus', hymns death as a
purification:

Sweet death, save us from humanity. Death, noble, unstainable death,
smash the glassy rind of humanity, as one would smash the brittle hide of
the insulated bug. . . . Let there emerge a few pure and single men—men
who give themselves to the unknown of life and death and are fulfilled.
(P 686–7)

When the duality of life is transcended, then man will be complete,
in true existence, 'a rose of lovely peace'. Lawrence sought to transcend
duality in the stability of what is not life, the 'living body of darkness'.
The underworld, conventionally associated with darkness, death and
demonic spirits was also for him associated with male being, especially
his father. Fleeing the 'frictional' and exhausting struggle with sex
and woman, he sought peace in a 'male womb', the death that is serene
being and power. This quest is the theme of the writings after
Women in Love, a novel that is still poised between two worlds and
takes its stand in the flux.

II
WOMEN IN LOVE

The novel (published 1921) begins with a discussion on the possibility of marriage, and ends with one on the possibility of a further relationship beyond marriage, between men. In each case the relationship is more than a private one, but has implications for society as a whole. The individual consciousness needs to be in harmonious relationship with the 'other'—the sensual being, the other person, society at large —distinct without being isolated, united without being absorbed; it seems that the society and values of early modern Europe offer only limited possibilities for life-enhancing relationship between men and women—and none for that between men.

The characters in the book revealed the world of early modern European culture, ranging from working class through professional people and bohemian artists to the nobility, and including many nationalities; they were based on real people, and many contemporaries read it almost as a *roman-à-clef*. Birkin may obviously be identified, to a large extent, with Lawrence himself, Ursula with Frieda, Hermione Roddice with Lady Ottoline Morell and Sir Joshua Mattheson with Bertrand Russell. Philip Heseltine (Peter Warlock), who had a mistress known as 'Puma' and whose subsequent wife was named Minnie, provided a model for Halliday, whose mistress was named Pussum (later changed to Minette), while Loerke owed something to the Jewish painter Mark Gertler (see CL 477). Gudrun derived partly from the short-story writer Katherine Mansfield. Gerald Crich owed much to John Middleton Murry, as well as to a Major Barber, who was blond, blue-eyed, had accidentally killed his brother, and was a modernising mine-owner in Eastwood, and also perhaps to Lawrence's older brother.

The symmetry of the opening and closing scenes is one indication of the remarkable formal control of the work. While there is a strong story-line—and the importance of the *sequence* of the events must be stressed—this is complicated and almost overlaid by the various patterns of the book. Chief of these is the pattern of relationships between characters, not only of the two main pairs but also of the various 'triangles': Birkin, Ursula and Hermione; Birkin, Ursula and Gerald; Gerald, Minette and Halliday; Gerald, Gudrun and Loerke. Other patterns include the interrelationships between various important symbolic scenes, and the patterns of repeated images (e.g. dark waters, white mountains, flaring yellow lights, various animals and reptiles) and key words (such as 'seething', 'corruption', 'demoniac', 'subtle').

This symbolic vocabulary can be so esoteric as to seem a jargon, and it is clear that certain speeches, notably by Birkin, were never imagined by Lawrence as spoken aloud. On the other hand, it is essential to realise that this extremely complex and close-textured novel 'works' primarily through its language. Repetition of key words and images cuts through individual personalities to the essential pulse of life (or death) within. By this means we are brought to see the essential identity of Hermione, Minette, the governess, the woman in the African carving, and the girl in that by Loerke; or to perceive the identity of Gerald and Bismarck the rabbit, or Birkin and the young man in the market, and Loerke; or how—perhaps less obviously— Gudrun embodies Birkin–Lawrence's homosexual impulses, responding to blond Gerald and dark Loerke much as Birkin, in the 'Prologue to *Women in Love*' (P2 92–108), responded to fair and dark men.

The basic paradoxes of the novel's theme are presented through the interaction of the ambiguities and connotations of its words. The Symbolist novel (and this is one of the greatest) works by the absolute organisation of its basic material: language.[6] The multiple meanings of the words coalesce in characters, scenes and incidents that are not simply set in the novel like plums in a pudding, but grow out of and are an intensification of their medium; character, event and scene are completely fused.

It is in fact through scene, or setting that the novel will be explored here.[7] There seem to be five main focal areas: the mining town of Beldover, the most obvious manifestation of Gerald Crich's industrial society; Shortlands, the Crich home, where the malaise of that society is perhaps more apparent; Breadalby, Hermione's country house, centre of sterile tradition and rationalism, built over Beldover, as it were; the Café de Pompadour, that presents the phosphorescent decadence of society; and beyond them all, the dead end of life, the holiday resort in the Tyrol. The sequence will be: first, Shortlands and Beldover; then Breadalby; then the Café de Pompadour; the 'water' chapters associated with Shortlands, and the coming together of the two main couples; and, finally, the Continental chapters.

Shortlands is in many ways the central area of the book, providing (with the adjoining lake) the setting of some of the most crucial episodes, a meeting-place for the characters, and the intersection of the industrial, managerial and intellectual-artistic sections of society. Lawrence very acutely shows the interrelationship between the industrial world and bourgeois relationships. Mr Crich's Christian-democrat philosophy of the essential equality of all men effectively denies individual uniqueness; his attitude is reflected in the 'anarchy' and egoistic wilfulness of his children, and the spiritual frustration and near madness of his wife, whom he sees as a 'white snowflower', but who is more like a 'broken wolf' and a 'caged eagle'. The workers share his values in a 'passion for equality' that leads to riots of 'seething mobs of men': 'seething' reveals their activity as part of the disintegrative process, the virulent energy associated with biochemical change. His denial of difference and uniqueness asserts only false life, and death for him is meaningless:

before the armour of his pity really broke, he would die as an insect when its shell is cracked . . . others would live on, and knew the ensuing process of hopeless chaos. He would not. He denied death its victory. (XVII)

His son Gerald also embodies a 'will for chaos' that produces the imposition of a mechanical, intellectual order upon human feeling and the family's business. He sees himself as 'the God of the machine' and the workmen as mere insignificant instruments, parts of 'a system, an activity of pure order, pure mechanical repetition, repetition ad infinitum, hence eternal and infinite'. He expresses this Hobbesian functionalism to Gudrun at Breadalby, who mocks him with their names, "Mrs Colliery-Manager Crich . . . Miss Art-Teacher Brangwen" (VIII), perceiving that he has effectively depersonalised sexuality and the individual. He is literally against the brotherhood of man (in the early killing, and his own eventual death, is perhaps Lawrence's guilt about the dead elder brother he felt he had replaced), and this spirit affects his work:

As soon as Gerald entered the firm, the convulsion of death ran through the old system. He had all his life been tortured by a furious and destructive demon [like the rabbit—a perversion of natural energy], which possessed him like an insanity [like his mother's]. This temper now entered like a virus into the firm, and there were cruel eruptions. (XVII)

The 'God' is also a 'demon'; 'temper' suggests not only a general tone but also his passion, and suggests a chemical hardening process, as of steel. It operates like a virus, while 'eruptions' suggests both volcanoes and skin disease: inhumanity and destruction have a paradoxical vitality (denied to the father), a *natural* disintegrative energy.

Once the men have submitted to perverse satisfaction in being part of the huge machine, and this is working perfectly, Gerald has no further purpose. He feels himself empty and meaningless, his face seems to him like a mask, his eyes

only bubbles of darkness. He was afraid that one day he would break down and be a purely meaningless bubble lapping round a darkness. (XVII)

The effect of such a disintegration between the conscious and emotional being, imaged in the bubble, has appeared earlier, in Gudrun's response to Beldover (I). The town seems 'amorphous', the buildings 'brittle', she herself is made to feel like a beetle. The workmen, Gerald, and Gudrun all feel the attraction of submission to this inhumanity. 'Why had she wanted to submit herself to it? It seems to her 'another world . . . an under world . . . a ghoulish replica of the real world'. Beldover has 'the glamour of blackness'.

This perverse complex is further explored in 'Coaldust' (IX). When Gudrun sees Gerald cruelly forcing his horse (the symbol of natural vitality, the libido) to confront the clanking chain of coal-wagons from his mine, she responds with sadomasochistic excitement to the vision of his 'loins and thighs and calves, enclosing and encompassing the mare heavily into unutterable subordination', and in a 'voice like a gull' (associated in *The Rainbow* with perverse feeling) shrieks the ambiguous reproach, "I should think you're proud".

Unlike Ursula, she and the degraded men of Beldover are in *rapport*; the town has for her 'a foul kind of beauty . . . a thick, hot attraction'. The voices of the miners

seemed to envelop Gudrun in a labourer's caress, there was in the whole atmosphere a resonance of physical men, a glamorous thickness of labour and maleness. . . . Now she realised that this was the world of powerful, underworld men who spent most of their time in the darkness. In their voices she could hear the voluptuous resonance of darkness, the strong, dangerous underworld, mindless, inhuman. The voluptuousness was like that of machinery, cold and iron. . . . Their voices were full of an intolerable deep resonance, like a machine's burring, a music more maddening than the sirens' long ago. . . . They aroused a strange, nostalgic ache of desire, something almost demonical, never to be fulfilled. (IX)

The appeal is to the depths of the psyche, to submission to 'inhuman' forces within, even the carbon of which Lawrence had written before; the response to this 'unnatural' energy is a perverse one, masochistic in Gudrun, equivalent to an unacceptable homosexual one in Lawrence.[8] Gudrun picks up with one of the products of this world, a young electrician, Palmer, in his way something of a 'dandy' like Hermione and herself. One is reminded of Baudelaire's cult of the dandy, by which man subjugates his nature by becoming artificial, an art-object, unnatural and so in a sense supernatural.

Gudrun sees Gerald as the apotheosis of the brute-mechanical ethos of Beldover; kissing him under the railway arch, she remembers that this was where

the colliers pressed their lovers to their breast. And now, under the bridge, the master of them all pressed her to himself! And how much more powerful and terrible was his embrace than theirs. (XXIV)

Later, when he is dressing after they have been to bed together, she thinks that he is like a workman getting up for work, and she like a workman's wife.

Two other areas that also reflect the disintegrative and sensationalist ethos of Beldover are the bohemian world of the Café Pompadour, and the great house of Breadalby, which have appeared in sequence immediately before 'Coaldust', so modifying the significance of that chapter. In fact, this sequence of five chapters is 'framed' by events on Willey Water ('Diver' and 'Sketchbook'), forming a lead-in to 'Water-party'. Birkin, Ursula and Gudrun all respond to Breadalby as the image of the beautiful but dead past;[9] the life there is the life of the mind, the talk like 'a rattle of small artillery', without warmth or humanity; the group there seem, when swimming, like dinosaurs, which suggests their inhumanity and imminent extinction.

Hermione Roddice, the dominant figure here, fears the power of feeling, whether in herself and others; armoured though she is by class, money, taste and intellectuality, yet she has an inner 'deficiency of being', a lack of integration between will and feelings, so that she is always self-conscious and perverse: 'a strange mass of thoughts coiled in the darkness within her, and she was never allowed to escape' (I). Though she repeats Birkin's words on spontaneity and instinct, this is merely theory and pretence for her, as he tells her:

"You'd be very deliberately spontaneous. . . . You want it all in that loathsome little skull of yours, that ought to be cracked like a nut. For you'll be the same till it *is* cracked, like an insect in its skin. If one cracked your skull perhaps one might get a spontaneous passionate woman out of you, with real sensuality." (III)

Here, nut and insect images combine, and the positivity of violent destruction is implied.

She and Birkin have been 'lovers' for some time. In 'Prologue to *Women in Love*' the mental, sterile nature of this relationship is outlined; their sexual relationship is unsuccessful, with her sacrificing herself to him like Miriam, on whom she is based in that early draft. Birkin is now attempting to break away, and the Breadalby chapter shows her last attempt to possess him. A crucial episode (both in their relationship, and in the book as a whole) is when she finds him copying a Chinese drawing of geese (a variation of the phallic swan in 'The Crown'). In his drawing Birkin intuitively apprehends 'unknown modes of being' in the Chinese artist and the geese:

"I know what centres they live from—what they perceive and feel—the hot, stinging centrality of a goose in the flux of cold water and mud—the curious bitter stinging heat of a goose's blood, entering their own blood like an inoculation of corruptive fire—fire of the cold-burning mud—the lotus mystery." (VIII)

The sliding syntax fuses together geese, Chinese and Birkin, in an intense awareness of relationship between the fire of passionate individual life and the fundamental non-living surrounding forces. These dark sources of life are themselves unliving: to be absorbed into them is to be destroyed, but to be, like geese and artist, in *rapport* with them is to be intensely alive, 'central' in a supporting cosmos. The goose's blood is a 'corruptive fire' in dissolving self-consciousness and uniting with the nonhuman, providing the exhilarating sensation (or even sensationalism) of the juxtaposition of the nonhuman flux with the individual and vital. The word 'inoculation' implies that such intuitive understanding, as in art, enables a controlled possession of what, directly confronted, would otherwise be deadly.[10] This account of artistic knowledge may be contrasted with that of Gudrun in 'Sketchbook' where she is

absorbed in a stupor of apprehension of surging water-plants . . . watery mud, and from its festering chill, water-plants . . . as in a sensuous vision, she *knew* how they rose out of the mud. (X)

Gudrun is *absorbed* by, not truly contemplative of, the phallic mystery here presented; though she sees more than does Ursula, her response is equally one-sided, seeing only subhuman sexual power, that culminates in Gerald.

Hermione, on the other hand, is unnerved by Birkin's account of the drawing, and his acceptance of unknown modes of being, that are impervious to intellectual possession such as hers. His later rejection of her cant about equality of spirit, implying the ultimate unknowableness of human beings, completes her feelings of helpless isolation:

her whole mind was a chaos, darkness breaking in upon it, and herself struggling to gain control with her will. . . . And then she realised that his presence was the wall. . . . Unless she could break out, she must die most fearfully, walled up in horror[11] . . . she must break him down before her . . . only this blotted out her mind . . . she was going to know her voluptuous consummation. (VIII)

Hermione's murderous assault on Birkin (as he sits quietly reading Thucydides' history of the Fall of Athens) is a release from inhibition, but into union with forces of deadly passion.[12] By his philosophy, Birkin cannot condemn her deadly blow for liberty, but after this crisis in human relations revives himself in a consummation with the natural world: 'Here was his world, he wanted nobody and nothing but the lovely, subtle, responsive vegetation, and himself, his own living self.' This reaction is clearly a regression from the dangers of human sexual involvement to hermit-like isolation and comfort in the body of nature.

The exhaustion and decay of humanity are blatant in the Café de Pompadour 'theme', that begins with the chapter 'In the Train', in the conversation between Birkin and Gerald. Birkin feels that modern life "is a blotch of filth, like insects scurrying in filth" and that "we've got to bust it completely, or shrivel inside it, as in a tight skin", while Gerald is simply interested in the sensation of destruction, to "just start and let fly". His answer is not revolution, but material amelioration and industrial efficiency. Entering London, Birkin mentally compares London with Sodom, before quoting from Browning's poem 'Love Among the Ruins', a story of love amidst a collapsing civilisation. They arrange to meet at the Café de Pompadour (the name evoking the civilisation overwhelmed by the French Revolution), later described as a 'bubble of pleasure' and a 'small, slow central whirlpool of disintegration and dissolution'. There Gerald begins an affair with Minette, upon whose eyes 'there seemed to float a curious iridescence, a sort of film of disintegration and sullenness, like oil on water' (VI).

Her response to black beetles suggests, as should now be obvious, her own disintegration and perversity. This beetle image should be linked with Minette and with the African and Pacific carvings.[13] One, in Halliday's flat, is of a woman in childbirth, grey-faced (like the Arab servant) and 'abstracted almost into meaninglessness by the weight of sensation beneath. [Gerald] saw Minette in it' (VIII). Birkin's interpretation of this figure as 'really ultimate physical consciousness, mindless, utterly sensual' should be considered with his exposition in 'Class-room' of how sensuality

"is a fulfilment—the great dark knowledge that you can't have in your head—the dark involuntary being. It is death to one's self—but it is the coming into being of another. . . . In the blood . . . there must be the deluge. Then you find yourself in a palpable body of darkness, a demon—" (III)

Even if the figure expresses only a partial experience, it contains considerable elements of the positive in its obliteration of consciousness by extreme sensation, in the 'opposite equivalent' of Birkin's underworld of the physical-intuitive being. Certainly it is better than the deliberate self-degradation in primitivism of which Birkin accuses Hermione: "You want to go back and be like a savage, without knowledge. You want a life of pure sensation [notice the Keats allusion] and 'passion'." Gerald consciously indulges in such disintegrated sensationalism with Minette.

The distinction between genuine sensual being and the thorough-going primitivism that may be beneficial through its destruction of consciousness and old forms of living, is a fine one. The problem appears in Birkin's letter, read aloud in the Café Pompadour by Halliday before being rescued by Gudrun (primarily because it speaks to her of her own condition). The language of the contemporary essays is not parodied, but (defensively) provided with a jeering commentary.[14] Here Birkin says that people are now filled with "the desire for reduction . . . a reducing back to the origin, a return along the Flux of Corruption to the rudimentary conditions of being . . ." and in this "reducing back of the created body of life, we get knowledge, and beyond knowledge, the phophorescent ecstasy of acute sensation . . .". This is a process of decivilisation, reducing the complexity of life and of man-woman relationship, to obtain more violent feeling in order to start again,

"reducing the two great elements of male and female from their highly complex unity—reducing the old ideas, going back to the savages for our sensations—always seeking to *lose* ourselves in some ultimate black sensation mindless and infinite." (XXVIII)

The fineness of the distinction is apparent in Birkin's use of the same vocabulary for the 'Class-room' speech and the account of the statuette. Persistence in such reduction to the absolute will, apparently, bring one round to the point of real sensual being again; Birkin has already told Halliday that he must continue his "ecstasy of reduction with Minette . . . till it is fulfilled", and then somehow "transcended".

Halliday is closely akin to Birkin: "He wants a pure lily, another girl, with a Botticelli face, on the one hand, and on the other, he *must* have Minette, just to defile himself with her." Likewise, the Birkin of the 'Prologue' had to 'have a Hermione, completely without desire; to be sensual, he must have a slightly bestial woman . . .' (P2 102). The Prologue continues with a discussion of Birkin's homosexual feelings; this, and the similarity with Halliday, emphasise Birkin's involvement in the corruption of this world.

The theme touched on here is presented more amply in 'Moony', which, however, should be considered as the culmination of the preceding 'water' chapters, 'Sketchbook', 'Island', and 'Water-party'. 'Sketchbook' begins with Gudrun 'absorbed' in her water-plants, while Ursula responds only to the butterflies and the 'nice' aspect of life, unlike Gudrun and Birkin. The plants, like 'pale, underworld, automatic colliers', culminate in Gerald who 'start[s] out of the mud', and floats with conscious sensuality upon the water 'like the rocking phosphorescence. . . . And the exquisite pleasure of slowly arresting the boat, in the heavy-soft water, was complete as a swoon'. Hermione's attempt to come between Gudrun and Gerald only makes them recognise that 'they were of the same kind, he and she, a sort of diabolic freemasonry subsisted between them'. 'Diabolic' is, of course, a negative form of the amoral 'demonic'.

Their relationship is developed in 'Water-party', but that of Ursula and Birkin makes a useful introduction. In their discussion, Birkin emphasises the corruption and deadness of the Sodom-world that he sees, where people are mere growths on a dead tree: what he prefers (especially after Hermione's assault) is

"grass and hares and adders, and the unseen hosts, actual angels that go about freely when a dirty humanity doesn't interrupt them—and good pure-tissued demons: very nice." (XI)

However, Ursula, with her 'diabolical knowledge of the horrors of persistence', insists that man and the present state of affairs will not disappear, and points out the inadequacy of his vision—"the end of the world and grass". The debate concludes with the image of Birkin's natural daisies and Ursula's romantic paper boat dancing on the water, 'in a slow, slow Dervish dance', naturally unborne by the dark forces of inhuman nature, in contrast to Gerald's deliberate sensual toying.

The exposition of Birkin's theories continues in the next two chapters; he uses the analogy of the horses to suggest that women have two wills, one for independence and one for submission—"the last, perhaps highest, love-impulse: resign your will to the higher being". Where the higher being is less than divine, this impulse seems suspect, even perhaps masochistic. Certainly it is not surprising that after her sight of Gerald on his mare, Ursula disagrees vigorously. Birkin then attempts to dismiss the merely human and conscious emotion of love in favour of the preconscious forces, and a non-merging confrontation of their ultimate selves, 'stark and impersonal and beyond responsibility', that is, beyond normal morality, to achieve a polarised relationship, "a pure balance of two beings—as the stars balance each other". Ursula determinedly interprets his rather apprehensive denial of love as merely an indirect and pretentious avowal of love. Frustrated by her imperviousness, Birkin again attempts allegory, interpreting the cat Mino's cuffing of its mate as an illustration of the stability brought about by male dominance (sliding from the stability of equilibrium to that of domination). The language describing the cats echoes that used of Gerald and Minette, and the similarity of the names Mino and Minette is suggestive. Ursula naturally howls him down, and he retreats to his earlier image of "two single equal stars balanced in conjunction". It can be seen that his arguments are not mere lumps of undigested 'pollyanalytics' but relative, conditioned by circumstances and expressive of changing relationships. Birkin makes a last attack on some cant talk of Ursula's about love, before she wins the battle, forcing him to submit to love, to her, and her 'strange golden-lighted eyes, very tender, but with a curious devilish look lurking underneath'. A yellow light in the eyes is frequently associated in Lawrence with self-assertive voluptuous sensuality. For Birkin, beyond such sensuous love there is male superiority, or at least equality, but within it there is insecurity, and the fear of a tendency to submission to the Magna Mater.

'Water-party' (XIV) is possibly the most brilliant chapter in the book, where character, event and setting coalesce in images that radiate throughout the novel. The world of the vulgar populace is dismissed with Gudrun's account (that betrays fascination in its horror) of the Thames pleasure-steamer. Retired to an island, Ursula sings serenely, while Gudrun attempts to obliterate self-consciousness in a quasi-ritualistic dance, culminating in a 'voluptuous ecstasy' when she attempts—as Gerald might—to cruelly subdue brute nature in the cattle. The consequent excitement makes her sexually aggressive towards Gerald when he appears, causing her to strike him. The description of his response—'it was as if some reservoir of black emotion had burst within him, and swamped him'—creates an identity between character and the setting, where flaring lights drift over black water (a physical representation of the phosphorescence-on-black-flood images)—black water which will kill, and then obliterate consciousness with a deafening boom.

Their words afterwards are, as Gudrun feels, absurdly melodramatic, but help to evoke the intensity of their confrontation. She is a *belle dame sans merci*, laughing 'a silvery little mockery', her voice 'crooning and witch-like'. Gerald is overwhelmed by intense emotion:

The terrible swooning burden on his mind, the awful swooning, the loss of all his control, was too much for him. . . . He walked on beside her, a striding, mindless body. But he recovered a little as he went. He suffered badly. He had killed his brother when a boy, and was set apart, like Cain. (XIV)

Briefly, he has the horror and pathos of Frankenstein's half-human monster. The reference to the childhood killing is brought in to 'explain' Gerald, who pathetically fears his own passions, that seem to him so dangerous that they must be suppressed; when someone at last seems prepared to accept them, he is overwhelmed by their unfamiliar and released power. It is convenient to refer here to the previous encounter between Gerald and Gudrun, in 'Rabbit' (XVIII),

when he subdues his nasty little sister's rabbit, Bismarck. The flail-
ing rabbit is 'demon-like . . . looking something like a dragon'
(Lawrence's symbol of the libido). This is the repressed and slightly
perverted passionate energy that Gerald excitedly recognises in
himself: in 'Industrial Magnate' (XVII) his former nurse described
how as a child he would "kick, and scream, and struggle like a demon.
Many's the time I've pinched his little bottom for him". Suppressed
passion becomes perverse, and it is this that excites Gerald and Gudrun.[15]

Birkin, meanwhile, is putting forward the ideas of 'The Crown' and
'The Reality of Peace'. While postulating two rivers of existence, "the
silver river of life" and "the black river of dissolution [and] corruption", he insists that the latter is "our real reality"; "it is the process
of creative destruction" in which everyone is involved. It produces in
the "spasm of universal dissolution" (a metaphor combining orgasm
and death) Aphrodite, the goddess of a purely erotic, unprocreative
sexuality, and "snakes and swans and lotus", all sexual-religious
symbols, and natural products of decay, like the marsh-flowers.
Ursula says that he "only want[s] to know death", which is a half-
truth, as Birkin–Lawrence asserts that decay and death are part of the
human condition, and need to be accepted for full existence. So, if
the silver river may be interpreted as the seminal flow, and the dark
river as the excremental, it means that Ursula and the conventional
idealists accept only 'normal' sexuality, while Birkin demands the
acceptance of the entire bodily process, particularly perhaps the
excremental, wherein lies 'the real reality'. Where the silver river is
conventional morality, Birkin insists that what is conventionally
regarded as morally corrupt is equally—and even pre-eminently—
part of man's nature, not to be suppressed, but accepted, if that nature
is to be fulfilled. Meanwhile, the 'ignis fatuus' and phosphorescence
of which he spoke appear in the lights on the water: 'Everywhere were
these noiseless ruddy creatures of fire drifting near the surface of the
water.'

The next episode, of the lanterns lit for Ursula and Gudrun, is
beautiful but rather portentously allegorical. Ursula receives a blue
lantern showing a flight of storks, presenting the element of air, and
then a lantern of 'flamy ruddiness' where the element of fire seems to
unite water and air: she is capable of resolving opposing elements.
The blue light makes Birkin's face look 'demoniacal. Ursula was dim
and veiled, looming over him', like some priestess or goddess: both
are charged with supernatural quality. Gerald and Gudrun are also
illuminated by her first lamp, a yellow one of flowers and butterflies,
emblematising earth, and a merely natural sexuality. Her next lantern,

of water, of a 'white cuttlefish flowing in white soft streams' staring 'straight from the heart of the light' (perhaps the 'opposite equivalent' of Joseph Conrad's 'Heart of Darkness') is associated with the moon-principle of deadly sterility. Gudrun's horror suggests that this is what she fears in herself, causing her to pass it to Ursula, who is indifferent to it.

Gerald and Gudrun then float in conscious sensuality on the dark water, until the cry of death rings out; "Di-Di-Di. . . ." Diving under the 'terrible, massive, cold, boundless surface' of the inhuman depths, Gerald is dehumanised (imaged as a seal and a water-rat). He describes it as "a whole universe under there; and as cold as hell, you're as helpless as if your head was cut off" (becoming again a 'mindless body'); the underworld is "so different really from what it is on top, so endless—you wonder how it is so many are alive, why we're up here". Gerald has known death, the underworld, 'the real reality', but for him the body of darkness is not fertilising, but wholly negative, opposed to the only reality that he can accept, that of individual consciousness.

This 'death by water' produces a rebirth only in Birkin. Observing that it was the girl who pulled the young man to his death (the consequence of female, natural love), and fascinated by the 'crushing boom' of the inhuman dark waters, he yearns for death, or a love like death, from which the individual may be reborn. Ursula, however, still insists on the individualistic 'hard flame of passionate desire', keeping him in the world of ordinary sexuality and life, though this is not what he really wants.

After their exciting though ultimately frustrating passion, comes the reaction. Ursula experiences an exhaustion, a weariness of life:

she was fulfilled in a kind of bitter ripeness, there remained only to fall from the tree into death . . . one was happiest falling into death, as a bitter fruit plunges in its ripeness downwards. Death is a great consummation, a consummating experience. It is a development from life . . . better die than live mechanically a life that is a repetition of repetitions. To die is to move on with the invisible. To die is also a joy, a joy of submitting to that which is greater than the known; namely the pure unknown . . . death is never a shame. Death itself, like the illimitable space, is beyond our sullying. . . . To know is human, and in death we do not know, we are not human. . . . The promise of this is our heritage, we look forward like heirs to their majority. (XV)

The change of tense indicates authorial agreement. Ursula is coming to accept Birkin's real reality, the inhuman unknown beneath consciousness, that is part of the rhythm of life.

In the meantime, Birkin revolts against her demands for love, "the

horrible privacy of domestic and connubial satisfaction", where (male)
individuality is smothered by feminine possessiveness, wanting instead

something clearer, more open, cooler as it were. . . . He wanted sex to revert
to the level of the other appetites, to be regarded as a functional process,
not a fulfilment . . . he wanted a further conjunction, where men had being
and women had being, two pure beings each constituting the freedom of
the other, balancing each other like two poles of one force, like two angels,
or two demons. . . . [Woman is the devouring mother:] By her very suffering
she bound her son with chains, she held him her everlasting prisoner. It
was intolerable, this possession at the hands of women. Always a man must
be considered as the broken-off fragment of a woman, and the sex was the
still aching scar of the laceration. . . . There is now to come the new day . . .
[when] there is no longer any of the horrible merging, mingling self-abnegation of love. There is only the pure duality of polarisation, each one free
from any contamination of the other. (XVI)

Behind this, clearly, is the frustration of Lawrence's sexual desire, in
his obsession with his mother; love is associated with self-denial, and
possession by the mother-woman, so that to remove the incestuous
inhibition sexuality must be without tenderness, functional—or even
detached altogether, into the homosexual.

Suddenly [Birkin] saw himself confronted with another problem—the
problem of love and eternal conjunction between two men. Of course this
was necessary—it had been a necessity inside himself all his life—to love
a man purely and fully. Of course he had been loving Gerald all along,
and all along denying it. (XVI)

Forgotten is the thought that love—for women—is horrible. He
even suggests *Blutbrüderschaft*, the mingling of blood—an equivalent
of sexual union. Gerald, apprehensive of how significant it might be
for him, fatally declines the relationship, which is presented in terms
of 'an impersonal union', with the overtly homosexual feeling played
down. That element appears in the 'Prologue' that explicitly discusses
Birkin's attraction to 'men of no very great intelligence, but of pleasant
appearance . . . who protected him in his delicate health more gently
than a woman', either blue-eyed blond 'northmen' or dark-eyed
'night-smelling men, who are the living substance of the viscous,
universal heavy darkness' (P2 105). Clearly this is the root of Gudrun's
attraction, first to Gerald and then to Loerke. It is regrettable that a
very just fear of public reaction obscured the presentation of Birkin's
nature: his theories of love and sex would have been more easily seen
as conditioned by his circumstances, and viewed more critically by
many readers, especially the inexperienced.

 This, then, is the context for 'Moony' (XIX); this great symbolic
D

chapter can only be fully responded to when its characters and images have been properly absorbed in the preparatory chapters. The chapter begins with Ursula in a state of withdrawal from life, a moon-like 'radiance . . . a luminousness of supreme radiation'. She feels the moon 'with its white and deathly smile' of sterile isolation watching her, and attempts to escape, turning to the shadowy pond, 'where the alders twisted their roots', in which organic underworld she sees Birkin stoning the moon's reflection. He speaks, to himself, of the moon as Cybele, which has led some commentators to interpret this as Birkin's attack on woman; while including this, the attack is on the moon-principle (which Ursula is also fleeing) of self-contained, sterile isolation and self-consciousness,[16] qualities that Lawrence regards as feminine, and which Birkin is fighting in himself. Throwing dead husks of flowers (imaging his own lifelessness) on the water, he says, "You can't go away. . . . There *is* no away. You only withdraw upon yourself." The magnificent account of the stoning of the moon's image reveals it as an act of creative violence, destroying congealed stillness to create the vitality of the active interchange between light and dark, male and female, that produces momentary peace. The moon's reflection, described at first as like a cuttle-fish (reminiscent of Gudrun's lantern), becomes at the end 'a ragged rose'. Two passages from essays of 1918 are relevant. First, that already quoted, from the 'Introduction to *New Poems*':

In the immediate present there is no perfection, no consummation, nothing finished. The strands are all flying, quivering, intermingling with the web, the waters are shaking the moon. There is no round, consummate moon on the face of the running waters...

The quivering nimble hour of the present, this is the quick of Time. This is the immanence. The quick of the universe is the *pulsating, carnal self*, mysterious and palpable. (P 218–20)

The other is from the essay 'Love':

We are like a rose. In the pure passion for oneness, [that is, unison] in the pure passion for distinctness and separateness, a dual passion of unutterable separation and lovely conjunction of the two, the new configuration takes place, the transcendence, the two in their perfect singleness, transported into one surpassing heaven of a rose-blossom. (P 154)

After this, Ursula and Birkin attempt a reconciliation, but her 'frightened apprehensive self-insistence' prevents it being more than a truce. Birkin reacts by turning again to the 'purely sensual, purely unspiritual knowledge' embodied in Halliday's West African statuette. The figure is distorted, so that there is emphasis on the weighty, protuberant buttocks; the nature of this 'inverted culture' where

mind and consciousness are annihilated, is 'beyond any phallic knowledge, sensual subtle realities far beyond the scope of phallic investi-
gation'. This is not literally true, as is hinted in 'Continental' (XXIX);
'phallic' here implies normal sexual experience, whereas the sensual
realities and knowledge referred to are knowledge of the corruption
at the centre of the body, that is, anal knowledge. There is an insistence
upon the 'great mysteries to be unsealed, sensual, mindless, dreadful
mysteries, far beyond the phallic cult'. 'Mysteries' implies profound
religious experience of esoteric knowledge, the plunge into the
'putrescent' black river of suppressed sensuality.

Birkin contemplates two modes of being: the north-European
'white' process, as seen in Gerald, of 'ice-destructive knowledge',
where the sensual being is sublimated, and the 'African' process of
submersion in dark sensuality, that destroys 'humanity' as he has
known it. This reflection may be seen as his reaction on two modes
of homosexual feeling, as in 'Prologue':

He could never acquiesce to his own feelings, to his own passion. He could
never grant that it should be so, that it was well for him to feel this keen
desire to have and to possess the bodies of such men, the passion to bathe
in the very substance of such men, the substance of living, eternal light,
like eternal snow, and the flux of heavy, rank-smelling darkness.

He wanted to cast out these desires, he wanted not to know them. (P2
106)

Separation and merging, sublimation and indulgence, seem equally
unacceptable, so that Birkin hopes irrationally for a 'paradisal entry
into pure, single being, the individual soul taking precedence over
love and desire for union . . . proud, individual singleness', and
in this unsatisfactory spirit goes off to propose to Ursula, and is
promptly rejected. This rejection is partly due to her father's bullying
that drives her back to the moon-spirit, 'radiant' in 'perfect hostility'.
This is followed by an inverted relationship with Gudrun (essentially a
repetition of that with Winifred Inger), achieving an almost obscene
intimacy. When she turns back to Birkin, she transfers this feeling to
him:

She was not at all sure that it was this mutual unison in separateness that
she wanted. She wanted unspeakable intimacies. She wanted to have him,
utterly, finally to have him as her own, oh, so unspeakably, in intimacy.
(XIX)

So the spirit of withdrawal from other life, in which she began the
chapter, has only modulated to the desire for devouring possession
of other life; the dark underworld remains unrecognised, unadmitted.

A perverse, reductive form of this appears in Birkin's consequent wrestling-match with Gerald, that is like a sexual encounter, the obliteration of consciousness and separation in physical sensation:

It was as if Birkin's whole physical intelligence interpenetrated into Gerald's body . . . like some potency . . . [they become] mindless at last, two essential white figures working into a tighter closer oneness of struggle, with a strange, octopus-like knotting . . . no head to be seen . . . the physical junction of two bodies clinched into oneness . . . a complete darkness was coming over [Birkin's] mind. . . . The world was sliding . . . (XX)

This is a dissolution of being in violence, 'experience all in one sort, mystically sensual' like the 'African' knowledge in corruption that Birkin had feared. This is the 'ecstasy of reduction' of Birkin's letter to Halliday, here 'fulfilled', and so enabling transcendence: having been *through* this experience, Birkin can now return to Ursula, this time successfully.

After Ursula had reacted against Birkin, she joined with Hermione in criticising him, until she realised how wrong they were, and what Birkin was really after:

He did not want an odalisk. He wanted a woman to *take* something from him, to give herself up so much that she could take the last realities, the last facts, the last physical facts, physical and unbearable.
And if she did, would he acknowledge her? (XXII)

This is still somewhat vaguely expressed, partly no doubt because of Ursula's rather vague comprehension; confirmation and clarification come in Birkin's thoughts in 'Excurse':

He had taken her as he had never been taken himself. He had taken her at the roots of her darkness and shame—like a demon, laughing over the fountain of mystic corruption which was one of the sources of her being, laughing, shrugging, accepting finally. As for her, when would she so much go beyond herself to accept him at the quick of death? (XXIII)

This root and fountain is the excremental flow of the black river, the '*quick* of death', where death and life are the same; the 'demon' exults in acceptance of the organic, living body of darkness, that promises fuller life. To take implies not only recognition, but also a sexual possession—which has not yet been enacted. Quite possibly, at this point Lawrence has forgotten his 'plot' and is writing of his relationship with Frieda, as in *Look! We Have Come Through!*

Ursula makes one last violent denunciation of his 'perversity', particularly as associated with Hermione, where sensuality was solely perverse. Having purged the sensual body of that unnaturalness, she is ready to accept him, to pluck the jewel of individual being from the muddy flux. Her embrace of Birkin is a culminating moment in the novel. Kneeling before him, like Lydia before Tom Brangwen, she puts her hands round his buttocks, sensing his anus, 'the dark river of corruption', 'the real reality';

It was a strange reality of his being, the very stuff of being, there in the straight downflow of the thighs. It was here she discovered him one of the sons of God such as were in the beginning of the world [of whom she had dreamed in *The Rainbow*], something other, something more [in that the excremental is not designed for her sexual service, and so is beyond her]. It was a perfect passing away for both of them, and at the same time the most intolerable accession into being, the marvellous fullness of immediate gratification, overwhelming outflooding from the deepest life-force, the darkest, deepest, strangest life-source of the human body, at the back and base of the loins...
She had thought there was no source deeper than the phallic source. And now, behold, from the smitten rock of the man's body, from the strange marvellous flanks and thighs, deeper, further in mystery than the phallic source, came the floods of ineffable darkness and ineffable riches. (XXIII)

The 'frictional sensationalism' of conventional sexuality is transcended in this—only apparently—perverse acceptance of the common human condition, prior to sexual difference, where 'we are of the earth, earthy'. By accepting the extremes of experience, especially that usually denied, the greatest 'access of being' is attained.

The account seems over-written and jargonistic, because Lawrence is trying to suggest what contemporary *mores* would not permit him to say openly. After this, the writing dips into bathos, first with the account of their tea—'there was a venison pasty, of all things, a large broad-faced cut ham . . . the teapot poured beautifully from a proud slender spout . . .'—and then in the description of Birkin driving them to Sherwood Forest,

like an Egyptian Pharaoh, driving the car. He felt as if he were seated in immemorial potency, like the great carven statues of real Egypt . . . potent in that other basic mind, the deepest physical mind. (XXIII)

Thus fundamentally enthroned, it is fortunate that he has the light of Greek intelligence to help him steer and change gear (though the symbolic and realistic modes of writing clash dreadfully). He and Ursula achieve consummation in 'pure night' and some obscurity:

The world was under a strange ban, a new mystery had supervened . . . his fingers upon her unrevealed nudity were the fingers of silence upon silence, the body of mysterious night upon mysterious night . . . only known as a palpable revelation of living otherness.
She had her desire of him, she touched, she received the maximum of

unspeakable communication in touch, dark, subtle, positively silent, a magnificent gift and give again . . . [the] living body of darkness and silence and subtlety, the mystic body of reality. (XXIII)

Conventional morality is under a 'ban', as the lovers achieve more than conventional sexual intercourse in mutual anal caresses such as they had anticipated she would repeat; afterwards, this experience, like her previous caress, is suppressed from conscious memory.

With the full acceptance of the body and of desire, they have achieved liberty, and a new commitment to each other. They consider marrying and settling down, and even get as far as buying a chair, before deciding that a fixed home, like all static formalisations of experience, is a constriction. They decide to give the chair to another young couple at the market, also setting up together, whose appearance suggests very strongly that they are 'parodies' of Frieda and Lawrence. The woman is the detested Magna Mater, full of her child, dominating the man, 'at once overbearing and very gentle'. He, on the other hand,

was a still, mindless creature, hardly a man at all, a creature . . . he had some of the fineness and stillness and silkiness of a dark-eyed silent rat. . . . He grinned sicklily, turning away his head. She had got his manhood, but Lord, what did he care! He had a strange furtive pride and slinking singleness. (XXVI)

The last words may be contrasted with Birkin's about 'proud, individual singleness' (XIX). This is the marriage that Birkin–Lawrence fears, where the sensual male is subordinated into perverse resentment by the pressure of the woman and society; but having displaced it on to this couple, Birkin can marry—so long as he can run away abroad, out of society.

Meanwhile the relationship between Gerald and Gudrun has developed—accelerated perhaps by his fear of the male relationship that Birkin offered. Unnerved by the slow dying of his father (reminiscent of that of Lawrence's mother) he turns to Gudrun for reassurance of his identity through passionate sensuality. For Gudrun, this sensuality is perversely exciting:

They were such strangers—and yet they were so frightfully, unthinkably near. It was like a madness. Yet it was what she wanted . . . (XXIV)

In their embrace in the dark underworld beneath the railway bridge, she submits to his power, in conscious dissolution, before swinging back to a feeling of possession of him: 'Ah, if she could have the precious *knowledge* of him, she would be filled. . . .' He does not stand up for himself, and she realises her power over him, anticipating when she can devour him: 'There were all the after days when her hands,

like birds, could feed upon the fields of his mystical plastic form. . . .'
When his father dies, Gerald is overwhelmed by his own insufficiency,
and runs to Gudrun for reinforcement. The clay on him from his
father's grave certainly makes him no less acceptable to her.

Into her he poured all his pent-up darkness and corrosive death, and he was
whole again. . . . The terrible frictional violence of death filled her, and she
received it in an ecstasy of subjection, in throes of acute, violent sensation.
(XXIV)

Their union (like that of Paul Morel with Clara, during his mother's
dying), far from denying death, is in fact the consummation of death.
For Gerald it is a regression to comfort in, and service of, the Magna
Mater. Gudrun, not having experienced any liberating submission
or union, is 'destroyed into perfect consciousness' in a vision of a
meaningless life.

Eventually they decide to go for a holiday in the Tyrol, as an
experiment, taking with them Ursula and Birkin. Like Lawrence and
Frieda, Birkin and Ursula can see no place in society, nor any way in
which their experience might help to modify society; instead they
intend to wander the earth in 'the quest of Rupert's Blessed Isles'.
Birkin hopes for somewhere[17]

"where we can be free—somewhere where one needn't wear much clothes
—none even—where one meets a few people who have gone through enough,
and can take things for granted—where you can be yourself . . ." (XXIII)

To Gudrun, who thinks that "the only thing to do with the world, is
see it through", Ursula says,

"One has no more connections here. One has a sort of other self, that
belongs to a new planet, not to this. You've got to hop off." (XXIX)

One is reminded of Donne's interest in life in other worlds—trans-
atlantic or extra-terrestrial—where lovers can be free. Fallen into a
new life, their first resting-place is far from ideal: the *cul-de-sac* of the
world, 'the flux of death'. In *Twilight in Italy* Lawrence had described
the Alpine mountain as 'the very quick of cold death . . . [the] radiant
nucleus of death in life . . . [whence] flows the great flux downwards
. . . [while] the people under the mountains, they seem to live in the
flux of death, the last, strange, overshadowed units of life'. The ice-
white mountains represent the inhuman abstraction associated with
Gerald and modern civilisation, that makes individual sensuality
hotter and more extreme by contrast. This sensuality is seen not only
in, say, the Pompadour 'set' or the orgiastic bohemians Gerald and
Gudrun met in Paris, but in both couples here.

After the hot Dionysiac dancing, Birkin becomes sardonic, satiric, suggestive and licentious, to which spirit Ursula submits herself. Afterwards she thinks of them as having been "bestial", yet also thinks,

"Why not be bestial, and go the whole round of experience? . . . How good it was to be really shameful! . . . She was free, when she knew everything, and no dark shameful things were denied her." (XXIX)

Ursula–Frieda has clearly been shocked by her experience of anal intercourse, a shock that still comes through Lawrence's attempt to present it as a liberation from bodily shame, a liberation that cannot but shock old preconceptions.

When Gudrun is tobogganing with Gerald, 'in pure white flame the white slope flew against her, and she fused like one molten, dancing globule, rushed through a white intensity'—an orgasmic ecstasy she describes as "the most perfect moment of my life". The description echoes that of the annihilation of Skrebensky's humanity, in the moonlight. After such experience, both Skrebensky and Gudrun can only respond to dark corruption and perversity—in her case, to Loerke.

Loerke, small, dark, lively, artistic, bisexual, his subhuman vitality evoked in images of mouse, bat, seal and water-rat, parodies Birkin— or presents those qualities that Lawrence most feared and disliked in himself (it is notable that Birkin has no direct confrontation with him). Lawrence makes Gerald less complex and initiate in corruption than he was before, and clumsy and insensitive, in order to emphasise Loerke's nature; Gerald becomes for Gudrun the epitome of the brute and mechanical, while he becomes obsessed with desire for sexual self-obliteration in her. She turns to Loerke: 'To Gudrun, there was in Loerke the rock bottom of life.' By using a pun (that is perhaps implicit), this may be set against Ursula's discovery of 'the smitten rock of [Birkin's] body' from which came dark fertilising floods that renewed Ursula's sense of the wholeness of life. For Gudrun, Loerke is the dark reality of utter negation, that makes 'life, seem naïve illusion:

There was no going beyond him . . . there *were* no new worlds, there were no more *men*, there were only creatures, little ultimate *creatures* like Loerke. The world was finished now, for her. There was only the inner, individual darkness, sensation within the ego, the obscene religious mystery of ultimate reduction, the mystic frictional activities of diabolic reducing down. . . . Of the last series of subtleties, Gerald was not capable. He could not touch the quick of her. But where his ruder blows could not penetrate, the fine insinu-ating blade of Loerke's insect-like comprehension could. (XXX)

The language again is suggestive of anal intercourse, that is 'diabolic'
—not 'demonic'—opening into no new world, but into 'the house of
[Gudrun's] soul [where]

there was a pungent atmosphere of corrosion, an inflamed darkness of
sensation, and a vivid, subtle, critical consciousness, that saw the world
distorted, horrific. (XXX)

Loerke and Gudrun share a freedom that is a parody of that of Birkin
and Ursula: while the latter, in relation with each other, seek further
life in the warm south, the former, bound in disjunction, drift like
parasites north to Germany and the bohemian world of Dresden.

The novel concludes with the destruction of Gerald, once a proud
Dionysiac figure. His attempt at self-obliteration in extreme sensation
with Gudrun blasts and shrivels him, making him look 'like a mask
used in ghastly religions of the barbarians'. He has been reduced,
made more intense and less human. In his attempt to strangle Gudrun,
sexuality and murder fuse in supreme assertion of his power over the
body of life (not unlike Paul's feelings when strangling Baxter Dawes).
Leaving her still alive, he climbs up into the moonlit icy mountains to
easeful death, with which he has always been in love. At the top, he
sees a small carving of Christ—the spirit crucified by the flesh. The
carvings described in *Twilight in Italy* (I) present his condition: one,
'the strong, virile life overcome by physical violence, the eyes still
looking back bloodshot in consummate hate and misery', the other's
limbs shattered pathetically 'so that they gave him a painful impression
there in the stark, sterile place of rock and cold'.

Gerald is the tragic hero of *Women in Love*, the epitome of his
civilisation, torn apart and destroyed by unrecognised contradictions
within, and his death is the death of his civilisation. Birkin comforts
himself with thoughts of nature's inexhaustible power of renewal,
but for him the loss is final.[18] He has lost his chance for relationship
not only with one man but man's society. Ursula believes the sexual
love of one couple is sufficient, but Birkin is sure it is not.[19] For Lawrence, too, the inability to solve the problem of the relationship
between men was crucial. In the novels of his next phase, he attempted
to rebuild a 'male' ethos, one transcending sexuality.

Women in Love is sometimes interpreted on narrowly moralistic
lines, making sharp distinctions between Birkin-and-Ursula and
Gerald-and-Gudrun. In fact, the characters are not clearly separable,
but enactments of Lawrence's own impulses, while all are caught up
in the flux of dissolution, which is morally ambivalent. The flow is of
death; dissolution may enable union; corruption may bring release
from isolation; reduction may enable a new start. The essential morality

of the novel is not that of conventional morality, nor its mere inversion, but the vitalist morality of truth to the self.

III

ENGLAND, MY ENGLAND

The next collection of stories (1922) grows out of the insights gained in the experience of the two great novels, and presents, in varying degree, the effects of the war, and of the warfare between the sexes. The link between the two wars is made explicit in 'Monkey Nuts': when the young soldier was rescued from the predatory female, he 'felt more relieved even than he had felt when he had heard the firing cease, after the news that the armistice had been signed'.

The title story, the most important, clearly presents the death of a culture (having something in common with the poems of Yeats, 'Ancestral Houses' and 'The Second Coming'[20]), and is closely related both in thought and imagery, to the essay 'The Crown' (both written in 1915; the story was revised for this collection). The protagonist is a young man of Lawrence's own age, an aesthete with a taste for expensively simple living, morris dancing and William Morris prints, who is parasitic upon his society and culture, as embodied in his father-in-law. For all his 'youth and health and passion and promise', he lives only on the bright surface of life, unaware of the violent forces in nature, that are the fount of vitality. The place where he and his young wife live should make them realise these forces:

Strange how the savage England lingers in patches: as here, amid these shaggy gorse commons, and marshy, snake-infested places near the foot of the south downs. The spirit of place lingering on primeval . . .

This spirit fills their old cottage (the property of her father), that is

dark, like a lair where strong beasts had lurked and mated. . . . They too felt they did not belong to the London world any more. Crockham had changed their blood: the sense of the snakes that lived and slept even in their own garden, in the sun.

One snake attacks a frog, causing it to emit 'the strangest scream, like the very soul of the dark past crying aloud';[21] this is the amoral savagery that Egbert ignores. Lacking this intensity, this creative-destructive energy, he is null and purposeless, incapable of ordering his garden, his children, or his work.

His wife respects her father more, 'a tough old barbarian fighting spirit' whose 'blood was strong even to coarseness. But that only made the home more vigorous, more robust and Christmassy.' His values, the structure of his morality, are now too weak to support the tree of life, and Egbert will not attempt to prolong them. As a result the old man seems only a persistent relic, while Egbert makes his 'old dark, Catholic blood-authority [seem] a sort of tyranny'. Egbert's anarchic reasonableness leads to an accident, when his daughter cuts her knee on a sickle he has left out. 'But then it was an accident—it was an accident. Why should he feel guilty?' The parallel with Gerald Crich's murderous rationalism is clear; Egbert, too, is a Cain, with the stigma cleft upon his forehead.

The child's leg is only saved from amputation by the authoritative intervention of the father-in-law. After this, the wife dies as an individual, and in her relationship with Egbert; love and passion are replaced by duty. Egbert's reaction against this leads him to the principle of corrupt vitality, the dispossessed man's yearning for sensual savagery, in a sophisticated and degenerate primitivism that apes the natural power of the previous generation.

His heart went back to the savage old spirit of the place: the desire for old gods, old, lost passions, the passion of the cold-blooded, darting snakes that hissed and shot away from him, the mystery of blood-sacrifices, all the lost, intense sensations of the primeval people of the place, whose passions seethed in the air still, from those long days before the Romans came. The seethe of a lost, dark passion in the air. The presence of unseen snakes.

Before the accident and his wife's stultifying 'duty' he was egoistic, irresponsible, incapable of seeing any significance in life; now he has a sense of a savage underworld, that gives him a perverse vitality. He and his daughter become snake-like, with flickering smiles, 'like members of some forbidden secret society. Knowledge they had in common, the same secret of life', like Gerald and Gudrun. Portentous references to Baal and Ashtaroth link with 'The Crown', that provides some illumination:

Aphrodite is, on one side, the great goddess of destruction in sex, Dionysus in the spirit. Moloch and some gods of Egypt are gods also of the knowledge of death. In the soft and shiny voluptuousness of decay, in the marshy chill heat of reptiles, there is the sign of the Godhead. It is the activity of departure. And departure is the opposite equivalent of coming together; decay, corruption, destruction, breaking down is the opposite equivalent of creation. In infinite going-apart there is revealed again the pure absolute, the absolute relation: this time truly as a Ghost: the ghost of what was. We who live, we can only live or die . . . (P2 402)

Egbert's ghost-like vitality cannot lead to anything positive, but a drift towards death, in the great machine of the war. His vitality was only the phosphorescent ghost of passionate being, mere sensationalism:

This is sensationalism, reduction, of the complex tissue back through rottenness to its elements. And this sensationalism, this reduction back, has
become our very life, our only form of life at all. We enjoy it, it is our lust.

It became at last a collective activity, a war, when, within the great
rind of virtue we thresh destruction further and further, till our whole
civilisation is like a great rind full of corruption, of breaking down, a
mere shell threatened with collapse upon itself. (P2 388)

. . . if we die sufficiently, the whole frame and form and edifice will collapse
upon itself. But it were much better to pull it down, than to have it collapse
upon itself. For we shall be like Samson, buried among the ruins. (P2 415)

Egbert was the last flicker of perverse vitality in the dying Christian-
rational-liberal culture, and parody of the new passionate and savage
culture that Lawrence believed would replace it: 'the reign of love is
passing, and the reign of power is coming again' (P2 436). The colossal
horse Egbert glimpses as he dies is more than German cavalry, but
rather another form of Yeats's apocalyptic

> . . . rough beast, its hour came round at last,
> Slouch[ing] towards Bethlehem to be born.

The other stories are concerned also with the effect of the war, and
the war of the sexes. The theme of female aggression is dealt with in
several more or less comic stories: 'Samson and Delilah', 'Monkey
Nuts', 'The White Peacock', 'Tickets Please'. In the first of these,
the wife, after throwing out her newly returned errant husband, so
asserting her dignity, then accepts him and submits to him, to their
mutual satisfaction. The story provides a light-hearted illustration of
Lawrence's dictum of five years later that

sex contact with another individual mean[s] a whole meeting, a contact
between two alien natures, a grim rencontre, half battle and half delight
always, and a sense of renewed and deeper being afterwards. (CL 725)

'Tickets Please' is a comic version of the nightmare of female sexual
aggression, a parody of the dismembering of Orpheus by the Thracian
Bacchantes. During the war, a group of 'fearless young hussies'
became ticket-collectors on some Midland trams; there is an atmosphere
of anarchic abandonment and barely-controlled energy, a 'certain
wild romance'. The young tram-inspector (significantly named John
Thomas—a popular euphemism for the phallus) is the Don Juan of
the line, and his latest girl is Annie, 'something of a tartar'. Their
initial flirtation is characterised by a 'subtle antagonism' but when they
meet at the—delightfully evoked—Fair that serves as a Dionysiac
festival, this is replaced by an erotic rapprochement. Annie wants to
develop the relationship on the conscious, personal level, but he insists

on remaining 'a mere nocturnal presence' (the god in the night); frustrated in her desire for a conventional human relationship, she becomes demanding and possessive, which makes him leave her. Vindictively, Annie and the other girls trap him one night, demanding that he choose one, and when he refuses, they attack him. 'He did not give in to them—no, not if they tore him to bits.' He 'chooses' Annie, who cannot now accept him, having overcome him, and she is left in a tortured frustration of hatred and desire.

'Monkey-Nuts' defeats expectations of one comic structure—in that the young man and woman are separated by the older man—replacing it with another, that of the expulsion of the intrusive outsider, with the strengthening of the original group's values. The older man, Albert, provides not wisdom but vulgar shrewdness and wit. He attempts to protect the immature young soldier Joe from the land-girl, Miss Stokes, who however manages to seduce him one moonlit night. The experience is for Joe one of dissolution of his integrity, and the situation and language indicate dangerous female domination; soon young Joe has almost the perverse vitality of Egbert, or the young man in the market in *Women in Love*. One evening Albert substitutes himself for Joe, so defeating her. Next morning, she attempts to re-assert her claim on Joe, who drives her off with the rude phrase that she herself had used before. Though Joe has escaped female domina-tion, it is hard not to prefer Miss Stokes to Albert's coarseness and emotional sterility. The story balances two negative impulses and two comic patterns in an interesting but not really comic or satisfying manner.

Three stories are concerned with the theme of 'touch'. In 'The Blind Man' Lawrence develops his aphorism 'The mind, that is the Light; the senses, they are the Darkness' (*Twilight in Italy* II). Maurice Pervin, scarred and blinded in the war that is also the sex war,[22] is immersed in the sensual physical-intuitive mode lived by the early Brangwen men, reduced and intensified to a phallic god of the nonhuman, passional underworld:

How near he was, and how invisible! The darkness seemed to be in a strange swirl of violent life, just upon her. She turned giddy . . . he was a tower of darkness to her, as if he rose out of the earth . . . when he stood up his face and neck were surcharged with blood, the veins stood out on his temples.

Their life is, however, a one-sided and unbalanced existence, and he and his wife sometimes find it claustrophobic. She consciously yearns for the social-intellectual values represented by a platonic admirer, Bertie, who fears direct feeling and close contact, being unable 'to approach women physically' (implying either psychic impotence or unrealised homosexuality). When Bertie visits them, Maurice withdraws from social chat into the mindless animal warmth of the dark barn (like the womb-barn of *The Rainbow*). When Bertie goes to fetch him back, the blind man feels Bertie's face, before making him feel his own blind, scarred eyes. The scene has sexual overtones (as in the similar—but heterosexual—scene in *The Lost Girl*); there is an element of the curative ritual of the laying-on of hands; Maurice feels that his physical nature and physical (psychical?) deformity have been accepted by the representative of civilised society. Afterwards Maurice feels reconciled with the world of light, exalted by 'the passion of friendship', his being enhanced. He is described as 'like a strange colossus', that is, the Samson who has destroyed an effete and decadent civilisation. The enforced physical contact[23] and awareness have annihilated Bertie: 'He was like a mollusc whose shell is broken.' The ending is, as Lawrence said, 'queer and ironical' (CL 566); the dark god has proved more powerful than the frail representative of light and the social world; but Maurice has not achieved the friendship, and the balanced relationship with the world, that he needs.

In 'The Horse-Dealer's Daughter' (originally entitled 'The Miracle') the young woman is literally, and the young man metaphorically, saved from death. The social, physical world is solidly presented, though charged with symbolic power: we see the collapse of a family's fortune and life, as their horses (the symbols of life-energy) depart. The young doctor sees the woman as 'intent and remote . . . like looking into another world'; this sense of an alien presence is part of his shock when he sees her attempt to drown herself; the impersonality of death increases the impersonal power of sexual need afterwards, when he has saved her, and she has assumed, and so forced into open being, his desire for her. The shock and pain of escape from death, of new life and commitment, are extreme—and sensitively portrayed.

'You Touched Me' is in a way transitional between 'The Daughters of the Vicar' and 'The Fox'. In the two later works, the reader may well have doubts about the socially-inferior and 'insouciant' young man, whose desire for material or social advancement is inseparable from his desire for the 'imprisoned' woman. While he provides a release for her from sterility, he is less obviously 'a heroic triumph of life';[24] there will be, one suspects, loss as well as gain, in terms of a full humanity. 'You Touched Me' also brushes the theme of unrealised incestuous desires, in the relationship between the young man and the women who had brought him up, and in the father (for whom she intended the caress that 'woke up' the young man) forcing the girl into marriage, and then to kiss him and her young husband, with whom he partially identifies.

The young man has some of the slinking courage and 'underground quality of the rat'. This demonic, amoral vitality is apparent in the young man in 'Fanny and Annie': 'Flame-lurid his face . . . the pulse and darkness of red fire from the furnace towers in the sky . . . lit him. . . .' This opening should qualify any interpretation of the story as a 'social-realist' tale of a snobbish young woman forced to make do with a lumpish and provincial Lothario. The story is certainly rooted firmly in the midland proletarian world, with a lively tone, and a good sense of character and of comedy. The harvest-festival service shows conventional forms charged with natural energy, while the lower-class young man is supremely indifferent when denounced in church by the coarse mother of the loose girl who claims he has fathered her child. Snobbery and conventional morality are defeated by the 'vulgar doom' of the heroine's submission to the young man's sexual power and to working-class-family solidarity. Again, Lawrence does not sentimentalise, and indicates the loss and diminishment for her, as well as suggesting the gain.

Incidentally, it is revealing to contrast Eliot's description of another young man given to illicit intercourse, in 'the young man carbuncular, One of the low on whom assurance sits Like a silk hat upon a Bradford millionaire'[25] with Lawrence's description of Harry:

He had even a kind of assurance on his face as he looked down from the choir gallery at her: the assurance of a common man deliberating entrenched in his commonness. . . . He sang . . . like a canary . . . with a certain defiant passion . . .

Lawrence sees the 'commonness' very clearly—and also something more; Eliot, by contrast, is supercilious and deficient in humanity and insight.

1. 'The Crown', P2 402.
2. cf. 'Nightmare', *Kangaroo* XII.
3. 'The conservative . . . the Liberal . . . Bertie Russell . . . all want the same thing: a continuing in this state of disintegration wherein each separate little ego is an independent little principality by itself . . . at the back of all international peace-for-ever and democratic control talks they want an outward system of nullity . . . so that in their own souls they can be independent little gods, referred to nowhere and to nothing, little mortal Absolutes' (CL 360).
4. W. B. Yeats, 'Crazy Jane Talks with the Bishop', *Collected Poems* (London 1952), p. 295. cf. G. Wilson Knight, Lawrence Joyce and Powys', *Essays in Criticism*, XI, no. 4 (1961).
5. The copulation of insects was associated for Lawrence with subhuman per-

versity, particularly homosexuality, as in this letter of 1915: 'Yesterday, at Worthing, there were many soldiers. Can I ever tell you how ugly they were. "To insects—sensual lust." I like sensual lust—but insectwise, no—it was obscene. I like men to be beasts—but insects—one insect mounted on another— oh God! . . . They will murder their officers one day' (CL 337).

6. Thus F. R. Leavis: 'A novel, like a poem, is made of words; there is nothing else one can point to. . . . The process of "creation" is one of putting words together'; and R. P. Blackmur: 'The reality you labour desperately or luckily to put into your words . . . you will actually have found there, deeply ready and innately informed to give you an objective being and specific idiom to what you knew and did not know that you knew.' Quoted by C. Feidelson Jr., *Symbolism and American Literature* (Chicago, 1953), p. 253 and p. 46 respectively.

7. A scheme adapted from that of H. Daleski, *The Forked Flame* (London, 1965).

8. cf. a letter of 1925, advising on a coal-mining novel: 'What was there in the miners that held the boy's feelings? The darkness, the otherworldness, the peculiar camaraderie, the sort of naked intimacy: men as gods in the underworld, or as elementals. . . . When we get inside ourselves, and away from the vanity of the ego . . . then things are symbols. Coal is a symbol of something in the soul, old and dark and silky and natural, and matrix of fire: and steel is a symbol of something else in the soul, hard and death-dealing, cutting, hurting, annihilating the living tissue forever' (CL 852). In *Women in Love* these two qualities fuse together, suggesting Lawrence's perverse and fearful desire of the male.

9. 'When I drive across this country, with autumn falling and rustling to pieces, I am so sad, for my country, for this great wave of civilisation, 2000 years, which is now collapsing, that it is hard to live. So much beauty and pathos of old things passing away and no new things coming: this house of the Ottoline's —it is England—my God, it breaks my soul—their England, these shafted windows, the elm-trees, the blue distance—the past, the great past, crumbling down' (1915; CL 378).

10. 'Knowledge, true knowledge, is like vaccination. It prevents the continuing of ghastly moral disease. . . . We have got to take the disease into our consciousness and let it go through our soul, like some virus. We have got to realise. And then we can surpass' (P2 358).

11. A metaphor based on Poe's story, 'The Black Cat'.

12. The nature of the revulsion from 'idealistic' self-denial, as in Hermione and Mrs Crich, is discussed in the essay 'Love': 'I love my neighbour as myself . . . until the unfulfilled passion for singleness drives me into action. Then I shall hate my neighbour as I hate myself. And then, woe betide my neighbour and me! Whom the gods wish to destroy they first make mad. . . . We are made mad by the split, the duality in ourselves . . .' (P 155).

13. There was great interest in primitive art in the decades around the turn of the century, not only among anthropologists (in whose work Lawrence was quite well read) but among artists such as Gauguin, Kirchner and Picasso, who responded both to its intensity and its extreme formalisation. By the time *Women in Love* was printed, the taste was somewhat vulgarised and *vieux jeu*. Lawrence saw primitivist art—that is, 'late' primitive or modern imitation—as a distortion of the intuitive understanding, equivalent to the perversion of true male sensuality: 'No man can look at the African grotesque carvings, for example, or the decorative patterns of the Oceanic islanders, without seeing in them the infinitely sophisticated soul which produces distortion from its own distorted psyche, a psyche distorted through myriad generations of degeneration. No one can fail to see the quenched spark of a once superb understanding' (SM 223).

14. 'In his most passionate moments of spiritual enlightenment, when like a saviour of mankind he would pour out his soul for the world, there was in him a capacity to jeer at all his own righteousness and spirituality, justly and sincerely to make a mock of it all. And the mockery was so true, it bit to the very core of his righteousness, and showed it rotten, shining with phosphorescence' ('Prologue' P2 103).

15. cf. the story of the rabbit 'Adolf' (P 7–13) and that of the puppy 'Rex' (P 14–21), that indicate Lawrence's mother's hostility to anarchic natural vitality. 'Rex' touches on Birkin's discussion of the struggle between independence and submission. 'Adolf' shows how love can be a smothering constriction; the rabbit's demonic energy and wild vitality depend on the stimulus of being hunted; 'It is agony. But it is also ecstasy. Ecstasy! . . . He is the unconquerable fugitive, the indomitable meek. No wonder the stoat becomes vindictive.' For this theme, of weakness desiring and stimulating cruelty, and that this is natural, see also 'Rabbit snared in the night' (CP 240).

16. cf. the passage quoted before: 'The moon is the centre of our terrestrial individuality . . . the fierce centre of retraction, of frictional withdrawal into separateness . . . [that] refuses to meet and mingle . . .' (*Fantasia*, p. 146).

17. This is Birkin's version of Lawrence's utopia, Rananim; cf. a letter of 1915: 'I want to gather together about twenty souls and sail away from this world of war and squalor and found a little colony where there shall be no money but a sort of communism as far as necessaries of life go, and some decency. . . . A community which is established upon the assumption of goodness in the members, instead of the assumption of badness' (CL 307). Lawrence was quite serious about this regressive dream of the *avant-garde* for some years. See also G. J. Zytaruk, *The Quest for Rananim* (Montreal and London, 1970).

18. When Birkin cries in his grief "I didn't want it to be like this", Ursula recalls the old Kaiser's words "*Ich habe es nicht gewollt*". These words were attributed to the old Emperor of Austria before his death during the war. While Lawrence may have heard of it during the war, it seems likely that this passage is a post-war addition; Lawrence might have known the great tragic-satiric drama by the Austrian writer Karl Kraus, *Die Letzten Tage der Menschheit* (*The Last Days of Mankind*), published in 1919. There, in the silence after mankind's destruction by the machinery of war, these words are spoken by God. Ursula, we are told, 'looked almost with horror on Birkin'.

19. The conclusion of 'The Education of the People' (1918); 'Marriage and deathless friendship, both should be inviolable and sacred: two great creative passions, separate, apart, but complementary: the one pivotal, the other adventurous: the one marriage, the centre of human life; and the other, the leap ahead' (P 665).

20. W. B. Yeats, op. cit., pp. 225 and 210.

21. The incident also appears in 'The Crown', where Lawrence comments, 'We were all white with fear. But why? In the world of twilight as in the world of light, one beast shall devour another. The world of corruption has its stages, where the lower shall devour the higher, *ad infinitum*' (P2 408).

22. 'I believe in the fight which is everything. And if it is a question of women, I believe in the fight of love, even if it blinds me' (*Aaron's Rod* XVIII).

23. 'No free thing can bear to be encompassed by the psyche of another being, save, perhaps in sheer fright or in sensual love. . . . No free creature willing yields itself to the touch of another being' (SM 60).

24. F. R. Leavis, *D. H. Lawrence: Novelist*, Peregrine ed., p. 98.

25. T. S. Eliot, 'The Waste Land', *Collected Poems* (1936).

4

FLIGHT TO POWER

I

THE DYNAMIC SELF

The death of Gerald in the icy mountains, symbolising man's self-destructive impulse, as seen in the war, announced Lawrence's belief in the impossibility of his finding love and common purpose with men, at least in the choking atmosphere of England. More and more, it seemed that the solution of his problems might be found in a new life elsewhere.

I *know* now, finally:
(a) That I want to go away from England for ever.
(b) That I want *ultimately* to go to a country of which I have hope, in which I feel the new unknown. . . . England has a long and awful process of corruption and death to go through. America has dry-rotted to a point where the final *seed* of the new is almost left ready to sprout. When I can, I shall go to America, and find a place. (CL 481–2)

This feeling was behind his latest work, written in 1917–18, the essays in American literature that were later, considerably emended, to become *Studies in Classic American Literature* (1923). In these essays, Lawrence presented the early Americans as seeking—like himself, though not consciously—new being in a new place. Combining theorising about individual and cultural psychology, he analyses the sickness of European civilisation (and implicitly of himself) and looks forward to a new world where the 'savage' passional being and the 'civilised' self will be reconciled, where male relationship will be liberated from fear and repression. The combination here of depth psychology, social theory, history and prophecy appears also in the other discursive works of the time, such as 'Education of the People', *Movements in European History* (1921), *Psychoanalysis and the Unconscious* (1921), and *Fantasia of the Unconscious* (1922):

the result of five years of persistent work. They contain a whole *weltan-schauung*—new, if old—even a new science of psychology—pure science. (CL 595)

As one would expect, Lawrence rejects formalistic literary theories; in his later essay on Galsworthy (1928; P 539) he wrote,

We judge a work of art by its effect on our sincere and vital emotion, and nothing else. All the critical twiddle-twaddle about style and form, all this pseudo-scientific classifying and analysing of books in an imitation-botanical fashion, is mere impertinence and mostly dull jargon. . . . A critic must be able to *feel* the impact of a work of art in all its complexity and force.

And in 'Morality and the Novel' (1925; P 527–32) he insisted,

The business of art is to reveal the relation between man and his circumambient universe, at the living moment. As mankind is always struggling in the toils of old relationships, art is always ahead of the "times" which themselves are always far in the rear of the living moment.

To discuss art is to discuss life; there are the same requirements: to abandon preconceptions and cliché responses, to grasp the individual essence. Discussing his own poetry, he wrote,

We can break the stiff neck of habit. We can be in ourselves spontaneous and flexible as flame, we can see that utterance rushes out without artificial form or artificial smoothness. But we cannot positively prescribe any emotion, any rhythm. (P 221)

So, he summed up the critic's duty: to ignore the artist's conscious intention, and to accurately register the essential meaning of the work itself, as presented to his own consciousness:

Never trust the artist. Trust the tale. The proper function of a critic is to save the tale from the artist who created it. (SCAM 9)

This may be achieved through a right understanding of symbolism, that is, the universal, 'archetypal' symbols unconsciously shared and recognised by all men. So, in his introduction to Frederick Carter's book on Apocalypse, he wrote, like a good Symbolist:

A complex of emotional experience is a symbol. And the power of the symbol is to arouse the deep emotional self, and the dynamic self, beyond comprehension. . . . No man can invent symbols. He can invent an emblem, made of images: or metaphors: or images: but not symbols carried on in the human consciousness for centuries. (P 296)

Likewise, in his first essay on Hawthorne, he writes:

Art-speech is . . . a language of pure symbols. But whereas the authorised symbol stands for a thought or an idea, some mental *concept*, the art-symbol or art-term stands for a pure experience, emotional and passional, spiritual and perceptual, all at once. (SM 19)

Such a theory *should* prevent merely personal interpretation; Lawrence certainly made his author's work his own, and the American literature essays are as personal and self-exploratory as any of his writing. In fact, many of his insights into American literature are upheld and developed in Leslie Fiedler's *Love and Death in the American Novel,* which is, indirectly, extremely illuminating about Lawrence. Fiedler's work reveals how the transcendental element in American literature—Lawrence's original title for the essays—answered a need in Lawrence's psyche. Lawrence's 'philosophy' of 'amoral' organic harmony seems most obviously a reaction against his mother's values, but Fiedler's brief synopsis of (American) nineteenth-century religion suggests how Lawrence's beliefs grew directly out of his mother's Puritanism.

By the late nineteenth century, according to Fiedler, Puritanism had split into two: one wing had passed via eighteenth-century "enthusiasm" and Methodism towards a hysterical evangelism—evoked briefly in the description of the tin chapels in the opening pages of *Apocalypse.* The impetus of

middlebrow, middle-class Puritanism . . . carries it, by way of rationalism and religious liberalism, to Unitarianism and beyond to a series of post-Christian, syncretistic beliefs. . . . Religion is finally defined as a vague call to social service and "duty", and as anti-materialism, which is to say a refusal to accept the body and its limitations (including death itself!) as real. Such a commitment to "spiritual" values leads, on the one hand, to a bland cosmic optimism, which denies "innate depravity" and considers evil an illusion or a mistake; and on the other hand, to a bloodless sort of asceticism, often combined with advanced social ideas.[1]

These are recognisably the values that Lawrence associated with his mother's civilisation, values that he fought against all his life.

The mid nineteenth-century culmination of that faith is, of course, Transcendentalism . . . [that] rests upon a series of assumptions sustained not by reason but by feeling and a home-made mythology. Some of the key assumptions are: that the real world is a world of ideas not apparent to the senses; that nature is beneficent and rational, and that man is, therefore, *at home* in the universe; that, in fact, both man and Nature participate in God, who is not finally separate from either; that consequently the fittest church is unadorned Nature itself and the truest Bible the heart of the lonely thinker; that a man alone with himself is closest to perfection and that mass society tends to corrupt him; that there is no evil illusion and distrust of the self. Such beliefs urge upon man as his essential duty the act of saying "Yea!" to everything, of crying out "I accept the Universe!"

The closeness of this position to Lawrence's does not require emphasis; what is missing appears in Fiedler's third line of development from Puritanism, what he terms 'tragic Humanism', as it appears in the works of Melville and Hawthorne. Among their assumptions, shared to some extent by Lawrence, especially in the early 1920s, are the following:

that the world of appearance is at once real and a mask through which we can dimly perceive more ultimate forces at work; that Nature is inscrutable, perhaps basically hostile to man, but certainly in some sense alien; that in man and Nature alike, there is a "diabolical" element, a "mystery of iniquity"; that it is impossible to know fully either God or ourselves, and that our only protection from destructive self-deceit is the pressure and presence of others; that to be alone is, therefore, to be lost; that evil is real, and that the thinking man breaks his heart trying to solve its compatibility with the existence of a good God or his own glimmering perceptions of goodness. From this it follows that the writer's duty is to say "Nay!", to deny the easy affirmations by which most men live, and to expose the blackness of life most men try deliberately to ignore. . . . In 1850 the sole name for what we would call the unconscious was "hell"; and forays into that region were therefore regarded as courting damnation.

This element is clearly very strong in Lawrence's writing, particularly, as noted above, in the early 1920s, with the culminating struggle of reconciliation, and consequent 'heartbreak', in the year of the writing of *The Plumed Serpent*, when he plunged deepest into 'the blackness of life', the 'living body of darkness', that proved ultimately beyond his possession.

Turning back, however, to the American essays, that are of crucial importance in the understanding of Lawrence: in the first essay, he discusses the strangulation of the 'pre-conscious' body of medieval Europe by modern civilisation, that is particularly opposed to the free play of the male sensual being. The early settlers, he claims,

lusted spiritually for utter repression in the sensual or passional self . . . cut and destroyed the living bond between men [the species or the sex?], the rich passional contact. And for this passional contact gradually was substituted the mechanical bond of purposive utility. (SM 27)

This conscious, 'civilising' purpose was however overborne by the unconscious desire for liberty, not just of the conscious ego but of the whole being, in a larger body:

Men are free when they are in a living homeland, not when they are struggling and breaking away. . . . Men are free when they belong to a living, organic, *believing* community, active in fulfilling some unfulfilled purpose. . . . Men are not free when they are doing just as they like. . . . Men are only free when they are doing what the deepest self likes. (SCAM 12)

The unfulfilled purpose of Lawrence's deepest self is to be in harmony
with a larger male body; in America, frustrating civilisation might
combine with the passional-homosexual self hitherto condemned and
feared as savage. This, he claimed, happened to the first settlers:

They breathed a savage air, and their blood was suffused and burnt . . .
their first and rarest life-stuff transmuted. (SM 29)

His first author is Benjamin Franklin, a little man who denies the
passionate vitality of nature, an imitation child (like the curate in
'Daughters of the Vicar'); though this writer embodies the principle
of the rationalistic, mechanistic control of nature, yet Lawrence recognises in Franklin his own first need for self-knowledge and self-control:

It is not until man has utterly seized power over himself, and gained complete
knowledge of himself, down to the most minute and shameful of his desires
and sensations, that he can really begin to be free. (SM 48)

Then, man does not have to commit himself to abstraction or to
barbarism, but can find 'the perfect *unique* self, incommutable; not in
any eternity, but in the sheer Now' (SM 44). Thus the next author,
Crèvecœur, is saved from his cliché mind by his glimpses of vivid
natural energy, symbolising the underlying passional self: birds and,
especially interesting to Lawrence, snakes. In the early version (SM)
Lawrence's hope of curing himself led him to credit Crèvecœur's
story of white children brought up by Indians being happiest with
them; by the time of the later version (SCAM), he rejects this, being
more aware of the power and regressive nature of the 'savage' impulse.
    Lawrence knew well enough how his problems arose from his
sensual inhibition by his mother; writing on Fenimore Cooper,
discussing the need of self-liberation from past guilts, he wrote that
his own dead (that is, his mother) lived on in him, unappeased and
demanding. The conflict of the two principles of love and desire,
civilisation and the savage, the deer and the tiger was the condition
of life—painful, intense, but life.
    First, absorption by women's love must be avoided, in the sexless
relationship of two men, as in that between Cooper's Natty and
Chingachgook:

They are the dual centre of all the whirl of life. . . . Two mature, silent,
expressionless men, they stand on opposite shores of being, and their love,
the inexpressible conjunction between them, is the bridge over the chasm
(SM 102–3)

—replacing the heterosexual rainbow. Such relationship is the source
of the future, while procreative sexuality is a mere 'mechanical
marking-time of the creative presence', and 'it is not in children that the

new takes place: it is in the mature, consummated men and women'.
So Frieda need not regret her lost or unconceived children: Lawrence
himself is the new birth. Marriage is just a seductive trap for cowards:

> Most men would rather have a home which is misery and torment than suffer
> from the sense of exposure to the winds of fate . . . it is a shrinking from the
> sheer communion in isolation which lies ahead, the mystic consummation
> of the White soul with the Red. (SM 105)

That is, of the civilised and rational with the savage and passional,
whether between two races or within one man. In the later version,
intercourse between the two sexes is regarded as self-destructive;
emotionless asexuality means integrity, as in Deerslayer:

> A man who turns his back on white society. A man who keeps his moral
> integrity hard and intact [by avoiding personal and sexual relations—and
> the phallic metaphor is clear]. An isolate, almost selfless, stoic, enduring
> man, who lives by death, by killing, but who is pure white . . . (SCAM 66)
> [the worst of both worlds!]

In the early version, Deerslayer (in many ways like Gerald Crich)
does not succumb to the woman, the Magna Mater of his shame, but
returns into the solitary womb-security of death: 'before him lies the
leap into space, into oblivion, into death. . . . For him the physical
consummation is a consummation into death' (SM 110–11).

Edgar Allan Poe's tales of murderously devouring incest are partly
concerned with self-destruction for self-recreation:

> This is how man must bury his own dead self: in pang after pang of vital
> explosive self-reduction, back to the elements. This is how the seed must
> fall into the ground and perish before it can bring forth new life . . . it is
> only perfect courage which can carry us through the extremity of death,
> through the crisis of our own nullification . . . (SM 117)

Poe's tales are the analysis of how the consciousness seeks to possess
and control the sensual being (that is, how Lawrence's mother attempted to possess him), in an unnatural urge for merging and identification.
Lawrence writes,

> But it is not enough to say, as Jung does, that all life is a matter of lapsing
> towards, or struggling away from, mother-incest. It is necessary to see what
> lies at the back of this . . . (SM 125)

but his analysis of this impulse towards conscious possession ends up
by saying only:

> It is the world-long incest problem, arising inevitably when man, through
> insistence of his will in one passion or aspiration, breaks the polarity of
> himself. (SM 128)

With the loss of a sense of real individual being, comes the sense of an animate, responsive womb-cosmos,

the special atmosphere in which alone the Ushers [Lawrence] could live. And it was this atmosphere which had moulded the destinies of his family. (SM 127)

The dialectic is of escape from the mother into independence, and the fearful return to security in the mother:

So the mystery goes on. La Bruyère says that all our human unhappiness *vient de ne pouvoir être seuls.* (SM 130)

This analysis of Poe has helped Lawrence, or so he hopes, to possess himself; Poe's tales

need to be written because old things need to die and disintegrate, because the old white psyche has to be gradually broken down before anything else can come to pass. . . . For the human soul must suffer its own disintegration, *consciously,* if ever it is to survive. (SCAM 67)

Such disintegration is the theme of the next study, of Hawthorne. *The Scarlet Letter* reveals the futility of men attempting to suppress the sensual being in themselves or in women (who are more threatening); man must combine the masculine (deep—even homosexual—desire) and the feminine (constricting, devouring consciousness and civilisation), as it is found in the Magna Mater:

Man must either lead or be destroyed. Woman cannot lead. She can only be at one with man in the creative union, whilst he leads; or failing this, she can destroy . . . it is the age of fatal, suffocating love . . . (SM 143–4)

Yet the essay is remarkable both for its fear of woman, the Magna Mater, and for its lack of confidence in male strength, which still needs woman's support to prevent collapse into perversion. In one passage, ostensibly about Hawthorne, Lawrence presents his own situation directly:

Hester . . . urges Dimmesdale to go away with her to a new country, to begin a new life. . . . When a man responds to the prompting of a woman to a new life, he has not only to face the world itself, but a great reaction in the very woman he takes. . . . If Dimmesdale had fled with Hester they would have felt themselves social outcasts. And they would have had to live in secret hatred of mankind, like criminal accomplices; or they would have felt isolated, cut off, two lost creatures, a man meaningless except as the agent, or tool, or creature of the possessive woman. . . . It would have been necessary for Dimmesdale in some way to conquer society with a new spirit and a new idea. And this was impossible. The time was by no means ripe. The old idea must be slowly undermined . . . (SM 145)

Here is Lawrence's fear of 'facing the world'; the woman has taken the initiative, and might overwhelm him; here is the fear of becoming the isolated outsider, excluded from normality, drifting into 'criminality' (a word suggestive of homosexuality, for Lawrence), and the realisation of the long campaign necessary to undermine society and prepare a new community.

The Magna Mater is then imaged as a witch, arousing unsatisfiable desires, thwarting the sensual impulses, turning the isolated individual, cut off from 'creative unison', into something perverse. Such an individual is Hester's daughter, Pearl (related to Egbert's daughter in 'England, My England'), with a spirit

"so perverse, sometimes so malicious, but generally expressed by a wild flow of spirits. . . ." She has a sort of reckless gallantry, the pride of her own deadly being. We cannot help regarding the phenomenon of Pearl with wonder, and fear, and amazement, and respect. (SM 149)

This is the spirit of Loerke, and anticipates Lawrence's attitude to Maurice Magnus—each of them the unnatural outsider he feared to become.

The second part of the Hawthorne discussion is concerned with attacking modern science, which subjects the individual to inexorable external laws, and with defending Lawrence's own science, derived from 'alchemy and astrology, and the Hermetic science', in which the individual's 'life-will' may control both physical and psychological nature. This comforting theory involves forbidden knowledge. One of Hawthorne's characters, Chillingworth, is apparently an exponent, and is described as a demonic magician, and associated with 'the Black Man that haunts the forest', the suppressed 'sensual male being in complete subordination, as we have him in modern life'. His spiritual descendant Hollingsworth is a 'dark, black-bearded monomaniac . . . Hephaestos of the underworld', with 'criminal' obsessions. When Hollingsworth nurses the sick Hawthorne (cf. Lilly nursing Aaron, *Aaron's Rod* IX), Hawthorne resists his lust for domination—that is, resists homosexual male power. The consequences of such a submission are seen in Hollingsworth's young wife Priscilla, who gives him

the last horrible thrills of sensual experience, in the direct *destruction* of the sensual body, pure prostitution . . . (SM 157)

She is reduced, dehumanised, acquiring an unnatural intensity, in

the infernal reality such as is suggested by the old legends of were-wolves and metamorphoses . . . the last processes of mystic disintegration out of being. The last lust is for this indescribable sensation—whose light we can see in the eyes of a tiger, or a wolf. (SM 158)

This is the self-destruction in submission to male sexuality that appears in *The Lost Girl*, that uses the same imagery.

The next essay, 'The Two Principles', presents Lawrence's 'pure science'. He posits the existence of two elemental principles, fire and water, male and female. When the sexes (actual men and women, or within one individual) meet in 'pure creation' in the 'youth of an era', they produce a soul 'harmonious and at one with itself'. They may, however, meet in

the tremendous conjunction of opposition, a vivid struggle, as fire struggles with water . . . it is the birth of a disintegrative soul, wherein the two principles wrestle in their eternal opposition . . . in the times of disintegration, the crumbling of an era. (SM 185)

Lawrence sees an imbalance in his parentage and in himself, and a movement towards abandonment of normal sexuality—'The sexes have no more dynamic connection, only a habitual or deliberate connection' —and towards isolation. From this unhappy position he turns to another scheme offering more hope, contrasting the upper 'spiritual' half of the body, source of the 'compulsion to equality and virtue', with the lower sensual half of the body (particularly the lower back and base of the spine, that is, the anus) where he finds

a magnificent central positivity . . . as a wheel sleeps in speed on its positive hub . . . a state portrayed in the great dark statues of the seated lords of Egypt. . . . there is the world of living dark waters, where the fire is quenched in the watery creation. Here, in the navel, flowers the water-born lotus, the soul of the water begotten by one germ of fire. And the lotus is the symbol of our perfected sensual first-being, which rises in blossom from the unfathomable waters . . . [where] we have our passionate self-possession, our unshakable and indomitable being. (SM 186–7)

So Lawrence swings back to find strength and reassurance in the male flower and the ultraphallic body of darkness.

Male divinity makes a violent appearance in the next essay, on Dana (of which only the later version is extant). Dana's voyages are interpreted as the individual's confrontation with man's basic elements, with the sea as the deadly-mother principle, the Magna Mater, destructive of man's 'integral being'. The isolated individual, like the solitary albatross or ship, struggles against the overwhelming, dehumanising friction of the female element. In Dana's story the tension of this struggle, and of that against repression by the forces of idealistic civilisation, 'machine-control, selfless, ideal control', is released by a flogging, which Lawrence interprets as the human equivalent of a thunder-storm that violently corrects the imbalance between fire and water (male and female). It is 'spontaneous passional morality, not the artificial ethical', and 'a natural form of human coition, interchange'. This symbol of the conflict between the thunderbolts of paternal deity and the drowning mother-element provide an insight into Lawrence's own state of tension at that time, that produced the blind, hysterical rages for which he later became notorious. After this confrontation with the mother element, Lawrence hopes for a new harmony, 'a winged centrality', like that of the sailing-ship:

It is this perfect adjusting of ourselves to the elements, the perfect equipoise between them and us, which gives us a great part of our life-joy. (SM 209)

This inner equipoise remained only a dream, and the Melville essays return to the struggle between the 'civilised' and the 'savage'. Melville, as the Viking Spirit, looks like Gerald, and acts like Loerke (Gerald's alter ego):

he has that strange inscrutable magic and mystery of the sea-creatures . . . the same curious repulsiveness, or inferiority of order . . . (SM 219)

His wanderings in the Pacific islands are a regression, a return into the womb-world, 'the heaven under the wave', 'the green Eden of the first, or last era, the valley of the timeless savages' that contains the last, somewhat degenerated remnants of 'the great sensual-mystic civilisations now gone'. The savages eat the flesh of other men, but when Melville has overcome his 'civilised' horror of this religious-magical means of assuming other men's power,

he finds himself at once in a pure, mysterious world, pristine . . . naked, simplicity of life, with subtle, non-mental understanding, rapport between human beings. (SM 225)

Yet he cannot indulge in deliberate primitivism (his horror at the shark-tattooed renegade Englishman anticipates Alvina's horror of the reptilian, tattooed Japanese in *The Lost Girl*), or regress to the 'savage', plunging into a male sensual world (however mystic). Modern 'progress' is some kind of 'life-development' and irreversible, just as Lawrence is terrified of abandoning his 'civilised' control over his (homosexual) passions.

We can't go back to the savages: not a stride. We can be in sympathy with them. We can take a great curve in their direction, onwards. But we cannot turn the current of our life backwards, back towards their soft warm twilight and uncreate mud. . . . We can only do it when we are renegade. (SCAM 138)

The inner struggle must continue. In the early version, Lawrence seems to think that some resolution is possible, but in the later one, he cannot envisage any perfect relationship or cessation of struggle, and settles for a stoic endurance.

Moby Dick sounds like a lost work by Lawrence himself, including as it does so many Lawrentian *motifs*. There is the lonely wanderer, Ishmael, briefly finding male love, with Queequeg; the solitary doomed idealist, Ahab, scarred with the scar of sexual agony, hunting down the embodiment of the phallic being, the libido (imaged elsewhere—e.g., *Apocalypse*—as a dragon); the solitary white albatross; the vision of 'the heaven beneath the wave' in the sight of the mother whales suckling their young, central in the clear depths; the terrifying aspect of the phallic being, in the appearance of the squid; the phallic being in peaceful, beneficent majesty, in the vision of the white whale on the surface; and the horror of the disastrous attempt to destroy 'the dragon of the primary self, the sensual psyche'—to quote the Hawthorne essay.

The last essay attempts a solution. Lawrence attacks Whitman's idealising, solipsist tendency, where independent being is swallowed up by the great body of life. Whitman's merging involves self-sacrifice,

the ecstasy of *giving himself*, and of being taken. . . . He knows nothing of the other sacrament, the sacrament in pride, where the communicant envelops the victim and host in a flame of ecstatic consuming, sensual gratification, and triumph. (SM 260)

This is the sacrifice of others for individual (sexual) satisfaction, that is very close to the Melville savages' cannibalism. Lawrence then takes up the theme of common male activity; when

man acts womanless it is no longer a question of race continuance. It is a question of sheer, ultimate being, the perfection of life, nearest to death. . . . And the polarity is between man and man . . . (SM 260–1)

as the plant in Whitman's poem 'Calamus' produces 'without the intervention of woman, the female. . . . It is the cohering principle of final unison in creative activity'.

The love between men is purged of its unacceptable 'savage' homosexuality, and made morally respectable, and superior to love for women:

true marriage is eternal; in it we have our consummation and our being. But the final consummation lies in that which is beyond marriage . . . then, at last, we shall know our starry maturity. (SM 264)

The essays display Lawrence's attempt to analyse and solve his personal problems. In the 'civilised' ethos of women and the masses he feels merely relative, inadequate and frustrated; he needs to assert his repressed sensual being without becoming isolated by becoming 'renegade', overtly homosexual. Knowledge of himself will, he hopes, bring power, integrated being, and the ability to relate harmoniously with other men (by the time of the later version, the male community has been replaced by a 'gladder worship of great and greater souls, because they are the only riches').

The other discursive non-fiction works of the time continue the attempt to universalise his own problems and, like Dimmesdale, to slowly undermine the old idea of civilisation, and 'conquer society with a new spirit and a new idea'. In *Psychoanalysis and the Unconscious* (1920) he continues his attack on modern science, in this case Freudian psychology. This theory he sees as implying that 'the unconscious' is not simply pre-conscious and pre-moral, but the locus of desires perverted and repressed by the consciousness, but which must be liberated. Lawrence dare not approve such a theory, fearing as he does the disastrous consequences of the enactment of such desires.

He displays considerable self-knowledge and frankness in a remarkable passage (the metaphor at the end is obviously derived from Poe's 'The Pit and the Pendulum', which shows a man trapped between terrifying vaginal and phallic symbols respectively):

A man finds it impossible to realise himself in marriage. He recognises the fact that his emotional, even passional regard for his mother is deeper than it ever could be for a wife. This makes him unhappy, for he knows that passional communion is not complete unless it be also sexual. He has a body of sexual passion which he cannot transfer to a wife. He has a profound love for his mother. Shut in between the walls of tortured and increasing passion, he must find some escape or fall down the pit of insanity or death. . . . And so the incest-motive is born . . .

—or the homosexual. Enactment is impossible, and sublimation futile:

We have still to find some way out. For there we are, all of us, trapped in a corner where we cannot, and simply do not know how to fulfil our own natures, passionally.

In *Fantasia of the Unconscious* (1922), Lawrence presents his familiar dualistic scheme of existence. On one side are moon, woman, (self-)consciousness, self-denying love and procreative sexuality; on the other side, sun, man, intuition, 'strong self-possession' and 'shared religious purpose'. These two groups of forces should not however be equal; the concept of balance has modulated into the concept of proportion: woman is in due proportion when subordinate to man, who may find renewal in sex (though this may be merely regressive,[2] the service of the Magna Mater), but achieves fulfilment only in 'religious' fulfilment in the world of men.

So, in ch. 1, Lawrence insists that the sex impulse is second to the religious or creative impulse, in ch. 7 that when woman is regarded as the prime being man finds no effective independent being, and in ch. 8, that when sex is seen as the prime motive in life, the world drifts into mechanical activity, despair and anarchy. Due 'proportion' must be kept, for wholeness of being:

The goal is *not* ideal. The aim is *not* mental consciousness. We want *effectual* human beings, not conscious ones. The final aim is not *to know*, but *to be*. (*Fantasia*, p. 60)

Lawrence again outlines his 'pseudo-science' or 'polly-analytics' as he defensively called them (p. 10). His theory is designed to dissolve the separation of mind and personality from body, by linking various emotions and values to various nerve-centres of the body. While the interrelationship of the physical and the psychological is more accepted now than in Lawrence's day, the elaborate system of ganglia and complexes remains rather unprepossessing, and it is hard to feel wholly persuaded by such statements as this:

Let us break the conscious, self-conscious love-ideal, and we shall grow strong, resistant teeth once more, and the teething of our young will not be the hell it is. (p. 54)

On the other hand, much of what the book says about the right upbringing of children for strength and self-confidence is, when considered in the context of its times, quite sensible—for example, the calm acceptance of childish sexual feelings, the avoidance of creating selfconscious, over-sensitive 'Christopher Robins'. However, the limitation of formal education for most children to the age of ten, with that education consisting largely of craft-work, physical training, household skills for the girls, and 'primitive forms of fighting' for the boys, is not likely to commend itself. The twentieth century is not going to go away yet, and at times the phoenix looks much like the ostrich with its head in the sand.

The work is concerned to reduce the effect of the mother's love-idealism, and increase the influence of the father's power and intuitive being. There are two passages in particular where Lawrence identifies intuitive wholeness with phallic, paternal power, identifying with it and desiring it. The first is in a superb description of the Black Forest[3] where the book is being written:

. . . big, tall-bodied trees, with a certain magnificent cruelty about them —or barbarity—I don't know why I should say cruelty. Their magnificent strong, round bodies! . . . it's no good looking at a tree to know it. The only thing is to sit among the roots and nestle against its strong trunk, and

not bother. . . . He towers, and I feel safe. I like to feel him towering round
me. I used to be afraid. I used to fear their lust, their rushing black lust.
But now I like it, I worship it. . . . But I can understand that Jesus was
crucified on a tree. (pp. 37–8)

The short sentences combine the childlike and the ecstatic. Spirit is
destroyed on the phallic trunk of the father, once resisted, now adored.
The second passage is the discussion of a dream of horses (the source
of Ursula's experience in *The Rainbow*), where the horses are identified
as 'male sensual nature', feared by the ego, but desired by the unconscious. The last sentences are revealing:

There may be an element of father-complex. The horse may also refer to
the powerful sensual being in the father. The dream may mean a love of
the dreamer for the sensual male who is his father. But it has nothing to
do with *incest*. The love is probably just love. (p. 155)

Inner conflict is caused when the mother turns to her child for
fulfilment, possessing and inhibiting the libido. This happens when the
woman is not satisfied by the man, who has failed to fulfil himself
(so Lawrence's father must also be held responsible):

When a man approaches the beginning of maturity and the fulfilment of
his individual self, about the age of thirty-five [Lawrence's age at the time
of writing] . . . he must now undertake the responsibility for the next step
into the future. . . . Till a man makes the great resolution of aloneness and
singleness of being, till he takes upon himself the silence and central appeased-
ness of maturity, *and then, after this*, assumes a sacred responsibility for the
next purposive step into the future, there is no rest . . . this is necessary to
every parent, every father, every husband, at a certain point. (pp. 111–12)

This, of course, is what Aaron attempts in *Aaron's Rod*. Without this,
the mother will over-stimulate and destroy her son.

Think of the power which a mature woman thus infuses into her boy. He
flares up like a flame in oxygen [An image dating back to *The Trespasser*].
No wonder they say geniuses mostly have great mothers. They mostly
have sad fates.
    And then?—and then, with this glamorous youth? What is he actually
to do with his sensual, sexual self? (pp. 114–15)

The quest for satisfaction in sexual love is doomed. Instead,

the central fulfilment, for a man, is that he possess his own soul in strength
within him, deep and alone . . . (p. 110) Retreat to the very centre and
there . . . be filled with a new strange stability, polarised in unfathomable
richness with the centre of centres . . . (p. 135)

—which sounds much like Birkin's 'real reality', the anal core. In
this way, man will also be in right relation with the cosmos, central

and powerful in an animate universe apprehended through the intuitive understanding of natural symbols (where, for example, as indicated before, sun and moon are aspects of his own being).

Few, however, are capable of this self-sufficient power, and they must be the priest-kings of the rest of humanity.

The secret is, to commit into the hands of the sacred few the responsibility which lies like torture on the mass. Let the few, the leaders, be increasingly responsible for the whole. And let the mass be free: free, save for the choice of leaders.

Leaders—this is what mankind is craving for.

But men must be prepared to obey, body and soul, once they have chosen the leader. And let them choose the leader for life's sake only. (pp. 78–9)

How these carefree children can judge of a leader is not explained. However, the identity of such a leader is made clear. It is Lawrence himself:[4]

There is no danger of the working man ever reading my books, so I shan't hurt him that way. But . . . I would like him to give me back the responsibility for general affairs . . . for the future . . . for thought, for direction. . . . And I would like to give him back, in return, his old insouciance, and rich, original spontaneity and fullness of life. (p. 103)

Woman's rationalist criticism must be overcome at all costs, to enable the fulfilment in faith, in the new life like death.

She'll never believe until you have your soul filled with a profound and absolutely unalterable purpose, that will yield to nothing, least of all to her. She'll never believe until, in your soul, you are cut off and gone ahead, into the dark. (p. 174)

So sex and love relationships with women are surpassed, in the apotheosis of the male principle, the phallus as bludgeon and idol.

Men have got to choose their leaders, and obey them to the death. And it must be a system of culminating aristocracy, society tapering like a pyramid to the supreme leader. (p. 165)

The nature of such a leader's amoral power appears again in an essay from the autumn of 1920, 'America, Listen to Your Own':

That which was abhorrent to the Pilgrim Fathers and to the Spaniards, that which was called the Devil, the black Demon of savage America, this great aboriginal spirit the Americans must recognise again, recognise and embrace. The devil and anathema of our forefathers hides the Godhead which we seek. (P 90)

II
BEYOND THE PALE

Such a devil-god, or demon, is the concern of *The Lost Girl* (1920), a novel begun before the war under the title *The Insurrection of Miss Houghton* as a counter-blast to Arnold Bennett's *Anna of the Five Towns*,[5] discontinued during the war, and completed in the period February to May 1920.

The protagonist, Alvina Houghton, was probably first thought of fairly simply as a 'nicely-brought-up' young girl who refuses to deny her passional self for provincial ethical values; however, Lawrence develops this self as a perverse one, that finds satisfaction in masochistic submission. The novel begins by outlining the values and social structure of the town in almost Dickensian vein:

A well-established society in Woodhouse, full of fine shades, ranging from the dark of coal-dust ... through the lustre of lard and butter and meat ... on to the serene gold-tarnish of bank-managers, cashiers for the firm, clergymen and such-like, as far as the automobile refulgence of the general-manager of all the collieries. (I)

Set amidst all this there is Alvina, whose values are not pious-Christian nor commercial, but barbaric; she has a sardonic, derisive attitude, 'a look of old knowledge' that can give her face 'a gargoyle look'.

Her first suitor is an Australian from down under, a dark demonic sensuous figure, with 'cruel, compact teeth', whom she does not 'love', in any sense that her governess, Miss Frost, or Alvina herself, would understand the word, but who excites in her a perverse sexuality. 'She felt him an outsider, an inferior', but when with him

found herself in a night where the little man loomed large, terribly potent, potent and magical, while Miss Frost had dwindled to nothingness. (II)

Miss Frost's sterile respectability stifles all her attempts at sexual liberation, particularly her taste for *fleurs du mal*:[6]

It was time now for Miss Frost to die. It was time for that perfected flower to be gathered to immortality. A lovely *immortel*. But an obstruction to other, purple and carmine blossoms which were in bud on the stem. . . . Black purple and red anemones were due, real Adonis blood, and strange individual orchids, spotted and fantastic. (III)

Her search for suppressed underworld experience leads her to a visit to a coal-mine: her response is like that of Gudrun, to Beldover. The coal-miner guide seems 'not human' and

E

there was a thickness in the air, a sense of dark, fluid presence in the thick atmosphere, the dark, fluid viscous voice of the collier making a broad-vowelled, clapping sound in her ear. He seemed to linger near her as if he knew—as if he knew—what? Something forever unknowable and inadmissible . . . knowledge humiliated, subjected, but ponderous and inevitable. (IV)

The surface, civilised world seems insubstantial as a bubble, and she imagines the revolutionary, apocalyptic eruption of this suppressed underworld force

of darkness which had no master and no control . . . it would be simply disastrous, because it had no master. There was no dark master in the world. The puerile world went on crying out for a new Jesus, another saviour from the sky, another heavenly superman. When what was wanted was a Dark Master from the underworld. (IV)

Here in Alvina is Lawrence's fearful desire for demonic male sexuality.

Alvina cannot be content with the petty little men produced by her civilisation. One, Arthur Witham, seems to her 'always a creature, never a man: an atrocious leprechaun from under the Chapel floor' (V)—the dispossessed and furtive man who cannot provide her with true oblivion from egoistic self-consciousness. She then goes to work in her father's little theatre, and this provides some titillation for her: she flirts with a middle-aged alcoholic flute-player (Aaron, no doubt), is fascinated by a figure of lewd, reptilian sexuality—a Japanese tattooed with an eagle on his shoulders and a serpent on his loins (the 'plumed serpent'), and becomes involved with a fantastic group of 'Red Indian' mime artists, the Natcha-Kee-Tawaras, who combine a court of love—complete with Magna Mater—with a rather absurd glimpse of barbaric splendour and quasi-religious ritual.

Here she meets her demon lover Cicio, the loutish, sensual Italian youth who is to be Dis to her Persephone. One of the virtues of this novel is that it does not lose touch with common sense as much as some later works, and Cicio's oafish vulgarity is never altogether forgotten, for all his other qualities of animal grace and passion. Though Alvina fears he may be simply 'stupid and bestial' yet she sees in his features 'a certain finesse . . . refined through ages of forgotten culture'. 'It was the clean modelling of his dark, other-world face that decided her—for it sent the deep spasm across her' (IX). Cicio soon establishes a worldless sexual dominance over her, that annihilates her consciousness through sexual power:

. . . the spell was on her of his darkness and unfathomed handsomeness. And he killed her. He simply took her and assassinated her. How she suffered no one can tell. Yet all the time, his lustrous dark beauty, unbearable. . . . He intended her to be his slave, she knew. (IX)

With her dark Italian she is like the woman with the Negro husband, 'beyond the pale' of normal civilisation:

Alvina felt herself swept—she knew not whither—but into a dusky region where men had dark faces and translucent yellow eyes, where all speech was foreign, and life was not her life. It was as if she had fallen from her own world on to another, darker star, where meanings were all changed. . . . In all the passion of her lover she had found a loneliness, beautiful, cool, like a shadow . . . (X)

After a separation, and last desperate attempt by Alvina to reconcile herself with the world of normality, the 'unintelligent forces' of nature (as a woman in the pangs of childbirth calls them) return in Cicio, who takes her again, and marries her.

There was no wonderful intimacy of speech, such as she had always imagined, and always craved for. . . . His love did not stimulate or excite her. It extinguished her. She had to be the quiescent, obscure woman . . . under all her questionings she felt well; a nonchalance deep as sleep, a passivity and indifference so dark and sweet she felt it must be evil. Evil! She was evil. And yet she had no power to be otherwise. (XIII)

As for Cicio (whose surname Marasca means 'bitter cherry'—or 'dark poison fruit' as Alvina interprets it), 'now something unfolded in him, he was a potent glamorous presence, people turned to watch him'. In him now appears the proud sensual male that Lawrence felt man (especially himself) might be, if women were completely subordinate. The central experience, however, is Alvina's: through her Lawrence explores the consequences of self-abandonment and submission to forbidden male sexuality.

When they go to Italy, leaving the coffin of England behind, it is to no easy, sun-drenched world that Cicio takes her, but a terrifyingly cold and bitter one: for the civilised person to go back to the primitive is to release inhuman terrors.

She seemed to feel in the air strange Furies, Lemures, things that had haunted her with their tomb-frenzied vindictiveness since she was a child and had pored over the illustrated Classical Dictionary. Black and cruel presences were in the under-air. They were furtive and slinking. They bewitched you with loveliness, and lurked with fangs to hurt you afterwards. There it was: the fangs sheathed in beauty—the beauty first, and then, horribly, inevitably, the fangs. (XV)

In his novel, Lawrence imagines the release of the power of male sexuality, both the passion that overwhelmed him, and the homosexuality that he feared. Alvina escapes the frustrations of conventionality, and briefly finds a new 'life' in the underworld, but as the imaginative living-out of experience continues, Lawrence sees that yielding to the tigerish savagery of mindless passion as embodied in a dark man is self-annihilation. The novel approaches tragedy, in Alvina's combined self-liberation and self-destruction; it is superior to much of the later writing in its realism, both in its setting, and in its grasp of how much is negative and destructive, as well as positive and enlivening, in the experience acted out by Alvina—the title is only partly ironic.

Certainly Lawrence dared not give himself over altogether to the furtive and slinking: the consequences of such a career were all too apparent in the life and death of Maurice Magnus, whom he had met in Florence (and who figured in *The Lost Girl* as Mr May, the theatre manager). In the winter of 1919–20 Lawrence was at first without Frieda, and felt very isolated: in the English colony in Florence he found himself in an *ambience* of parasitic bohemianism and homosexuality (evoked in *Aaron's Rod*). Here he met Magnus, and in this cosmopolitan *poseur*, bisexual dandy, and parasitic con-man found an affinity, an affinity with that element in himself portrayed in Loerke. He recognised their common condition as perverse outsiders, and though he condemned much in Magnus, yet he respected in him 'the terrified courage of the isolated Spirit' exploring 'the boundaries of human experience'.

Lawrence's 'Introduction to *Memoirs of the Foreign Legion* by M[aurice] M[agnus]' (P2 303–61), written in January 1922, but based on experiences of 1919–20, is a brilliant little piece, ranging from comedy to hysterical rage, from travel-writing to keen insight. After the light comedy of the opening where Lawrence recounts how he met Magnus with the writer Norman Douglas in Florence, and briefly and with uncertain disapproval shared their bohemian life, comes the account of his visit to Magnus (without Frieda—for Magnus himself is separated from his wife and does not care for women) at the monastery of Monte Cassino, where he is staying, and which Magnus claims, preposterously, to intend joining.

Magnus receives him almost wooingly in the ice-cold monastery, set high above 'the gulf where the world's valley was' (the scheme of *Twilight in Italy*). It is so bitterly cold that, to make their tour of the monastery, Magnus persuades Lawrence to wear his enormous expensive overcoat that is lined with black sealskin and has a collar of black sealskin (fitting perfectly into Lawrence's private symbolism). So they make their tour, before returning to Magnus's room, where he shows Lawrence a photograph of 'a lovely lady' (the hostility in the phrase appears in the later story of that title), whom Lawrence tells him looks 'a bit cheap, trivial'; unfortunately, it is Magnus's mother.

The morning after, Lawrence looks out over the valley and is overcome with yearning for the passion and religious intensity of the outgrown past.

I looked down on the farm cluster and the brown fields and the sere oaks of the hill-crown, and the rocks and bushes savagely bordering it round. And the poignant grip of the past, the grandiose violent past of the Middle Ages, when blood was strong and unquenched and life was flamboyant with splendours and horrible miseries, took hold of me till I could hardly bear it. It was really agony to me to be in the monastery and to see . . . all that lingering nonchalance and wildness of the Middle Ages, and yet to know that I was myself, child of the present. It was so strange from M—'s window to look down on the plain. . . . To see the trains stop in the station and tiny people swarming like flies! . . . This was almost a violation to my soul, made almost a wound. (P2 318–19)

Language and imagery combine to reveal this viewpoint as sterile and perverse regression and assertion of the 'savage', essentially homosexual, sensual being. Magnus, whose views parody Lawrence's, approves of the isolated 'aristocratic' mode, but Lawrence realises that, bitter and frustrating though modern civilisation may be,

here on the mountain-top was worst: the past, the poignancy of the not-quite-dead past. . . . "I think one's got to go through with the life down there—get somehow beyond it. One can't go back," I said to him. (P2 325)

This self-denial, and commitment to struggle, leave him heart-broken, and he leaves Magnus to return to his wife. However, Magnus later turns up again, begging help and money. The next section is filled with the painful comedy of the struggle between Magnus's effrontery, parasitism and pathetic pride, and Lawrence's scrupulous-ness and lower-middle-class carefulness with money. Eventually Magnus's demanding submissiveness seems a threat, and Lawrence refuses more help: Magnus must be self-responsible. Lawrence then outlines Magnus's further brief career of cheeky parasitism and fraud before, cornered by the police on the barren island of Malta, he commits suicide. His death-note is characteristic: "I want to be buried first-class, my wife will pay."

Lawrence feels guilty at having said, in effect, "yes, he must die if he cannot find his own way", but insists on the rightness of this judgment. Magnus was a Judas betraying everyone's trust (but Lilly, in *Aaron's Rod*, says: "A Jesus makes a Judas inevitable. A man should remain himself, not try to spread himself over humanity. He should pivot himself on his own pride."). Yet Lawrence also commends his perverse integrity as a

courageous isolated little devil, facing his risks, and like a good rat, *determined* not to be trapped. . . . He went through vile experiences: he looked them in the face, braved them through, and kept his manhood in spite of them. For manhood is a strange quality, to be found in human rats as well as in hot-blooded men. M— carried the human consciousness through circumstances which would have been too much for me. (P2 357)

Lawrence implicitly identifies with Magnus, and his 'fear of his own self and its consequences'; the recent inhuman mechanical war, against which he rages hysterically, is the hopeless struggle against both the inhumanity of (homosexual) passion, and the inhumanity of suppression of feeling. The dehumanising influences in man can only be conquered by understanding:

This is true of all the great terrors and agonies and anguishes of life: sex, and war, and even crime . . . it is the great command *Know Thyself.* We've got to *know* what sex is, let the sentimentalists wriggle as they like. . . . We've got to know the greatest, and most shattering human passions, let the puritans squeal as they like for screens. And we've got to know humanity's criminal tendency, look straight at humanity's deeds of crime against the soul. . . . Knowledge, true knowledge, is like vaccination. It prevents the continuing of ghastly moral disease. (P2 358)

Magnus, according to Lawrence, had the courage to confront his own 'criminality' and 'disease' (that is, particularly, his homosexuality) and to overcome and surpass them. That this was in fact so is not very apparent, even from Lawrence's account; but this is how Lawrence was determined to see him, as a model for himself. So Lawrence greets a kindred spirit who, like Alvina, Dana and Loerke, had ventured on his behalf where he dared not go himself, and accords him a generous elegiac farewell, as a self-destroyed hero of the human spirit—'a strange, quaking little star'.

Lawrence himself was not so alone, with Frieda to support him; yet at this time, beginning another new life of wandering, he felt very solitary and exposed, desperate for new identity. This feeling appears in several of the 'thought-adventures' of the time—to use the term he applied to *Kangaroo.* In all, the distinction between fiction and non-fiction is blurred, as Lawrence wanders through the world seeing only himself. Characteristic are the vivid but impalpable settings, the creation of allegorical scene or character from recent experience, and the basing of the main character upon Lawrence himself, who intrudes upon the work with chatty commentary. This intrusion, the loose repetitive structure and the apparent digressions deny the novel-form as self-contained art-work, detached from 'real life'. Conventional form is for Lawrence an equivalent of civilisation's conscious distortion and repression of feelings. The new works are self-exploratory, the form inseparable from content; the effort is to enable the 'spontaneous' volcanic release of hitherto repressed libidinal energy, that will surcharge man (Lawrence) with potency. Self-expression and free form, the recovery of primary being and of male potency belong together in these works.

The close relationship between the fiction and non-fiction is apparent in the juxtaposition of the essay 'David' (1920; P 60–4) with *Aaron's Rod* (especially ch. XVI). The essay is concerned with Michelangelo's statue of David (with whom David Lawrence identified) in Florence. Here is the opposed duality of the fire of intense male individuality and the water of smothering woman. By day the rain seems to drench the city, but at night the flood-water howls with cat-like passion. In the midst is the corpse-white sensitive figure of David, not altogether quenched but tensely awaiting renewal in the miraculous New Year's Eve orgasm that popular myth accords him. He is the embodiment of Florence (the city of the flower of manhood), the lily, 'the flower of adolescence, of incipient sexuality':

> Too naked, too exposed . . . half self-conscious all the time . . . stripped so bare, the very kernel of youth. Stripped even to the adolescent orgasm of New Year's night—at midwinter. Unbearable.

The favourite image of the nut fallen open to the fearful possibilities of life is implicit in this dream-like vision of self-exposure in the crucifixion of sexuality (an image found in the roughly contemporary 'Tortoise' poems). As a figure of doomed male sexuality, David is the 'Dionysus and Christ of Florence', filled with male fire that maternal waters almost quenched. Dionysus is in some myths the son of Persephone (always associated for Lawrence with his mother); twice born, he is also the son of Semele, who was destroyed by the divine sexual power of Zeus.

> Semele, scarred by lightning, gave birth prematurely to her child. The Cinque-Cento. Too fierce a mating, too fiery and potent a sire. The child was sewn again into the loins of the lightning. So the brief firebrand. It was fire over-whelming, over-weening, briefly married to the dew, that begot this child. The South to the North. Married! The child, the fire-dew, Iacchus, David.

In the lightning-scar, Lawrence sees male sexuality as frighteningly powerful; his own parentage was a mis-mating between divine and human; his mother pushed him too early into conscious life, and he must return into the phallic body of the divine father, that provides a new cosmic womb, security and identification with the potent male.

Adolescence is the moment before the 'Fall' into sexual maturity: in Lawrence's historical myth, the very beginning of the Renaissance, the Cinque-Cento. Three art-works figure the fall: David, poised on the brink of sexuality, Botticelli's Venus on her scallop-shell (born of the white foam of her divine father's castration), and John the Baptist, head separated from body because of woman.

Fire and dew one moment proportionate, immediately falling into dispro-portion ... [Then comes the modern world,] morality, chastity ... equality, democracy, the masses, like drops of water in one sea, overwhelming all outstanding loveliness of the individual soul.

This flood has prevented the full growth of the bud of the immature phallus and being, but David, still unquenched, will one day complete his development and receive recognition. 'One day he reaps his mates' (not female, but male companions) to achieve 'the pride of the fulfilled self. . . . Not the frail lily. . . . But the full tree of life in blossom' of which Lilly speaks at the end of *Aaron's Rod*. The essay seems the kernel of the novel.

In *Aaron's Rod* (1922), Lawrence is split into Lilly, whose name identifies him with 'spontaneous' male power, and Aaron, who synthe-sises manhood and art in his phallic flute, and who as ex-working-class artist and husband seeks to escape psychological and financial parasi-tism on his wife and society, and to achieve independence and maturity in the world of men. The initial breaking of Aaron's blue ball by the destructive feminine wilfulness of his daughter symbolises the shatter-ing of his own brittle, hollow being. At the pub, he is incapable of melting into sensual bonhomie, inhibited by his 'strained unacknow-ledged opposition to his surroundings, a hard core of irrational, exhausting withholding of himself'; in argument with the Indian doctor (an improbable occupant of a workman's pub) the thought of large numbers of independent self-responsible people (in an independent India) threatens his own shaky self-confidence. A few nights later he retreats to the dark night outside his home, whence the human domes-tic world seems threatening and smothering, and the solitary outsider runs away.

In London, he is taken up by an arty-literary set; a tiresome con-versation one evening provides important thematic material. Here, the love-impulse is seen as a mere boost for an inadequate personality. The *motif* of breath also appears here: for Jim Bricknell, the proponent of tender love, "Love is the soul's respiration"—but he only wants to breathe in; Lilly, the eventual proponent of singleness, declares, "When your soul breathes out, it's a bloody revolution". Bricknell's love is consuming—to achieve true being, it seems, one must renounce and expel breath and love, just as Aaron ran away from his wife for "a breath of fresh air", as he tells the girl Josephine. Later, when Lilly is denouncing love and Jim Bricknell, Jim punches him in the stomach, causing him to lose breath and the impulse to love, and driving him towards isolation.

Aaron's seduction by the primitivist-passionate Josephine induces extreme psychosomatic illness in him. From this he is rescued by Lilly who restores him in a ritual rubbing and anointing (a version of Lawrence's 'bath of life'), "as mothers do their babies whose bowels don't work", which eventually releases Aaron's 'hard core of irrational, exhausting witholding of himself'. Aaron wants to be left alone, but is overborne by quasi-parental authority. On his recovery, Aaron and motherly little Lilly unite in mutually consoling criticism of marriage, and of women who possess and dispossess their men. They agree that "marriage wants readjusting—or extending—to get men on their own legs once more . . ."; men must "stick together". An extended interruption by a visiting officer-friend of Lilly's, about the horrors of the war, allegorises the obsessive agonising over sexual conflicts that must be transcended if new being is to be attained.

The ensuing dialogue is essentially internal; Aaron, as realist-principle, criticises Lilly the idealist who expresses a theory of self-possession, like being in Nirvana:

to be quite alone, and possess your own soul in isolation—and at the same time, to be perfectly *with* someone else. (X)

Aaron acutely derides this as being like sitting "on a mountain top, back to back with somebody else, like a couple of idols", and accuses Lilly of being his own "idol on the mountain top, worshipping yourself". Such criticism is unacceptable, and Lilly drives him away.

Having refused submission, Aaron returns home to attempt reconciliation, only to find his wife, still unhumbled, accusing him of being "too weak to love a woman and give her what she wants: too weak. Unmanly and cowardly, he runs away." Impotence, physical or psychological, is indicated. Aaron will not remain as an unsatisfied sexual tool, but runs away to the characteristic Lawrentian union with nature.

To be alone, to be oneself, not to be driven or violated into something which is not oneself, surely it is better than anything. . . . As for future unions, too soon to think about it. Let there be clean and pure division first, perfected singleness. (XI)

So Lawrence abandons relationship for self-preservation; which is about as far as he had got by 1919, when the work was discontinued, and he went off to Italy. There the thinking about society, isolation, and male love were developed; in *The Lost Girl* he imagined how it would be to submit to, and lose identity in, the sexual power of the

demonic 'underworld' male; here he imagines a conquering of sexuality
and the attainment of strength in male love. Aaron now follows
Lawrence to Italy. There, at the home of a rich patron, Sir William
Franks, he defends his chosen course of spontaneity and trust in
providence, while Sir William indicates the difficulty of independence
and the threat of parasitism. Aaron escapes into the town, which is
dominated by 'tiger-like Alps', an image suggesting returning self-
assertion; the dangers in the resurgence of suppressed passions are
implicit in Lady Franks's dream (displaced from Aaron) of mob
revolution.

   Aaron–Lawrence now relives the fight with himself and his wife.
She sees his fulfilment as being service of herself, but he will neither
submit nor give himself to her, in spite of their unusual sexual intimacy
(the description of which seems to suggest anal intercourse, but with
Aaron withholding 'the very centre of himself'). Aaron abandons the
struggle, again choosing to be alone: 'His intrinsic and central aloneness was the very centre of his being. Break it, and he broke his
being.' With this full realisation, the old conception of self and reality
disappears in an apprehension of 'a-social' being:

. . . the accepted idea of himself cracked and rolled aside like a broken
chestnut-burr, the mask split and shattered, he was at last quiet and free.
He had dreaded exposure: and behold we cannot be exposed, for we are
invisible [like Wells's *Invisible Man*, to which Lawrence refers]. We cannot
he exposed to the looks of others, for our very being is night-lustrous and
invisible. (XIII)

Man must not give away this self, in love, but remain in loneliness—
immediately redefined as singleness—and so find fulfilment: the lily
reappears as an image of such 'life-rooted, life-central' singleness,
untroubled by care, even about love. Aaron can now even contemplate
sexual relations of a more passionate kind than Lilly's, like Whitman's
Dalliance of Eagles, where there is no loss of self-control or self-
possession.

   Aaron moves on to Milan, where he actually sees Lady Franks's
allegorical rebellious mob. Here is male force, inhuman, demon-
looking and vicious; out of this mass springs a youth who is watched
admiringly as he climbs up a building to snatch a flag in 'one unending
wriggling movement' like a lizard (a smaller version of Lawrence's
libido-dragon of *Apocalypse*, 'the fluid, rapid, invincible, even clair-
voyant potency that can surge through the whole body and spirit of
a man'); when the police, as representatives of conventional order,
return, the youth is left exposed, alone and deflated. Likewise in
Florence the statue of adolescent David is contrasted with the

statues of the 'big lumpy Bandinelli men'. The desire is to assert and
to be recognised by the male, the fear is of inadequacy and isolation.
Aaron senses in cold, dark Florence and in himself 'the end of the
old world and the beginning of the new' and contemplates the manly
Florentines,

red lilies . . . flowers with good roots in the mud and muck, as should be:
and fearless blossoms in the air, like the cathedral and the tower and the
David. (XVI)

In this male world, even the stripes on the tower are likened to the
stripes on the tiger-lily, by Lilly, who now reappears.

Lilly is still arguing for an easy indifference and isolation, but
Aaron still has to make one last attempt at relation with a woman.
The old Marchese's wife cannot submit to her husband, and is imaged
as the beauty imprisoned in self-will and egoism. Aaron's phallic
flute dominates her, releasing her from inhibition, and enabling her
to sing freely for the first time. Filled with eagle-like self-confidence,
Aaron enacts the sexual metaphor in their *affaire*. At first the Marchesa
is slightly frightening, her full, mature figure evoking the Magna
Mater, her cosmetics the Scarlet Woman, yet Aaron dominates her
sexually, so that she becomes like a child to him. Soon however her
dependence seems threatening, her sexual demands make him feel
used, the God who is sacrificed and torn apart by sexuality, and once
again he withdraws from involvement with women.

He returns to Lilly, whose fascistic political arguments in a café
reveal the same compensation for inadequacy:

"People are not *men*: they are insects and instruments, and their destiny is
slavery. They are too many for me, and so what I think is ineffectual. But
ultimately they will be brought to agree—after sufficient extermination—
and then they will elect for themselves a proper and healthy and energetic
slavery." (XX)

Also sprach Hitler. Lilly–Lawrence sheers away from the implications
of this, into cant about hatred of bullying, when the discussion is
interrupted by the anarchists' bomb-explosion, that destroys Aaron's
rod: self-assertion, whether sexual or artistic, must now be abandoned.
In Aaron's ensuing dream, he is split in two: the invisible self sits in
front of a boat on the lake in the underworld, contemplating the deep
blue water of the unconscious and the fish of the individual phallic
self. When the boat enters white shallow water, the other, palpable
Aaron is struck on an exposed limb by three posts (allegorising the
harm done to his phallic self by his three heterosexual encounters),
but when he changes his position the invisible Aaron can breathe

freely again. The boat can then return to 'deep, unfathomable' water, in the womb of serene, unconscious being, as in the egg with which the dream concludes.

The parent will be Lilly; together they experience quiet, almost foetal centrality in the Italian countryside, 'not passivity, but alert enjoyment of being central, life-central in one's own little circumambient world', before the concluding dialogue. Here Lilly tells Aaron to cease trying to affect, or be affected by, other people, but to concentrate on "the precious Easter egg of your own soul" which will eventually produce the "one-and-only phoenix", so that the buried self will eventually grow into the "Tree of Life, roots and limbs and trunk". This will be achieved by developing his own inherent male power, "a vast dark source of life and strength . . . waiting either to issue into true action, or to burst into cataclysm" (like the bomb): he will achieve true being and liberty by finding power in himself, or by submitting to greater power in other men.

There was a long pause. Then Aaron looked up into Lilly's face. It was dark and remote-seeming. It was like a Byzantine eikon at the moment.
    "And whom shall I submit to?" he said.
    "Your soul will tell you," replied the other. (XXI)

There was at the time a cult of Byzantine art as the fusion of the physical and spiritual (most familiar in the poetry of Yeats); here, however, the inhumanity is pompous, arrogant and absurd, and confirms most readers in a dislike of the novel. Certainly the novel is flawed by the casual treatment of the realistic level, which is choked by the psychological conflict and allegory; furthermore the psychological inadequacy of the protagonist(s) is never fully admitted, which vitiates the prophetic, didactic argument. The novel traces a progress from jealous resentment of woman as life-creator and sexual being, to a state of frail isolation and of being able to 'stand up for oneself'; however, this soon slips back into a perverse submission to stronger male power, presented more acceptably in the father-figure of Lilly than in the furtive animation of Cicio. Singleness appears as inhibition, as self-responsibility, as loneliness, and as a quasi-foetal security in a greater male, when Semele's child returns to the body of his divine father.

The struggle against feminine inhibition appears in the three long tales of this period—'The Fox', 'The Captain's Doll', and 'The Ladybird'. The first of these was originally written about the same time as 'You Touched Me' and was a variation on that theme, of the lower-class younger man enforcing the submission of one of two women. Here the two women, Bamford and March, are in escape from society on a remote chicken-farm, engaged in a sterile lesbian relationship. Bamford is white, frail and nervous (the social, selfconscious self) while March, in trousers, is the stronger passionate being; her repressed sexual desires appear in her obsession with a thieving fox, the precursor of the young man (Lawrence's modulation between the realistic and symbolic levels is very well done here). The difference between the first and the final version, which has much greater intensity and savagery (indicating perhaps Lawrence's own more desperate situation) is revealed by indicating what incidents are missing from the first version.[7] It does not show the young man assuming the fox's power by killing and crucifying it; nor March's repeated caresses of the dead fox's (phallic) brush, even getting blood on her hand, like Gudrun; nor the young man's killing of Bamford, employing her own feminine, perverse resistance, so that the dead tree of her withered passional self falls on her, smashing her head; while, at the end, instead of a simple anticipation of new life, Lawrence eventually added a passage implicitly admitting the impossibility of attaining the ideal. There he suggests that the ideal is like death, and to strain for it perverse, because at the centre of (his own?) being was something fearful, horrible, essentially null:

The more you reached after the fatal flower of happiness, which trembles so blue and lovely in a crevice just beyond your grasp, the more fearfully you become aware of the ghastly gulf of the precipice below you, into which you will immediately plunge, as into the bottomless pit, if you reach any further. You pluck flower after flower—it is never *the* flower. The flower itself—its calyx is a horrible gulf, it is the bottomless pit.

Lawrence's ideal is, he senses, regressive and self-destructive: within the flower, associated with spontaneity and maleness (perhaps its blueness links it with his mother, also) is the gulf, the pit of unthinkable and terrifying desires. In Alvina Houghton, he had expressed even greater horror at the consequences of abandonment to a lower male being of intense sexuality.

'*The Fox* belongs more to the old world' (CL 569) wrote Lawrence, expressing the view that the other two tales were more exploratory; certainly in them the fantasy becomes more extreme. In 'The Captain's Doll' the protagonist, Captain Hepburn, has the perverse, diabolic charm of the man dispossessed by conventional social forms and a 'lovely lady' Magna Mater wife. However, she is got rid of by a possibly accidental but fatal fall from a hotel window. The horror of this is partially suppressed by Hepburn's disgust, and also by an uneasy attempt at a comic tone. Liberated from her domination, he now attempts a new relation with life:

All our troubles, says somebody wise, come upon us because we cannot be alone [that is, because men have lost sexual self-confidence, as Josephine told Aaron]. And that is all very well. We must all be *able* to be alone, otherwise we are just victims. But when we are *able* to be alone, then we realise that the only thing to do is to start a new relationship with another— or even with the same human being. That people should all be stuck apart, like so many telegraph poles, is nonsense.

In this spirit he sets off to subdue and marry his former German mistress, Hannele (perhaps related to Frieda?), whose doll-portraits are a miniaturising, satiric art, like Gudrun's; having made a doll-portrait of him, she had effectively diminished him as much as his wife had done:

"The most loving and adoring woman today could any minute start and make a doll of her husband—as you made of me. . . . And when she's got your doll, that's all she wants. And that's what love means. And so, I won't be loved. And I won't love."

So Hepburn repossesses the image of himself (in a painting made of the doll) and takes Hannele away from a proposed 'decadent' marriage. The description of his quest through Europe is akin to Lawrence's travel writing, penetrating appearances to find the 'spirit of place', that is, symbols of his own condition. The tale concludes with the familiar juxtaposition of the valley of warm life with the icy mountains of sterile sublimation and isolation.

Hepburn crosses a lake in a small boat, like Aaron in his dream; all around swim lively insouciant youths, and ahead he sees Hannele also swimming. 'Round the boat fishes were suddenly jumping.' After this vision of resurgent sexuality, comes the account of the climb up the mountain and glacier, where fear of sexuality has to be conquered. There is a terrified mare galloping down the road; a cleft in the earth, 'a secret naked place of the earth'; at the summit is the 'grand beast', the 'immense sky-bear' of the glacier. Hepburn comically struggles over the white body of the glacier (like Ahab mounting the white phallic body of Moby Dick) that 'looked so pure, like flesh. . . . But pure ice, away down to immense depths.' The 'huge body of the soft-fleshed ice' is full of clefts through which the dead underworld breathes, intensely blue (the terrifying blue depths parallels the conclusion of 'The Fox'), a sterile deadly existence: 'A world sufficient unto itself in lifelessness. . . .' Having surmounted the neuter appeals of homosexuality and sublimation, he can return to life, to demand submission from the woman, in a comic battle in a swaying bus taking them downhill.

In *Fantasia* and elsewhere, Lawrence had demanded woman's

submission to the greater purpose in man; but Hepburn, not being Lawrence, only intends to farm in Africa (the flight from civilisation) and to study the moon (still the obsession with withdrawal and the isolate self). After her last Frieda-like criticisms, Hannele seems prepared to accept him, and Hepburn withdraws mysteriously over the water into the darkness. For all its penetration, the story is loosely constructed, and the struggle between realistic comedy and psychological allegory is not resolved wholly successfully.

The failure to make the realistic and mythical cohere is even more apparent in 'The Ladybird'. Worth noting are the motifs of the implicit connivance of the husband in his wife's seduction by the young man (a displaced Oedipal fantasy), and the dark demonic outsider, Count Dionys, who dominates woman in the world of darkness and night, and offers fulfilment only in death; but the story is not worth serious or extensive discussion.

Healthier, and more successful, are the poems of the years 1920–1, gathered in *Birds, Beasts and Flowers* (1923), the most successful volume of his verse. Though he presents the appearance of the plants and creatures with great vividness, the nature that he apprehends is his own. These poems' colloquial ease and vigour, sensuous apprehension, and wit manifesting serious intelligence, make them reminiscent of seventeenth-century poetry (and truer equivalents than the dry, clever verse of Eliot and Empson), particularly of the emblem poems, where objects are interpreted by ingenious allegorisation.

The first poem defends Lawrence's method; 'Pomegranate' (CP 278) has the authentic arrogant opening of a Donne poem:

> You tell me I am wrong,
> Who are you, who is anybody to tell me I am wrong?
> I am not wrong.

'Peach' (CP 279) wittily emblematises the female sexual parts.

> Would you like to throw a stone at me?
> Here, take all that's left of my peach.

A cool offer of the peach-stone. Sensuously, he evokes a fresh rounded body—of the peach; blandly, he explains, "I am thinking, of course, of the peach before I ate it". What else? He of course has had the 'fruit', and 'you' have not. Why is the peach so round, and grooved, if not, as he insinuates, as a female emblem? Desexualising man would prefer it mathematically perfect, smooth

> . . . as a billiard ball.

And because I say so, you would like to throw something at me.

> Here, you can have my peach stone.

Donne would have loved this. Other poems are more ponderous:
'Medlars and Sorb-apples' (CP 280) embody Lawrence's principle
of experience in corruption that produces the perfection of the phallic
being:

> Autumnal excrementa;
> What is it that reminds us of white gods?
>
> Gods nude as blanched nut-kernels,
> Strangely, half-sinisterly flesh-fragrant
> As if with sweat,
> And drenched with mystery.
>
> Sorb-apples, medlars with dead crowns.
> I say, wonderful are the hellish experiences,
> Orphic, delicate
> Dionysos of the Underworld.

To go 'down the strange lanes of hell, more and more intensely alone'
creates the fullness of individual being, 'Intoxication of final loneliness'.
Lawrence is going a strange way, where Frieda cannot follow. In
'Cypresses' (CP 296) he finds his underworld companions—the
archaic Etruscans:

> Vicious, dark cypresses:
> Vicious, you supple, brooding, softly-swaying pillars of dark flame.
> Monumental to a dead, dead race
> Embowered in you!
>
> Were they then vicious, the slender, tender-footed
> Long-nosed men of Etruria?
> Or was their way only evasive and different, dark, like cypress-trees in
>   a wind?

The trees are Lawrence's phallic god again; 'vicious' is what conventional ethics would consider male love to be, that did not deny itself
for civic virtue; 'evasive and different' directly parallels the 'furtive
pride and slinking singleness' of the dispossessed and perverse man.
Lawrence concludes by anticipating his two great fantasies of male
religious community, *The Plumed Serpent* and *Etruscan Places*:

> There is only one evil, to deny life
> As Rome denied Etruria
> And mechanical America Montezuma still.

In 'St Matthew' (CP 320) his theme is that man must not deny, but
accept all his life, that man's nature demands he oscillate between
and include extremes of being, going to the limit of the spiritual
before turning to the 'opposite equivalent' of the animal-demonic.

Man may spring up like the lark at heaven's gate singing, but must fall back as the blood-spirit, the bat:

> Bat-winged heart of man,
> Reversed flame
> Shuddering a strange way down to the bottomless pit . . .

The reversed flame and the pit indicate that this is the 'unnatural' natural of perversity and homosexuality, the bat of diabolic darkness, the obscene spirit that repels him to the frenzy so brilliantly and comically evoked in 'Man and Bat' (CP 342); there he wants to expel the diabolic parody of man, for 'the human soul is fated to responsibility In life'. The 'subhuman' depths that Matthew says man must sink to are presented more sympathetically as the fish 'sinking down the dark reversion of night. . . . Beyond everything, except itself.' This solitary self-sufficient phallic being appears in 'Fish' (CP 334). Here alliteration and assonance evoke the sensuous quality of fish-life:

> Your life a sluice of sensation along your sides,
> A flush at the flails of your fins, down the whorl of your tail,
> And water wetly on fire in the grates of your gills;
> Fixed water-eyes.

Here is loveless life-energy disporting itself in its cold mother-element.

> Who is it ejects his sperm to the naked flood?
> In the wave-mother?
> Who swims enwombed?
> Who lies with the waters of his silent passion, womb-element?
> —Fish in the waters under the earth.

The leaping fish is the divine phallus he hymned in 'Virgin Youth', the being beyond his conscious power. When he held it in his hand, he

> . . . felt him beat in my hand, with his mucous, leaping life-throb.
> And my heart accused itself
> Thinking: *I am not the measure of creation.*
> *This is beyond me, this fish.*
> *His God stands outside my God.*

This respect for the unknown phallic being that implicitly asserts his own appears in his most famous poem, 'Snake' (CP 349). Lawrence, here the uncertain representative of civilised consciousness, confronts the god of the underworld, the representative of the libido. Out of the fissure of the earth's body the snake comes to drink, silently

asserting priority as an elemental being. Apprehended first as harm-
lessly slack-bodied and as unthreatening as cattle, his—not 'its'—
forked tongue gives him demonic connotations, coming from the
'burning bowels' and overseen by the volcanic mountain of contained
fire. Only when the long body turns to re-enter the body from which
it came (the hole now seems horrible: the image implies unnatural
or incestuous practice) does the spirit of conditioned hostility to
natural power escape from the trance, to provoke an ineffectual
attack, and make the god seem convulsed, obscene and absurd. 'King
in exile, uncrowned in the underworld, Now due to be crowned
again', he is the phallic self, the god Dis, the father-King that Lawrence
has recognised and must identify with.

Such identification is not yet possible: in the Tortoise poems,
Lawrence presents his own situation. The baby tortoise is the self-
sufficient spark of life, enviably indifferent to his indifferent mother.
The lightness of Lawrence's humour comes out in the lines—

> It is no use my saying to him in an emotional voice:
> "This is your Mother, she laid you when you were an egg."

The tortoise is in his way insouciant, 'young gaiety':

> He doesn't know he is alone;
> Isolation is his birthright,
> This atom. (CP 357)

'Lui et Elle' (CP 358) presents the male's sexual need as absurd, even
degrading. The female is literally the Magna Mater, larger than him;
'And he has a cruel scar on his shell'—the wound of sex. In the male
tortoise, Lawrence mocks his own pretensions and exposes his plight.

> The lonely rambler, the stoic, dignified stalker through chaos,
> The immune, the animate,
> Enveloped in isolation,
> Fore-runner.
> Now look at him!
> Alas, the spear is through the side of his isolation.
> His adolescence saw him crucified into sex,
> Doomed, in the long crucifixion of desire to seek his consummation
>   beyond himself.
> Divided into passionate duality,
> He, so finished and immune, now broken into desirous fragmentariness,
> Doomed to make an intolerable fool of himself
> In his effort towards completion again.

> Poor little earthy house-inhabiting Osiris . . .

'Tortoise Shout' (CP 368) is a magnificent reverent presentation of

the mystery of coition, the self-destructive self-fulfilling crucifixion of
sexual union, the sexual struggle which urges life into articulation:

> Sex, which breaks us into voice . . .

> The same cry from the tortoise as from Christ, the Osiris-cry
>   of abandonment,
> That which is whole, torn asunder,
> That which is in part, finding its whole again throughout
>   the universe.

Sexual agony is for Lawrence the origin and essence of self-expression;
we may turn back again to the 'Study of Thomas Hardy':

> It is only a disproportion [of the male and female], or a dissatisfaction,
> which makes the man struggle into articulation. And the articulation is of
> two sorts, the cry of desire or the cry of realisation, the cry of satisfaction,
> the effort to prolong the sense of satisfaction, to prolong the moment of
> consummation. (P 460)

These poems, in their intelligence, wit and humanity are far more
successful and mature than the obsession and self-inflation of much
of the contemporary fiction. Another pleasant and honest piece,
written while composing *Aaron's Rod*, is the volume *Sea and Sardinia*
(1921), where Lawrence appears, not as a Byzantine eikon, but as a
rather wistful, sensitive married man in search of spontaneous sensual
life and precivilised male community.

The journey to Sardinia is not only a quest, but also a flight—from
what is embodied in Mount Etna, near where the Lawrences have
been living: the deadly Magna Mater, arousing and frustrating desires,
creating intense, unnatural and dehumanising passions.

> Ah, what a mistress, this Etna! with her strange winds prowling round her
> like Circe's panthers . . . her strange, remote exhalations [the breath of the
> sensual underworld that Lawrence had discovered]. She makes men mad.
> Such terrible vibrations and beautiful electricity she throws about her like
> a deadly net! [So Clytemnestra destroyed Agamemnon.] Nay, sometimes,
> verily, one can feel a new current of her demon magnetism seize one's living
> tissue and change the peaceful life of one's active cells . . . unless a man is
> very strong, she takes his soul away from him and leaves him not a beast,
> but an elemental creature, intelligent and soulless . . . like the Etna Sicilians
> [or Melville, or Loerke, or Birkin in 'Prologue to *Women in Love*' P2 103].
> Intelligent daimons, and humanly, according to us, the most stupid people
> on earth. Ach, horror! How many men, how many races, has Etna put
> to flight? (I)

So, with Frieda (resentfully nicknamed 'the queen bee') Lawrence
sets off into the interior of Sardinia, seeking not frightening individual

passion, but soothing communal being. He only finds a brutal and degenerated existence, and the only life is in his own engaging personality and lively observation. Male vitality is not found until the end, at a puppet-show in Palermo. Here, in the all-male audience, and the medieval romance legend of the play, he finds the male energy he had sought,

the massive, brilliant, outflinging recklessness in the male soul, summed up in the sudden word: *Andiamo! Andiamo!* Let us go on[8] . . . the splendid recklessness and passion that knows no precept and no school-teacher, whose very molten spontaneity is its own guide. (VIII)

Male spirit spurts out of female constriction. Even more significant is the account of the conquest of the play's wicked witch (akin to the spirit of Etna):

Hear her horrible female voice with its scraping yells of evil lustfulness. Yes, she fills me with horror. And I am staggered to find how I believe in her as *the* evil principle . . . this white, submerged *idea* of woman which rules from the deep of the unconscious. Behold, the reckless, untamable male knights will do for it. As the statue goes up in flames [perhaps reminding Lawrence of the burning of the doll in *Sons and Lovers*]—it is only paper over wires—the audience yells! And yells again. And would God the symbolic act were really achieved. It is only little boys who yell. Men merely smile at the trick. They know well enough the white image endures. (VIII)

In reality, Lawrence decides, the male unconscious being cannot overcome 'female' frustration and self-division. Whatever his fantasies of male power and unconscious blood-being in a paternal cosmic womb, and his fears of dispossessed unnaturalness in 'furtive pride and slinking singleness', he would have to continue to struggle with with himself and the world, a 'stoic [more-or-less] dignified stalker through chaos'.

Such was his 'savage pilgrimage' of travel through the world, seeking self-integration and an ideal community; the futility of this search he sometimes admitted:

Perhaps it is necessary for me to try these places, perhaps it is my destiny to know the world. It only excites the outside of me. The inside it leaves more isolated and stoic than ever. That's how it is. It is all a form of running away from oneself and the great problems. (CL 723)

In these years he felt pulled in two: Mabel Dodge wanted him to go west to 'write up' New Mexico, while Witter Bynner beckoned to a Buddhistic Nirvana in Ceylon. In fact, he felt the east meant passivity and regression, and that he must go west to life:

More and more I feel that meditation and the inner life are not my aim, but some sort of action and strenuousness and pain and frustration and struggling through. . . . I have decided to go to Taos in New Mexico. . . . I want to fight and to feel new gods in the flesh. (CL 681)

Instead he went to Ceylon, fell ill, and moved on promptly to Australia, a substitute for his new world.

1. Quotations from Leslie Fiedler, *Love and Death in the American Novel* (London, 1967) ch. XIII, pp. 431–3.

2. 'At certain periods the man has a desire and a tendency to return to the woman, make her his goal and his end, find his justification in her. In this way he casts himself as it were into her womb, and she, the Magna Mater, receives him with gratification. This is a kind of incest. . . . I have done it, and now struggle with all my might to get out. In a way, Frieda is the devouring mother' CL 565).

3. cf. the description of savage cults in the forest of pre-Christian Europe: 'The dark groves with their blood-stained altars terrified and haunted the Romans. . . . The tree-worship, the worship of the Tree of Life seems always to have entailed human sacrifice. Life is the fruit of that Tree. But the Tree is dark and terrible, it demands life back again.' *Movements in European History* (1921), p. 59.

4. Another demonic leader, and admired man of destiny and savage power, is Attila the Hun. 'His little eyes sparkled with tremendous passions, his body had great nervous energy. A haughty little creature, he had a prancing way of walking, and he rolled his eyes fiercely, filling the onlookers with terror, and enjoying the terror he inspired' (*Movements*, p. 83). Following Gibbon, Lawrence relates how Attila was destroyed by sexual passion, marrying a fair princess and dying in a blood-soaked bridal bed. Attila also appears in the essay 'Blessed are the Powerful': 'True destructive power is power just the same as constructive. . . . The moment the divine power manifests itself, it is right: whether it be Attila or Napoleon or George Washington' (P2 442). Power and vitality are wholly amoral; and, it seems, the greater the amorality, the greater the power.

5. See CL 150–1.

6. cf. 'Purple Anemones' (CP 307). There Lawrence asserts that flowers (especially the male flower) are the gift of Dis,/The Dark one./Prosperpine's master . . ./She thought she had left him;/But opened around her purple anemones, /Caverns, little hells of colour, caves of darkness,/Hell, risen in pursuit of her; royal, sumptuous,/Pitfalls.'

7. 'The Fox' in H. T. Moore (Ed.), *A D. H. Lawrence Miscellany* (London, 1961), pp. 26–46.

8. cf. '*Allons*, there is no road yet, but we are all Aarons with rods of our own (*Fantasia*, p. 18).

5

BEHIND THE FIERCE SUN

The Lawrences stayed in Australia only a short time before continuing their widdershins circumnavigation; considering it was written in only about six weeks, *Kangaroo* (1923) is a remarkable work. Lawrence dignified it with the appellation 'thought-adventure', but his other description, 'this gramophone of a novel' seems more appropriate. There is little in it that is new, and the story and to a large extent the setting are only backcloths.

Poor Richard Lovat wearied himself to death struggling with the problem of himself, and calling it Australia. (II)

The central characters Richard Lovat Somers and his wife Harriet are transparently Lawrence and Frieda. Somers is constantly attempting to achieve ascendancy over Harriet by entering upon 'impersonal' male activity in society, beyond her reach. Their arguments, drawn from life, have considerable honesty and vigour:

"I want to do something with living people, somewhere, somehow, while I live on the earth. I write, but I write alone. And I live alone. Without any connection whatever with the rest of men."

"Don't swank, you don't live alone. You've got *me* there safe enough, to support you. Don't swank to me about being alone, because it insults me, you see. I know how much alone you are, with me always there keeping you together. . . . Besides, you liar, haven't you your writing? Isn't that all you want, isn't that *doing* all there is to be done? Men! Much *men* there is about them! Bah, when it comes to that, I have to be even the only man as well as the only woman."

"That's the whole trouble," said he bitingly. (IV)

Somers dreams of a woman, combining his mother and his wife, filled with grief and accusation at his attempt to 'betray her love' by going on to achieve this independence among men. "They neither of them believed in me," he said to himself—which is not surprising, as even he has to admit his

ingrained instinct or habit of thought which made him feel that he could never take the move into activity unless Harriet and his dead mother believed in him. (V)

He is presented with two ways to this activity with men. One is in male love—or being 'mates'—with an ex-serviceman, Jack Callcott, who seems the embodiment of rude male vigour, the 'he-man', to Somers's 'she-man' as Lawrence puts it towards the end, when Somers has withdrawn from the relationship, and is subjected to the charge usually directed at the outsider, of betrayal (reminiscent of Magnus). Callcott introduces him to a revolutionary quasi-fascist ex-servicemen's league, the Diggers, that provides a form of brutal 'manly' activity, and enables Lawrence to play his schoolboy game of planning the organisation of a secret society. This male society culminates in the somewhat androgynous figure of Ben Cooley, known as Kangaroo, whose almost marsupial paunch offers a paternal womb.

"Man needs a quiet, gentle father who uses his authority in the name of living life, and who is absolutely stern against anti-life. I [Kangaroo] offer no creed. I offer myself, my heart of wisdom, strange warm cavern . . ." (VI)

However, his is the principle of deliberate smothering 'love' that absorbs every individual ego. Somers of course cannot submit to this force, which refusal induces in Kangaroo an almost murderous rage (as we would expect, from the early essay 'Love'). When Kangaroo is shot in a political brawl, it is allegorically in his male womb, his 'bowels of compassion' which go rotten in a liquefying putrefaction.

The other alternative is the socialist workers' movement, embodied in a shrewd dry leathery little man, Willie Struthers. This movement seems to Somers merely "the brotherhood of man on a wage basis", destructive of difference, order and hierarchy, substituting a levelling-down egalitarianism in a dusty aggregation of egos; it is merely an intensification of the spirit of modern Australia, evidenced in the Sydney suburb's 'little square bungalows dot-dot-dot close together and yet apart, like modern democracy' (I)—something that Lawrence regards as akin to anarchy. Against these principles of absorption and fragmentation, Somers sets 'the principle of lordship', and 'the great God who enters us from below, not above. . . . Enters us from the lower self, the dark self, the phallic self . . .' (VII). This is the

condition when man is by himself but responsive to supernatural-
subliminal forces, 'like the oracle above the fissure into the unknown.
The oracle, the fissure down into the unknown, the strange exhalations
from the dark' (XIV). This is the power from man's inner core,
erupting through the encrustation of civilised consciousness, culminating in one single all-powerful being (and we know who):

the true majesty of the single soul which has all its own weaknesses, but its
strength in spite of them, its own lovableness, as well as its might and
dread. The single soul that stands naked between the dark God and the
dark-blooded masses of men . . . (XIV)

—like the David in Florence. This principle of power is frequently
expressed with some defensiveness, and does not receive much
emphasis in the novel as a whole, certainly not as much as the theme
of isolation, of withdrawal from the human world altogether.

The novel is famous—or notorious—for the chapter 'The Nightmare', where Lawrence recounts his wartime persecution in Cornwall
by the police and military authorities (on suspicion of spying and
treachery—the charges levelled against Somers here). The account
provides a further explanation of Lawrence's fear and hatred of the
masses and external authority, and provides considerable insight into
his state of mind when writing *Women in Love*. It would appear also
that at this period Lawrence was engaged in a quasi-homosexual
romance with a Cornishman, here named, with unfortunate significance,
John Thomas. Certainly a considerable element in this chapter, that is
relevant not only to *Kangaroo* but also *Women in Love* and 'England,
My England', is a revulsion from normal humanity and a reversion
to the 'savage', as when Somers

felt that he was over the border, in another world. . . . The spirit of the
ancient, pre-Christian world, which lingers still in the truly Celtic places,
he could feel it invade him in the savage dusk, making him savage too, and
at the same time, strangely sensitive and subtle, understanding the mystery
of the blood-sacrifice . . . with his soul departed back, back into the
blood-sacrificial pre-world . . . away from his own white world, his own
white, conscious day. Away from the burden of intensive mental consciousness. (XII)

It is notable that one of the few characters with whom Somers has
any real rapport is a Cornishman, William James, another of Lawrence's
cynical subtle outsiders, who recognises Somers's lack of real desire
to commit himself to anything beyond himself, and preference for
remaining perversely isolate.

The novel vividly presents a bitty, casually egalitarian petit-
bourgeois society, without purpose or significance, and even more

vividly what Lawrence really responded to in Australia: the emptiness
of the vast land and its surrounding ocean. Here is the objective,
external world, devoid of human presence and human pressure, where
the solitary can feel free. Again and again come scenes where Somers
withdraws from the problems of human involvement to contemplation
of the natural world,

The strange, as it were, *invisible* beauty of Australia, which is undeniably
there, but which seems to lurk just beyond the range of our white vision.
(V)

The sea is a neutral body of massive force wherein plunge phallic
creatures like diving gannets and porpoises, fulfilling themselves
instinctively, exuberantly and lovelessly; or else the sea casts up
strange solitary creatures, like jelly-fish; or crashes against his body,
sweeping him up, and increasing his awareness of energetic individuality. So, when Jack Callcott's wife offers herself to him with Jack's
tacit connivance (he later attempts to prise Harriet away) Somers
retreats from 'the bright, swift, weapon-like Bacchic occasion',
preferring to wait for 'a vast, phallic sacred darkness'; the next day he
runs naked in the rain and plunges into the powerful sea, before
returning to a 'wondering' Harriet 'straight from the sea, like another
creature'.

The empty land is not energising but pacifying; one walk into the
outback, in particular, is a regression to the pre-human world:

The lonely, lonely world that had waited, it seemed, since the coal age. . . .
What was the good of trying to be an alert, conscious man here? You
couldn't. Drift, drift into a sort of obscurity, backwards into a nameless
past, hoary as the country is hoary. Strange old feelings wake in the soul:
old, non-human feelings. And an old, old indifference, like a torpor, invades
the spirit. . . . Even the never-slumbering urge of sex sinks down into
something darker, more monotonous, incapable of caring—like sex in trees.
The dark world before conscious responsibility was born. (X)

So the solitary male returns to a pre-adult, prehuman passivity; the
sea, too, can provide such an influence, such a soothing escape from
conscious life:

The thud, the pulse of the waves: that was his nearest throb of emotion.
The other emotions seemed to abandon him. Like a stone that has fallen
into the sea, his old life, the old meaning, fell, and rippled, and there was
vacancy, with the sea and the Australian shore in it. Far-off, far-off, as if
he had landed on another planet, as a man might land after death. Leaving
behind the body of care. Even the body of desire. Shed . . . [it is] only in
this pause that one finds the meaninglessness of meanings and the other
dimension, the reality of timelessness and nowhere. (XVII)

Through Harriet, Lawrence expresses an apprehension of how this mood is taking Somers away from life to 'non-human gods, non-human being', reducing him to subhumanity. She acquires a horror of the land:

Sometimes a heavy, reptile-hostility came off the sombre land, something gruesome and infinitely repulsive. . . . It was as if the silvery freedom suddenly turned, and showed the scaly back of a reptile, and the horrible jaws. (XVIII)

This passage was written in Lawrence's early days in New Mexico, and displays the spirit of that place: the degeneration into brutal inhumanity (associated with homosexual feeling) that appears in *The Plumed Serpent*. In the meantime, he is aware that this regression is deadly. In the Somers' last walk in the bush they find a stream that does not flow out into the sea, but plunges back into a 'gruesome' hole in the ground, without apparent outlet: this is inversion, negation, the end. Lawrence found no possibility of building a new life or new world in Australia; instead he was presented only with his own ineffectual isolation. It was time to move on before he gave up altogether, to try again in his long-deferred dream-land of the west.

In America he found a similar contrast between a mechanical civilisation and the primitive past, which was here still alive. At first all of it seemed unreal, a phantasmagoria. So, in 'Indians and an Englishman' (P 92–9) he wrote:

. . . here am I, a lone lorn Englishman, tumbled out of the known world of the British Empire onto this stage: for it persists in seeming like a stage to me, and not like the proper world . . . as for me, poor lamb, if I bleat at all in the circus ring, it will be my own shorn lonely bleat of a man who's lost his mother.

However he responded to, and brilliantly evoked, the primitive culture of the Indians of the southwest, sensing a quality of savagery hostile to modern consciousness. In the Indians' war-whoop he can hear

the humanness, the playfulness, and then, beyond that, the mockery and the diabolical, pre-human, pine-tree fun of cutting dusky throats and letting the blood spurt out unconfined.

He is aware—but accepts—that his yearning for this mode of being is regressive,

a pungent awakening to the lost past, old darkness, new terror, new root-griefs, old root-richnesses.

The pueblo (in 'Taos', P 100–3) even reminds him of 'one of the

monasteries of Europe' (Monte Cassino) that on the collapse of the
Roman Empire 'in a world flooded with devastation . . . alone kept
the human spirit from disintegration'—a mode of being from which
he is now separated:

> There it is, then, the pueblo, as it has been since heaven knows when.
> And the slow dark weaving of the Indian life going on still, though perhaps
> more waveringly. And oneself, sitting there on a pony, a far-off stranger
> with gulfs of time between me and this.

Wandering alone in the dark (in 'Indians and an Englishman') he
stands wistfully outside a ring of ritually chanting Indians, where the
old priest is a voice 'from the bristling darkness of the far past';
however, he knows that he cannot regress to primitivist savagery,
but continue the struggle with the complexity of real life.

> I never want to deny them or break with them. But there is no going back.
> Always onward, still further. The great devious onward-flowing stream of
> conscious human blood. From them to me, and from me on.
>   I don't want to live again the tribal mysteries my blood has lived long
> since. I don't want to know as I have known, in the tribal exclusiveness.
> But every drop of me trembles still alive to the old sound, every thread in
> my body quivers to the frenzy of the old mystery. I know my derivation.
> I was born of no virgin, of no Holy Ghost. Ah, no, these old men telling the
> tribal tale were my fathers. I have a dark-faced, bronze-voiced father far
> back in the resinous ages. My mother was no virgin. She lay in her hour with
> this dusky-lipped tribe-father. And I have not forgotten him. But he, like
> many an old father with a changeling son, he would like to deny me. But I
> stand on the far edge of their firelight, and am neither denied nor accepted.
> My way is my own, old red father; I can't cluster at the drum any more.

The origin in the past is acknowledged, individual maturity claimed.
There can be no regression into primitivism or a child-state; he
recognises the sexual relationship between his father and mother
(which the Oedipally-jealous child cannot admit); though different
from his father, he is also a man among men.
   But almost at once, anxiety over this independence returns, and in
the poem 'Spirits Summoned West' (CP 410–12) he cancels this
achievement, entreats his dead mother's spirit to be his bride and
comfort:

> Come back then, mother, my love, whom I told to die.
> It was only I who saw the virgin you
> That had no home . . .
>   .   .   .
>
> *Come, delicate, overlooked virgin, come back to me*
> *And be still,*
> *Be glad . . .*

At this time Lawrence's sense of isolation and of crisis increases: in this world he has only himself to rely on. In the critical writing of the time there is a new note of strident personality-display, of aggressive flippancy, especially about ideas, particularly other peoples'. The revision of the American Literature essays, *Studies in Classic American Literature* (1923), displays a hysterical flippancy; brutality comes out in the harsher, more physical images, and the greater emphasis on male power. For example, in the description of sexless male love (in the essay on Fenimore Cooper), where in the early version they are

Two mature, silent, expressionless men, they stand on opposite shores of being, and their love, the inexpressible conjunction between them, is the bridge over the chasm (SM 105)

in the final version their relationship is

a great release into a new world, a new moral, a new landscape. . . . And each is stark and dumb in the other's presence, starkly himself, without illusion created. Each is just the crude pillar of a man, the crude living column of his own manhood. And each knows the godhead of this crude column of manhood. (SCAM 57)

Man is only an erect phallus. Continually the book advocates the destruction of an effete and frustrating civilisation, and erection of harsh male power, as in the 'great souls' requiring acknowledgment and submission, with which the book ends.

With Lawrence in this state, it is not surprising that his marriage went through a period of strain. Frieda insisted on a return to England, where Middleton Murry was prepared to set up a magazine to promote Lawrence's ideas. Lawrence went with her as far as New York, and then balked; Frieda went on alone, leaving Lawrence in a state of acute tension, which eventually drove him to follow her to England in the December of 1923. In his absence Frieda apparently proposed an *affaire* to Murry, whose wife had just died, but he declined, out of a sense of loyalty to Lawrence. Lawrence on his arrival acquired some knowledge of this, and at the notorious 'Last Supper' at the Café Royal spoke much of 'betrayal', before collapsing.

This was a crucial episode in Lawrence's life; at a time when he felt most isolated, and was desperately struggling for a sense of mature independent manhood, he was effectually betrayed by the woman and the man he loved. His sense of his own inadequacy was intensified, while the phallic power he lacked seemed all the more threatening and terrifying, and the male love he desired was prevented him by a woman. The writing that follows[1] is almost entirely a reaction to this experience, confronting the nature of male sexuality and his

own nature. What was this nature, how could he make himself strong?
The old civilisation must be replaced by barbaric strength. So in the
'Letter from Germany' (P 107) based on his visit in February 1924,
he says that

The old spell of the old world has broken and the old, bristling, savage
spirit has set in. . . . And it is a happening of far more profound import
than any actual *event*. It is the father of the next phase of events. . . . The
human soul recoiling now from unison, and making itself strong elsewhere.
. . . And the whole stream of feeling is reversed.

Whatever prophetic insight Lawrence might have about Germany in
the early 1920s, he is chiefly writing of his own condition. Returned
to America with Frieda, he plunged into work and the creation of
loveless male power.

The most famous work from this period, worth close examination,
is 'St Mawr' (1925), a work of great power but of uncertain meaning
and doubtful success. Perhaps its most apparent weakness lies in the
uneasy relationship between symbolic action and realistic surface:
certainly both plot and characters are improbable. The tale is partly
Lawrence's reply to Forster's *Passage to India*, which he was reading
that summer,[2] with the last section the equivalent of Forster's 'lump'
at the end, where Lawrence's empty desert answers Forster's temple
as a vision of what underlies appearance. More obviously, the tale is
Lawrence's reaction to the disastrous visit to England.

He himself appears in various forms: the protagonist Lou Carring-
ton, with her 'lurking sense of being an outsider everywhere', and her
sense of unfulfilment and dissatisfaction with life, has something in
common with Lawrence. Her absurd elegant *poseur* husband Rico
owes much to Murry, but as another drifting outsider shares Lawrence's
fear of other people:

this defenceless man-to-man business . . . was bad for his nerves. For he
was *also* an artist. He bore up against it in a kind of desperation, and was
easily moved to rancorous resentment. . . . He really was aware that he
would have to hold his own all alone, thrown alone on his own defences in
the universe. The extreme democracy of the Colonies [Australia] had taught
him this.

In Rico the passional male body has been almost completely suppressed ('If his head had been cut off, like John the Baptist, it would
have been a thing complete in itself, would not have missed the body
in the least.'); though this makes him seem effete and trivial, yet the
suppressed being, perverted by its suppression, constantly threatens
violent eruption. He is very like the fierce and deadly stallion St
Mawr:

He didn't want to erupt like some suddenly wicked horse—Rico was really more like a horse than a dog, a horse that might go nasty any moment.

The stallion also has a

dangerous, half-revealed resentment, a diffused sense of hostility . . . sensitive . . . and nervous with a touchy uneasiness that might make him vindictive.

For all Rico's lonely defensiveness he lacks the wild animal's

courage, the wild thing's courage to maintain itself alone and living in the midst of a diverse universe,

being only one of those

who conspire to live in absolute physical safety, whilst willing the minor disintegration of all positive being.

But St Mawr? Was it the natural wild thing in him which caused these disasters? Or was it the slave asserting himself for vengeance?

This is indeed Lawrence's crucial problem: what is the nature of the suppressed passional being? Does self-fulfilment necessarily involve savagery and cruelty, or is this only the quality of the oppressed and hence somewhat perverted being?

The stallion is partly defined by juxtaposition with Rico, who epitomises the remorselessly trivial and unnatural society that Lawrence considered the England of the 1920s. Lou's discontent with this society and her marriage is reinforced by her battle-axe mother Mrs Witt (a nastier Mrs Moore) who, it is notable,

would almost rather have preferred Lou to elope with one of the great, evil porters at Les Halles. Mrs Witt was at the age when the malevolent male in man, the old Adam, begins to loom above all the social tailoring.[3]

For Mrs Witt, the sensual male power she had always denied now seems 'malevolent' and perversely, masochistically, desirable: this is much how Lou feels, and mother and daughter are very intimate and similar, not least in their sardonic strength. Mrs Witt is one of Lawrence's most memorable and least pleasant creations—not least because of his evident approval of her continual sarcasm, which is intended as brilliant and crushing, but is liable to strike most readers as crass malevolence.

Her continual challenge of society, attempting and failing to find the glamour of civilisation as presented by European high society, takes her, her daughter, and eventually Rico to ride in Hyde Park; as a result, Lou finds and buys for her husband the dangerous stallion St Mawr. The stallion signifies more for Lou than phallic energy. It is somewhat perverse, refusing to mate with the mares; it fears human contact, springing away 'as if lightning exploded in his four hoofs'; it has already killed two men. What draws Lou is a masochistic impulse to submit to dangerous, deadly male sexuality that is destructive of normal civilised life:

... his great body glowed red with power. . . . What was his non-human question, and his uncanny threat? She didn't know. He was some splendid demon and she must worship him. . . . What did it mean, and what ban did it put upon her? She felt it put a ban on her heart: wielded some uncanny authority over her, that she dared not, could not understand. . . . Master of doom, he seemed to be!

Such a ban and authority appeared in 'Excurse', in *Women in Love*. St Mawr's abnormal power appears in his men attendants, so that Lou detects in the Indian groom Phoenix (whose name links him with Lawrence) 'an unyielding resistance and cruelty: yes, even cruelty'. The other groom, a bearded Celt, Lewis, is about forty (Lawrence was thirty-nine at the time of writing) with 'eyes that looked phosphorescent, and suggested the eyes of a wild cat' (Lawrence's signals of suppressed mindless sensuality since *Twilight in Italy*), and who appears to Lou and her mother to possess the qualities of St Mawr. There is also Dean Vyner (a combination of Lawrence and his friend Frederick Carter) an artist,

about thirty-eight, and poor, just beginning to accept himself as a failure, as far as making money goes. But he worked at his etchings and studied esoteric matters like astrology and alchemy.

He looks like the goat-god Pan (as Lawrence liked to think that he did) and helps to indicate the nature of St Mawr in his account of Pan:[4]

"the god that is hidden in everything. In those days you saw the thing, you never saw the god in it: I mean in the tree, or the fountain or the animal. If you ever saw the God instead of the thing, you died. . . . But in the night you might see the God . . ."
    "Do you think I might see Pan in a horse, for example?"
    "Easily. In St Mawr!"

Down in Shropshire Lou, Rico, Mrs Witt, the grooms and the local gentry go riding in the hills ('like great shut fingers', reminiscent of Forster's Marabar Hills), that are on the border of the savage world. Here the stallion is frightened by a dead snake (symbolising crushed phallic being), rears up, and is pulled back over by Rico on to his rider, seriously injuring him. For Lou, the horror is in the horse's plunging, thrashing movements that, with the images of fish and lizard (associated for Lawrence with subhuman phallicism), present a vision of coitus and male sexual power and activity as horrific and terrifying. Rico's attempt to restrain this power causes only greater frenzy, and 'reverses' or perverts this passion. Lou now becomes the vehicle for an extended hysterical discourse on the dehumanising evil of modern civilisation, and Rico–Murry.

> She saw the same in people. They were thrown backwards, and writhing with evil. And the rider, crushed, was still reining them down . . .
> Mankind no longer its own master. Ridden by this pseudo-handsome ghoul of outward loyalty, inward treachery, in a game of betrayal, betrayal, betrayal. The last of the gods of our era, Judas supreme!
> People performing outward acts of loyalty, piety, self-sacrifice. But inwardly bent on undermining, betraying. Directing all their subtle evil will against any positive living thing [*etcetera*]. . . . The individual can but depart from the mass, and try to cleanse himself. Try to hold fast to the living thing, which destroys as it goes, but remains sweet. And in his soul fight, fight, fight to preserve that which is life in him from the ghastly kisses and poison-bites of the myriad evil ones. Retreat to the desert, and fight.

The sexual horror, and horror of betrayal, derive from Lawrence's own recent experience with Frieda and Murry, which motivates this vision of bland idealism threatening the solitary being who must retreat into further isolation to protect himself.

After this accident the forces of civilisation gather to have St Mawr killed or at least gelded, though real county, horsy people would have approved Mrs Witt's defence of the horse and condemnation of the rider. Mrs Witt, impatient of half-hearted living, and yearning for painful experience—especially painful death—as evidence of existence (almost a definition of masochism), contemptuously drives them off, and then takes St Mawr away, in the sole company of Lewis.

This simple misogynist indulges in fantasies of power and revenge, in his folk-myth of the people of the moon (the planet of inhuman isolation): "If you want to matter, you must become a moon-boy. Then all your life, fire can't blind you [sexual passion: cf. 'The Blind Man'] and people can't hurt you." His naïve integrity so impresses Mrs Witt that she proposes marriage to him, but the domineering female is decisively humiliated:

> "No woman who I touched with my body should ever speak to me as you speak to me, or think of me as you think of me. . . . Nothing in the world," he said, "would make me feel such shame as to have a woman shouting at me, or mocking at me, as I see women mocking and despising the men they marry. No woman shall touch my body, and mock me or despise me."

So Frieda is firmly put in her place. It is time now for sexual quiescence and separation, as Lou says afterwards to Lewis:

"It seems to me that men and women have really hurt one another so much, nowadays, that they had better stay apart till they have learned to be gentle with one another again. Not all this forced passion and destructive philandering."

The movement towards isolation in the desert develops. In America, Mrs Witt and St Mawr drop out of the story, the former because female aggression has been defeated, the latter because dangerous male sexuality has been transcended. The magnificent last section displays the inhuman world to which Lou–Lawrence has retreated.

The landscape lived, and lived as the world of the gods, unsullied and unconcerned. The great circling landscape lived its own life, sumptuous and uncaring. Man did not exist for it.

For Lou, this magnificent mountain landscape has replaced St Mawr as the more than human power to which she can submit—but safely. At the beginning she thinks,

". . . sex, mere sex, is repellent to me. I will never prostitute myself again. Unless something touches my very spirit, the very quick of me, I will stay alone, just alone. Alone, and give myself only to the unseen presences . . ."

However, absolute inhumanity produces furtive subhumanity and degeneracy, in Lawrence's familiar pattern. The desert is also populated by goats and rats (creatures associated with degenerate sexuality); cruelty, savagery, and 'unnatural' desires, cluster together. One is reminded of the glacier in 'The Captain's Doll':

A strange invisible influence coming out of the livid rock-fastnesses in the bowels of those uncreated Rocky Mountains, preying upon the will of man, and slowly wearing down his resistance, his onward-pushing spirit.

The little woman who was one of Lou's predecessors in the lonely farm also senses this:

Especially she was conscious of the prowling, intense aerial electricity all the summer, after June . . . moving invisible, with strange menace. . . . And then, most mysterious but worst of all, the animosity of the spirit of place: the crude, half-created spirit of place, like some serpent-bird for ever attacking man, in a hatred of man's onward-struggle towards further creation.

The phrasing suggests that 'the spirit of place' is not just the natural condition of the place, but implies a savage subhuman condition, akin to the plumed serpent.

The seething cauldron of lower life, seething on the very tissue of the higher life, seething the soul away, seething at the marrow. . . . The gods of those inner mountains were grim and invidious and relentless, huger than man, and lower than man. Yet man could never master them.

F

The image-cluster from *The Lost Girl* and the Etna passage in *Sea and Sardinia* are familiar; Lawrence is aware of the degradation consequent upon such a withdrawal from sexual normality. He has attempted to see this mode of being as the state of assured potency, as in the pine tree near the cabin:

A passionless, non-phallic column, rising in the shadows of the pre-sexual world, before the hot-blooded ithyphallic column ever erected itself.

This soon modulates into an abnormal, sadistic sexuality:

A cold, blossomless, resinous sap surging and oozing gum, from that pallid brownish bark. And the wind hissing in the needles, like a vast nest of serpents. . . . [The pine trees in the forest behind rise] in blind assertiveness . . . their needles glistened like polished steel . . . the tufts would be dark, alert tufts like a wolf's tail touching the air . . . they hedged one in with the aroma and the power and the slight horror of the pre-sexual primeval world.

That is, the devouring sexuality prior to civilised 'feminine' sexuality. Later, a pine-tree is scarred by lightning, causing the woman to think

"There is no Almighty loving God. The God there is shaggy as the pine-trees, and horrible as the lightning. . . . What nonsense about Jesus and a God of Love, in a place like this! This is more awful and more splendid. I like it better."

Retirement from civilisation has not brought calm power: the ultimate self, the heart of nature, has an intense energy, amoral and possibly even evil in so far as it is inimical to normal humanity. Lou concludes,

"I am here, right deep in America, where there's a wild spirit wants me, a wild spirit more than men. And it doesn't want to save me either. It needs me. It craves for me. And to it, my sex is deep and sacred, deeper than I am, with a deep nature aware deep down of my sex. It saves me from cheapness, mother."

Flight from the demands, threats and competition of other people does not bring assured power; isolation and withdrawal brings rapport with nature, but a nature that reflects the bitterness, malevolence and unnaturalness of the fugitive dispossessed, just like Rico and St Mawr. Lawrence 'tips the balance' in this story, attempting to suppress his awareness that Lou is like Alvina Houghton, a 'lost girl'; the plumed serpent is nearly hatched.

'The Woman Who Rode Away' may have been the first violent reaction to the European experience; it displays a similar ambivalence, where fulfilment of the protagonist's essential nature demands sub-mission and destruction. The 'Woman' is an almost characterless middle-class American. As a girl she had hoped her marriage would be an adventure, but at thirty-three she had not developed during her marriage to a much older man, who loathes the physicality of life, redirects his passion into idealism and frenetic activity, and keeps her an adored prisoner in his home deep in the Sierra Madre.

The tale is concerned with her next attempt at self-fulfilling adventure, in her escape from her barren life to seek a mysterious, sacred Indian tribe, the Chilcuis, descendants of the Aztecs. She is content to be intercepted on her journey by the Indians who lead her, as she is thrillingly aware, into doom and death (her primary desire is for masochistic self-abandonment and a yearning for painful annihilating sensation—like Mrs Witt). They ascend high over the barren rocky mountains above the world, before dropping into the hidden haven of the Chilcuis. Here she is fearfully satisfied to be in the absolute power of the dark alien priests, who strip her and prepare her for sacrifice: in their myth, their gods must be liberated from the white races' captivity by the (self) sacrifice of a white woman. Lawrence offers an interpretation: 'feminine' self-consciousness is to give away to primitive integrity of being.

Her kind of womanhood, intensely personal and individual was to be obliterated again, and the great primeval symbols were to tower once more over the fallen individual independence of woman. The sharpness and the quivering nervous consciousness of the highly-bred white woman was to be destroyed again, womanhood was to be cast once more into the great stream of impersonal sex and impersonal passion.

For 'woman' read 'Lawrence'—in the second sentence, at least.

A young man who plays the part of a hostile if intermittently sympathetic son eases her passage into annihilation (he has been to America, and must watch over her: it is all preparation for maturity). Under the influence of drugs she attains a 'passional cosmic consciousness', an 'exquisite sense of bleeding out into the higher beauty and harmony of things'. When fully prepared she is taken into an orifice in the body of the mountain, stripped and spread-eagled (the crucifixion of the spirit on barbaric flesh envisaged in *Fantasia*). When the sun shines blood-red through the savage phallic icicle over the cave-mouth (again the pattern of Poe's 'The Pit and the Pendulum') then the old priest 'would strike, and strike home, accomplish the sacrifice and achieve the power. The mastery that man must hold, and that passes from race to race.' The action is not completed in the story, which halts in horrified fascination at this ultimate sexual conquest and destruction. The woman here (as in the other contemporary fiction) is not merely the women in Lawrence's life, on whom he is revenging himself, but the female element of self-consciousness and 'civilisation' in his own psyche, which he contemplates destroying in order to release the savage, sacred male power in himself. More and more in his isolated fantasies he sees essential being and Nature, with which he seeks to identify, as inhuman and deadly.

This is particularly apparent in the next fable—almost equally fantastic and unhappy—'The Princess'. Dollie Urquhart was brought up by an incestuously doting father as a fairy princess, one of "the last of the royal race of the old people". After his death she needs another man, and at a dude ranch in New Mexico is attracted to a young Indian guide, also a dispossessed member of a pre-Christian nobility.

He gave her the feeling that death was not far from him. Perhaps he too was half in love with death. However that may be, the sense she had that death was not far from him made him "possible" to her.

She makes him take her up into the mountains, where they leave behind the 'tangle of decay and despair [that] lay in the virgin forests' (the frustration in natural life) to enter an inhuman world above and beyond life.

In front now was nothing but mountains, ponderous, massive, down-sitting mountains, in a huge and intricate knot, empty of life or soul. Under the bristling black feathers of spruce nearby lay patches of white snow . . .
    It frightened the Princess, it was *so* inhuman. She had not thought it could be so inhuman, so, as it were, anti-life. And yet now one of her desires was fulfilled. She had seen it, the massive, gruesome, repellent core of the Rockies. She saw it there beneath her eyes, in its gigantic heavy gruesomeness.
    And she wanted to go back. At this moment she wanted to turn back. She had looked down into the intestinal knot of these mountains [cf. the description of the Alpine valley in *Women in Love* as the 'navel of the earth']. She was frightened. She wanted to go back.
    But Romero was riding on . . .

As in *Women in Love* the entry into the body of inhuman male power culminates in sexual brutality. Dollie seduces Romero into sexual intercourse, but her subsequent disgust and contempt drive him into frenzies of violence, attempting to break her will; in the end her absolute passive resistance breaks him, and they are both spiritually nullified. Brutal male primitivism can neither liberate nor conquer female consciousness, and is punished for the attempt. Dollie is rescued by Forest Rangers, who kill Romero. With her return to civilised nonentity and marriage to an older man, the story indeed ends in stalemate (though a happier ending, with the couple separated but the woman liberated and pregnant, is provided in *Lady Chatter-ley's Lover*).

The horrific sexual fantasies, ambivalence and self-negation of these stories indicate Lawrence's plight, torn between sexual roles; 'female' civilisation is self-denial, but male assertion seems disastrous. Somehow he must assume the male role and power, but also control it.

This is largely the concern of *Mornings in Mexico* (1927), a series of essays written concurrently with the tales. With their fresh, supple and colloquial style they seem at first simply brilliant reports of experience, but have been carefully ordered to make a significant unity. The first four essays were in fact written slightly later, during the second draft of *The Plumed Serpent*, to which they seem to constitute a reaction, being very unpretentious and human; the next three belong to the summer of 1924, and reflect the novel more directly.

The first essay mocks the pretensions of authors, of humanity and of white civilisation: reality escapes our limitations and prejudices, there are modes of being different to ours. Next Lawrence provides an example of such difference. The imperviousness of the Indians to European responses and civilisation can even seem horrible, but it is simply difference and indifference, which should be appreciated, as Lawrence appreciates the body of the naked Indian youth whom he comes upon unawares. Throughout the book he plays the Indian myth and year against the Christian, which seem half-hearted in comparison. The third essay contrasts the birth of Christ with the Indian myth (horrifically satisfying for Lawrence) where the mother,

the goddess of love is a goddess of dirt and prostitution, a dirt-eater, a horror, without a touch of tenderness. (III)

Her degrading coupling brings forth, not an idealist or self-conscious being like Christ or Lawrence, but a stone knife: this is true (Indian) nature, hard, strong and cruel, single and self-contained, indifferent to other people and times, but living *now*:

For the *moment* is as changeless as an obsidian knife, and the heart of the Indian is as keen as the moment that divided past from future, and sacrifices them both. (III)

Lawrence however has more in common with the subject of the essay, the servant Rosalino, a sensitive self-conscious 'mother's boy', emotionally scarred by the attempt to force him into military service: for all his frailty and intermittent gaiety, he resists humanity, and being 'caught'.

The relationships between such cautious self-contained people can only be brief: a swift movement, centripetal as it were, into warm human contact, followed by a centrifugal movement

on a strong swerve of repulsion, curved out and away again, into space.

Nothing but the touch, the spark, of contact. . . . Like the evening star, between the sun and the moon, and swayed by neither of them. The flashing intermediary, the evening star that is seen only at the dividing of the day and the night, but then is more wonderful than either. (IV)

Lawrence cannot commit himself to either isolation or communion, to male or female, but only to an intermediate condition of 'touch and go'.

'Indians and Entertainment' develops the nature of the Indians difference. Where the European's drama and ritual implies a spectator, an observing consciousness detached from action and experience as in self-conscious living, the Indian is not so divided, being

completely embedded in the wonder of his own drama. . . . They are not representing something, not even playing. It is a soft, subtle *being* something. The mind is there merely as a servant, to keep a man pure and true to the mystery, which is always present. The mind bows down before the creative mystery, even of the atrocious Apache warrior. It judges, not the good and the bad, but the lie and the true. (V)

This is of course a restatement of Lawrence's own aesthetic theory, discussed in a previous chapter. Without the self-conscious intellect the dance is simply the welling-up and bodying-forth of essential nature, the ambivalent amoral source of all living forms, that are not good or bad, but more or less true to that ultimate source. There is no sense of separation and conflict. So the dance may be of the return to the source, 'the downward rhythm, the rhythm of pure forgetting and pure renewal), or of the pride of life,

the dance of the naked blood-being, defending his own isolation in the rhythm of the universe. Not skill nor prowess, not heroism. Not man to man. The creature of the isolated, circulating blood-stream dancing in the peril of his own isolation, in the overweening of his own singleness. The glory in power of the man of single existence. The peril of the man whose heart is suspended like a single red star, in a great and complex universe, following its own lone course round the invisible sun of our own being, amid the strange wandering array of other hearts. (V)

From the source of life, the amoral Unconscious, comes the energy to fulfil individual being, without fear of competition from others.

The next two essays present two of the dances. The Spring Corn Dance takes place on 'the Wednesday after Easter, after Christ Risen and the corn germinated . . . green resurrection'. The men and women in separate groups are the two complementary principles, of the sexes, or of sky and earth; and between them are 'the hopping Koshare, the jesters, the Delight-Makers', not belonging to either, on whom Lawrence focusses and with whom he identifies. Extraordinarily painted, 'they are anything but natural', pure spirit, essential beings, outsider artist-priests like himself, dancing between the great opposites, calling forth life.

Between them all, the little seed: and also man, like a seed that is busy and aware. And from the heights and from the depths man, the caller, calls: man, the knower, brings down the influences and brings up the influences, with his knowledge: man, so vulnerable, so subject, and yet even in his vulnerability and subjection, a master, commands the invisible influences and is obeyed. Commands in that song, in that rhythmic energy of dance, in that still-submissive mockery of the Koshare. And he accomplishes his end, as master . . . recovers all he once sent forth, and partakes again of the energy he called to the corn, from out of the wide universe. (VI)

The next essay, on the Hopi Snake Dance, sums it up. Lawrence gives his version of the Indians' belief: the individual Father-God is replaced by a 'dark sun', a primary source of energy and life, throwing forth the various individual forms, human and nonhuman. The need is to tap this power, that is the Unconscious, the great prehuman potencies within oneself, that cannot be deliberately channelled, but may, with courage, be ridden. The passional forces in oneself must not be seen as the monsters that fear and conscious repression make them seem (thus for the Oedipal son, maternal tenderness is a devouring witch, the libido a deadly dragon), but transformed into forces for the fulfilment of one's own nature: it is thus man becomes a god.

The only gods on earth are men. For gods, like man, do not exist beforehand* They are created and evolved gradually . . . smelted between the furnace of the Life-Sun, and beaten on the anvil of the rain. . . . The cosmos is a great furnace, a dragon's den, where the heroes and demi-gods, men, forge themselves into being. It is a vast and violent matrix, where souls form like diamonds in earth, under extreme pressure. . . . But gods frail as flowers; which have also the godliness of things that have won perfection out of the terrific dragon-clutch of the cosmos. (VII)

He suggests that this central energy contains duality, the male and female, but there is as yet no balance in Lawrence's psyche: the male is still identified with deadly force, thunder, the dragon, the serpent, and the inward sterility of his self-denial must be enlivened.

Some inward fate drove him [the Hopi Indian—and Lawrence] to the top of these parched mesas, all rocks and eagles, sand and snakes, the wind and sun and alkali. These he had to conquer. Not merely, as we should put it, the natural conditions of the place. But the mysterious life-spirit that reigned there. The eagle and the snake [the plumed serpent that is 'the spirit of place']. (VIII)

This the Indian does through the ritual dance with the libido-symbolic snakes; by soothing them, and dancing with them in their mouths, the Hopi dancers both assuage and assume their powers. The phallus, embodied in the snake, loses its terrifying hardness. The snakes hang

very still and docile. Docile, almost sympathetic, so that one was struck only by their clean, slim length of snake nudity, their beauty, like soft, quiescent lightning. (VII)

Afterwards the snakes are returned to the earth, and 'the source of all things, which we call sun because the other name is too fearful'; their return to the source is equivalent to man's possession and com- prehension of his essential being. Primal fears have been confronted and partially overcome, primal energy tapped; the snake's poison has been drawn, and Lawrence briefly can dare to be himself and be a man.

Further insight into the impulses behind *The Plumed Serpent*, particularly perhaps the less appealing impulses, can be gained from the essays collected under the title *Reflections on the Death of a Porcu- pine* (1925; P2 363–484), that relate closely to the other writings of 1924–5. Lawrence begins by contemptuously dismissing other novelists as idealistic betrayers of their true 'passional inspiration [in which] they are all phallic worshippers'; their 'morality' is merely fear and hatred of the phallic being:

Secretly, Leo [Tolstoy] worshipped the human male, man as a column of rapacious and living blood. He could hardly meet three lusty, roisterous young guardsmen in the street, without crying with envy: and ten minutes later, fulminating on them black oblivion and annihilation, utmost moral thunder-bolts. (P2 423)

The honourable novel and novelist (such as Lawrence) will not be self-crucifyingly idealistic, but express the impulses of the phallic self, that transcend conventional ethical limitations:

This we know, now, for good and all: that which is good, and moral, is that which brings into us a stronger deeper flow of life and life-energy: evil is that which impairs the life-flow. (P2 428)

It is time for the overthrow of self-denying idealism by self-fulfilling passion, now called 'power':

The reign of love is passing, and the reign of power is coming again. . . . We want to feel the power of life in ourselves.
We're sick of being soft, and amiable, and harmless. (P2 436–8)

Such power is not the conscious will to domination, but potency, that stems from primary being: God, or the unconscious. It is uncontrollable and amoral.

For power is the first and greatest of all mysteries. It is the mystery that is behind all our being, even behind all our existence. Even the phallic erection is a first blind movement of power. Love is said to call the power into motion: but it is probably the reverse: that the slumbering *power* calls love into being . . . true destructive power is power just the same as constructive. . . . The moment the divine power manifests itself, it is right. (P2 442)

Which is a comforting thought, except for anyone in the way. 'Love' is a function of egoistic individualism, to be supplanted by the more fundamental, unwilled power of 'desire'.

The ego is always concerned in Love. But in the frail, subtle desirousness of the true male, towards everything female, and the equally frail, indescribable desirability of every female for every male [note: the phrasing does not accord desire to the female], lies the real clue to the equating, or the *relating*, of things which otherwise are incommensurable . . .
   The two individuals stay apart, for ever and ever. But the two streams of desire, like the Blue Nile and the White Nile, from the mountains one and from the low hot lake the other, meet and at length mix their strange and alien waters . . . (P2 452–3)

The two individuals must not make demands, whether for conscious intimacy or sexual union, but leave each other alone, and wait upon desire (one seems to overhear an argument with Frieda):

The living stream of sexual desire itself does not often in any man, find its object, its confluent, the stream of desire in a woman into which it can flow. The two streams flow together, spontaneously, not often, in the life of any man or woman. Mostly, men and women alike rush into a sort of prostitution, because our idiotic civilisation has never learned to hold in reverence the true desire-stream. We force our desire from our ego: and this is deadly. (P2 455)

After this somewhat unhappy consideration of power as desire, Lawrence turns to power as conquest, and the prose no longer stumbles defensively, but quickens and lightens. Lawrence has brought himself to kill a porcupine, that seems a degraded being: 'all savagery has a touch of squalor, that makes one a little sick at the stomach' (P2 460). As in 'St Mawr', such creatures embody the degenerate aspect of male savage power, that he must overcome: so he insists, 'Wherever man establishes himself upon the earth, he has to fight for his place, against the lower orders of life'; 'If the lower cycles of life are not *mastered*, there can be no higher cycle'. Vital energy is attained by drawing the energy from lower orders of being, that are proved

F*

lower because they can be so overcome. From the struggle between higher and lower comes the divine energy of life, as in the dandelion flower produced by the struggle between the sun and the cold dark earth:

Till the two fall in one strange embrace, and from the centre the long flower-stem lifts like a phallus, budded with a bud. And out of the bud the voice of the Holy Ghost is heard crying: "*I am lifted up! Lo! I am lifted up! I am here!*" (P2 470)

(cf. the similarly entertaining climax in 'The Man Who Died'). Lawrence, somewhat uneasy perhaps, wants to suggest that the mastering and domination is a two-way process, that the mastered desire to be so, that submission is liberty:

There will be conquest, always. But the aim of conquest is a perfect relation of conquerors with conquered, for a new blossoming. . . . Freedom, sacrifice, almightiness, these are all human side-tracks, cul-de-sacs, bunk. All that is real is the over-whelmingness of a new inspirational command, a new relationship with all things . . . every man, in the struggle of conquest towards his own consummation, must master the inferior cycles of life, and never relinquish his mastery. Also, if there be men beyond him, moving on to a newer consummation than his own, he must yield to their greater demand, and serve their greater mystery, and so be faithful to the kingdom of heaven which is within him, which is gained by conquest and by loyal service. (P2 472–3)

Such greater men, prophet-artists with a vision of greater vitality, plugging man in to the cosmic womb, are the true aristocrats:

Whoever can establish, or initiate, a new connection between mankind and the circumambient universe is, in his own degree, a saviour. Because mankind is always exhausting its human possibilities, always degenerating into repetition, torpor, *ennui*, lifelessness. When *ennui* sets in, it is a sign that human vitality is waning, and the human connection with the universe is gone stale. (P2 478)

Lawrence's tone, which up to now has been his perky slangy style, with only a hint of condescension, now becomes hysterical, and abusive of any reader not wholeheartedly supporting him. Fighting against a sense of waning energy, whipping up his sense of possible vitality, he insists on an animate, vibrant universe in relation with man, the power of which he can merge with and assume. The work concludes with an ascension from mundane reality. First comes union with the Almighty:

. . . no man is man in all his splendour till he passes further than any relationship: further than mankind and womankind, in the last leap to the sun, to the night . . . with the sun he has his final and ultimate relationship, beyond man or woman, or anything human or created. And in this final relation is he most intensely alive, surpassing. (P2 483)

One might accept this combination of Icarus and Empedocles leaping into Etna, as the self-destructive return to the Unconscious, for rebirth and self-transcendence; but he goes on, almost pitiably:

Enough of the squalor of democratic humanity.

It is time to begin to recognise the aristocracy of the sun. The children of the sun shall be lords of the earth. . . . And in the coming era they will rule the world, a confraternity of the living sun, making the embers of financial internationalism and industrial internationalism pale upon the hearth of the earth. (P2 484)

Which brings us to the novel at which most readers, and even Lawrentians, balk. *The Plumed Serpent* (1926) has been resisted and rejected by most critics, though it is perhaps Lawrence's most ambitious attempt to solve the fundamental problems of his being, and is certainly not the aberration in his development that several critics see it as.

In the story, Kate Leslie, a twice-married widow aged forty, visiting Mexico, abandons the 'civilised' city in disgust, drawn to the interior by her fascination with two revolutionary leaders and their revival of the ancient Aztec religion, which is to supplant the cult of Mary and Jesus. The novel outlines the nature and development of the religious movement, and Kate's half-reluctant submission to the two men, until one, Don Ramon, becomes spiritual leader of Mexico, and Kate has married the other, the general Don Cipriano, and committed herself to this world.

In spite of vivid scene-painting and the use of material from *Mornings in Mexico*, *The Plumed Serpent* is not realistic, but a psycho-drama set in the country of the mind.[5] The main characters—all, like Lawrence, about forty, at the crisis of middle age—and events, which when considered realistically are often grotesque, absurd and monstrous, are not apprehended by Lawrence as real or autonomous, but as mere shadows of the struggle in his own psyche, a struggle dating back to his adolescent years, the world of *Sons and Lovers*. This absence of the reality-principle accounts for the work's ultimate failure both as novel and as personal therapy. It is a romance of psychic death and rebirth acted out for Lawrence by Kate, who provides the feminine response (of Frieda and of his own feminine 'anima') to the growth of the 'power' principle discussed previously. As in *Reflections*, part of the trouble is due to Lawrence's confusion between power as potency, life-energy and fulfilment, and power as 'conquest', masculine harshness and domination.

Frieda appears in Kate, widowed from her second marriage to Joachim Leslie, who is clearly the 'idealist' Lawrence who had struggled with the world; his death indicates abandonment of this exhausted former self (which had been appearing in the stories as a weak older man), while the name Joachim presents him as a prophet of Apocalypse,[6] of the death of one spiritual order and birth of a new. He has no single successor, but the duality of 'soul' (Ramon) and rampant flesh (Cipriano) mediated by the third member of the trinity, Kate herself: there is to be no one 'absolute' but a constant interaction between the various elements in the psyche.

Kate finds herself in 'Mexico', a degenerate state, where exhausted, irritable 'civilisation' masks a death-wish. This 'civilisation' is epitomised in the 'beetle-trap' bull-ring where a loutish mob relishes the spectacle of a maddened bull thrusting its horn into the anus of a horse, disembowelling it. In hysterical flight from this emblem of degenerate coitus, and of the destruction of the libido by brute phallic being, Kate is rescued by Don Cipriano, who later introduces her to Don Ramon, the reviver of the cult of Quetzalcoatl, the eagle-serpent God.

Under their influence she decides to abandon this death-in-life and visit the interior of the country and of the self, to die to the old life and seek the new:

Ye must be born again. Out of the fight with the octopus of life, the dragon of degenerate or of incomplete existence, one must win this soft bloom of being, that is damaged with a touch . . .

She was forty, and in the rare, lingering dawn of maturity, the flower of her soul was opening . . .

The thing called "Life" is just a mistake we have made in our own minds. Why persist in the mistake any further? (III)

So Kate goes to Lake Sayula, the water of death and rebirth, ferried over the sperm-white water by a crippled Charon, in whom she sees the

gentleness between a scylla and charybdis of violence. . . . The magnificence of the watchful morning-star, that watches between the night and the day, the gleaming clue to the two opposites. (V)

This world at first seems terrifying (the dead man with his genitals thrust in his mouth is the negative of the Hopi Snake Dancers) but she presses on up the lake, rowed now by two men (possibly precursors of Ramon and Cipriano) with whom she feels herself to be in a sexually quiescent relationship preferable to her love-relationship with Joachim. In the interior she feels that

Concrete, jarring, exasperating reality had melted away, and a soft world
of potency stood in its place, the velvety dark flux of the earth, the delicate
yet supreme life-breath in the inner air. Behind the fierce sun the dark eyes
of a deeper sun were watching ... (VI)

At the villa Kate has rented, the quester meets her 'double' in the
servant Juana, another passionate and unstable widow aged forty,
who acts chiefly as her tester, attempting to provoke or drag her into
negative responses. Her next step into the living underworld is when
she takes part in an almost hypnotic Quetzalcoatl dance,[7] clearly the
dance of the downward rhythm in *Mornings in Mexico* V, where
conscious individuality is merged in a sense of larger being emanating
from the preconscious. After this first experience there naturally
follows a reaction of fear of the forces in the Indians and in herself,
that may overwhelm her. In an image significant for Lawrence she
imagines Jesus as a miner crushed underground, and also remembers
Joachim defining evil as the return to the past, and to superseded
states of being. In the irrational impulse of faith, she decides that this
return is merely to achieve a reconnection with the energising forces
of primary being, so that one is no longer merely self-dependent and
isolated (a condition that perhaps caused Joachim's exhaustion), but
in a wider relationship. Certainly she hopes, rather oddly for a woman,
that this religion will enable a better relationship between men.

After this resolution—and first third of the novel—Kate can proceed
further, to the inner sanctum of Ramon's villa. Here she meets his
wife Dona Carlota, an idealist adorer of Mary, who regards men as
wayward children, and who after adoring Ramon (like his aunt and
his next wife) has become deeply hostile to this new development in
him. Carlota's passive resistance drives Ramon to prayer, in order to
obliterate consciousness and increase emotional self-confidence. He
then goes on a little self-comforting tour of his estate where everyone
is engaged on art and craft-work (anticipating Mellors's scheme in
Lady Chatterley's Lover) to the greater glory of the movement and
Ramon in particular, before concluding with a religious ceremony
when he anticipates escaping from time and consciousness.

Feminine criticism is then rebuked by the spectacle of an embrace
between Ramon and Cipriano, intended as an example of non-
possessive love, but chiefly remarkable for its intimacy, and Cipriano's
filial submissiveness. Cipriano afterwards makes explicit the two kinds
of power, in explaining to Kate the two states of man. One is like the
dewy morning, with the flower of the self in blossom, when man
desires woman; the other is the burning heat that withers up sexual
desire and the flower, when the self is a coiling serpent, and a man
wants to be "a very big man and master of all the people". Cipriano

attempts to balance this latter (and for him, stronger) impulse by proposing marriage to Kate; Ramon at this stage is complete in him-self—heavy breasted, yet with majestic fatherliness for them both.

At the mid-point of the book Cipriano tempts Ramon to turn his religious potency into destructive self-assertion, "to be a serpent, and be big enough to wrap one's folds around the globe of the world, and crush it like an egg". Ramon resists the impulse to negation, and insti-tutes perhaps the best of the Quetzalcoatl rituals, where the principles appear most clearly. First he invokes the snake from the earth's centre, the libido, to come and kiss his "inner thigh" (his genitals) to regenerate his manhood, and then invites the eagle, the thunderer, to rest on his arm; man will exist between and reconcile the opposing forces in creation, like the Morning Star; the old self will die and the new be born. The chapter culminates in the thunder and torrential rain of the new birth.

After this comes a slack period of uncertainty, awaiting new develop-ments. Ramon describes to Kate his vision of the new international aristocrats (as in the essay 'Aristocracy') of god-men and god-women; this is accompanied, as in the essay, by disgust of ordinary humanity and revulsion from human intimacy, expressed by Kate and Ramon respectively—or interchangeably. He admits the loneliness of being a trail-breaker for humanity, but Kate's suggestion that he rest from this task only results in his fourth Hymn, a hymn of hate for 'white' civilisation, its women, and the dead (presumably the spirit of Law-rence's mother) that would prevent the growth of the new man and new world. From this comes his next step of taking over the Church.

Chapter XVIII, two thirds through the book, is in a sense climactic. After Ramon's talk of the horror of men and women "ravishing" each other (the emotional and sexual demands upon himself that Lawrence loathed), and of the need to conquer the dragons of self-inhibition, comes the culminating moment: the burning of the effigies of Mary and Jesus. The immediate analogy with this powerful scene is the burning of the white witch-puppet in *Sea and Sardinia*, but an earlier instance is in *Sons and Lovers*, when Paul ritually burns the doll that has caused him to feel such guilt. So the tender love and mother-child complex is destroyed in fierce self-assertion. Lawrence's sense of guilt at this, and fear of the demonic male energy he has released, produces a savage attack upon Ramon by a gang of men who indeed seem demonic in their almost irresistible power. The sexual implications of this assault are very apparent: knives in the groin, and jerking buttocks. He survives this horrific assault partly through the assistance of Kate (either as his protective woman, or as his 'civilised' anima).

The feminine principle, having asserted itself, must again be suppressed by the male, so suddenly Kate is overwhelmed by a vision of Cipriano's phallic power:

She could see the skies grow dark, and the phallic mystery rearing itself like a whirling dark cloud, to the zenith, till it pierced the sombre, twilit zenith; the old, supreme phallic mystery . . .

Ah! and what a mystery of prone submission, on her part, this huge erection would imply! Submission absolute, like the earth under the sky. Beneath an over-arching absolute.

Ah! what a marriage! How terrible! and how complete! With the finality of death, and yet more than death. The arms of the twilit Pan. And the awful, half-intelligible voice from the cloud . . .

Ah, what an abandon, what an abandon, what an abandon!—of so many things she wanted to abandon. (XX)

Lawrence had more sense, and wrote better, in *The Lost Girl*. Kate realises that Ramon, having survived the attack, is now beyond her, 'remote, remote from any woman'; but his other self, Cipriano, takes her and envelops her in 'the inaccessible, voluptuous mystery of man's physical consummation', and they are 'married' by Ramon.

Ramon is now ready to assume divinity as the living Quetzalcoatl. At the ceremony, Carlota interrupts desperately, and collapses. Afterwards the dying woman, now clearly Lawrence's mother, is reviled for having been cold-hearted and life-destroying:

"You stale virgin, you spinster, you born widow, you weeping mother, you impeccable wife, you just woman. You stole the very sunshine out of the sky and the sap out of the earth. . . . Die and be a thousand times dead! Do nothing but utterly die!" (XXI)

After this exorcism, Ramon's last encounter with his sons, alienated from him by Carlota, illustrates the agony of choosing between father and mother. His sons are replaced by Cipriano, and after a ritual anointing (similar to that of Aaron by Lilly, in *Aaron's Rod*) Cipriano is symbolically reborn from his 'father' Ramon.

The son can now avenge the father, and ritually executes the surviving 'traitors' who had attacked Ramon. Again a certain fear is felt, expressed by Kate, who thinks that Cipriano 'seemed to be driving the male significance to its utmost, and beyond, with a sort of demonism' (XXIV); however she persuades herself that there will be a reciprocity in their relationship, that each needs the other. Cipriano is indeed not self-sufficient, and feels he cannot fulfil his conception of himself—become the war-god Huitzilopochtli—without her: he presents himself to her like a boy seeking his mother's approval, asking Kate to join him in the ritual and be his bride Malintzi, the

fertility goddess. In the church they achieve apotheosis and rebirth in
sexual union, and 'regain' their adolescence and virginity. In effect
Lawrence cancels the previous twenty-five years of his adult life, and
returns to his adolescent years to possess the woman, magically made
younger and virginal, whom he then desired (cf. the poem 'Spirits
Summoned West').

Another woman from the past must also be possessed: Ramon
suddenly marries Teresa, whose nun-like intensity and adoration, and
bullying brothers, identify her as Miriam, of *Sons and Lovers*. If
Lawrence had married Miriam his true religious self would have
developed, he suspects, unhindered by the inhibitory criticism of his
mother and Frieda. Teresa is a better wife than Kate because she
makes no demands, and completely subjugates herself, so that Ramon's
spiritual-sexual being develops without the need for self-assertion.

Meanwhile Kate has to forgo any self-assertion. She has no 'personal
intimacy' with Cipriano, who, in their love-making, denies her her
orgasm, her 'satisfaction'; what she achieves is

So different from the beak-like friction of Aphrodite of the foam, the
friction which flares out in circles of phosphorescent ecstasy, to the last
wild spasm which utters the involuntary cry, the final love-cry. This she
had known to the end, with Joachim. And now this too was removed from
her. What she had with Cipriano was curiously beyond her knowing: so
deep and hot and flowing, as it were subterranean. She had to yield before
it. She could not grip it into one final spasm of white ecstasy which was like
sheer knowing. (XXVI)

This is not only compensatory for Lawrence, subordinating the
woman to the man, and preventing her from 'using' and possessing
him; it is also the subordination of 'feminine' will, for the release of
the whole being. Kate is an exemplar of civilised self-inhibition, where
will confines the body's capacity for sensuous pleasure to solely
genital excitation and orgasm, a sensationalism that manifests rather
than threatens the will's control. (The line of thought and imagery here
date back to *Women in Love*). Cipriano prevents this narrow focus,
to achieve not merely genital but total orgasm, submerging the will
in the whole body's pleasure.[8] So the taming of the shrew is completed.

In the last chapter, Kate's lingering anxieties—emblematised in a
lost horse—are assuaged by various sights symbolic of psychic integration and reborn life, as of a bull gently eased into an enclosed boat
with a cow, to sail out on the waters of a lake, and of a newly born
ass with its mother (traditionally associated with Christ and his
mother). For all this, Ramon confesses his loneliness and fear of
inadequacy; Kate covertly offers herself, but her 'motherly touch'

arouses his resistance again. Teresa, in conversation with Kate, confuses their ritual robes, imagining herself in Kate's green dress of Malintzi. However, the exchange of partners is averted (as it was in *Kangaroo*). The psychological 'allegory' is somewhat complex. Lawrence's 'anima' Kate cannot unite with his true self, Ramon; as Ramon, Lawrence turns away from a mother figure, and being a mature man does not usurp his predecessor (Lawrence's own father, or Frieda's first husband); he rejects Frieda–Kate and stays with his soul-bride Miriam–Teresa; the dark woman, the sacred prostitute, is preferred to the fair representative of white consciousness. Kate, both as mother and as Frieda, remains subject to male power, and does not betray her husband for another man. So, some old wounds are plastered over.

Kate cannot leave Mexico for her old home and children, so cancelling Frieda's earlier return to Europe; but Kate's failure to return from the 'interior' world to the world of normality blocks the mythical pattern that demands, after psychic death and reintegration, a return into life and renewed activity. The novel cannot complete this essential pattern, thus further preventing its success, because Lawrence has not, in spite of his appalling efforts, conquered his 'dragons'. This is further revealed in his failure to integrate true manhood in one figure, keeping it split into transcendent, rather frail soul, and harsh, dominating flesh.

The total effort was nearly fatal; the day he completed the main work on the book he collapsed with malaria and dysentery, which revived his tuberculosis; with ironic symbolism, as he lay helpless, there was a great thunderstorm and earthquake; Frieda had to take him away, back to Europe and the old world, desire and reality still unreconciled.

---

1. The stories of the time are satiric of Murry. 'The Border Line' uses the imagery of 'Letter from Germany', where Lawrence returns as from the dead to kill the usurper and reclaim his wife. In 'Jimmy and the Desperate Woman', wife-seduction and mother-seduction fuse. Jimmy–Murry–Lawrence takes away the dour tartar of a wife (Lawrence's mother's situation, with some of Frieda's fierceness) of a miner (Lawrence's father giving him extra strength). Apart from Oedipal fantasy of the father condoning the seduction, there is a homosexual element in the tale, as Jimmy feels himself united with the miner in embracing the woman, and wonders which of them he will possess first.

2. 'Am reading *Passage to India*. It's good, but makes one wish a bomb would fall and end everything. Life is more interesting in its undercurrents than in its obvious; and E. M. does see people, people and nothing but people; *ad nauseam*' (CL 799).

3. So was Lawrence: 'You have to have something vicious in you to be a creative writer. It is the something vicious, old-adamish, incompatible to the

"ordinary" world, inside a man, which gives an edge to his awareness' (P 373).

4. cf. a letter to the editor of *The Laughing Horse* magazine: 'Two-legged man is no good. If he's going to stand steady, he must stand on four feet. Like the Centaur. When Jesus was born, the spirits wailed round the Mediterranean: *Pan is dead. Great Pan is dead.* And at the Renaissance the Centaur gave a final groan, and expired. . . . It would be a terrible thing if the horse in us died for ever, as he seems to have died in Europe. . . . Horse sense, I tell you. That's the Centaur. . . . After that, these same passions, glossy and dangerous in the flanks. And after these again, hoofs, irresistible, splintering hoofs, that can kick the walls of the world down' (CL 768–9). See also 'Pan in America' (P 22–31).

5. In my interpretation, much is owed to two works: J. Kessler, 'Descent in Darkness: The Myth of *The Plumed Serpent*' in H. T. Moore, *A D. H. Lawrence Miscellany* (London, 1961), pp. 239–59; and C. Jung, *Symbols of Transformation, Collected Works*, vol. V, (London, 1956).

6. Not only was this an old obsession of Lawrence's, but while writing the first draft of *The Plumed Serpent*, he had read the MS of Frederick Carter's *The Dragon of the Apocalypse*. See CL 744–7.

7. The dark, chanting Indians echo the blackened, singing miners of Lawrence's youth: the homeward-trooping of the colliers in 'Return to Bestwood' (1926; P2 257–66) and the drunken hymn-singing miners in ch. I of *Sons and Lovers*; see also 'Hymns in a Man's Life' (1928; P2 597–601). At least one Hymn of Quetzalcoatl owes something to the hymns Lawrence sang when a child—further evidence of his imaginative return to these formative years.

8. See Wilhelm Reich, *The Theory of Orgasm*.

6

TOMORROW IS ANOTHER DAY

I

A RETURN TO THE ANCIENT FORMS

While recuperating from the collapse consequent upon the writing of *The Plumed Serpent*, Lawrence dictated to Frieda the fragment called 'The Flying Fish' (P 780–98), which forms the pattern for much of his later work. The parallel with Lawrence and his mother is clear in the story of the malaria-ridden Gethin Day called home from Mexico by the death of his much older sister Lydia (Lawrence's mother's name), whose criticisms have always unnerved him. Now the perturbed spirit is at rest, and he can return, 'come into his own'— womb and tomb.

Preparing to do so, he recalls several long passages from an Elizabethan metaphysical chronicle of his family, 'The Book of Days', that contrasts the lesser day of ordinary life with the greater day of life in death. This greater day he had glimpsed in his illness in Mexico, when the lesser day

had cracked like some great bubble, and to his uneasiness and terror, he had seemed to see through the fissures the deeper blue of the other Greater Day where moved the other sun shaking its dark blue wings. . . . He was ill, and he felt as if at the very middle of him, beneath his navel, some membrane were torn, some membrane which had connected him with the world and its day.

The Elizabethan book advocates the abandonment of ordinary living, and acceptance of death, and joyful reunion with the great womb prior to life. Man is imaged as a flying fish:

For it is on wings of fear, sped from the mouth of death, that the flying fish riseth twinkling in the air and, rustles in astonishment silvery through the thin small day. But he dives again into the peace of the deeper day, and under the belly of death, and passes into his own. . . . Cease then the struggle of the flight, and fall back into the deep element where death is and is not, and life is not a fleeing away.

There must be no more straining at ejaculation, but an acceptance of quiescence, and an unforced insouciant spontaneity:

Wrap thyself in patience, shroud thyself in peace, as the tall volcano clothes himself in snow. Yet he looks down in him, and sees wet sun in him molten and of great force, stirring with the scald sperm of life. Be still, above the sperm of life, which spills alone in its hour. Be still . . . [T]o the nightingale his song is Nemesis, and unsung songs are the Erinyes, the impure Furies of vengeance. And thy sun in thee is thy all in all, so be patient, and take no care. Take no care, for what thou knowest is ever less than what thou art . . .

The strain of independent manhood melts in his contemplation of the untouchable purity of the sea, just in front of his homeward-bound ship, in which porpoises disport themselves.

And below, as yet untouched, a moment ahead, always a moment ahead and perfectly untouched, was the lovely green depth of the water . . . so serene, fathomless and pure and free of time . . . the body was cradled in the sway of timeless life, the soul lay in the jewel-coloured moment, the jewel pure eternity of this gulf of nowhere [wherein the porpoise mingle] among themselves in some strange single laughter of multiple consciousness, giving off the joy of life, sheer joy of life, togetherness in complete motion, many lusty-bodied fish enjoying one laugh of life, sheer togetherness, perfect as passion . . . what civilisation will bring us to such a pitch of swift laughing togetherness, as these fish have reached?

Two of Lawrence's letters of 1927, to Trigant Burrow, show the dismissal of the old effort and strain, and the hopeless yearning for the new corporate communion, the 'single laughter of multiple consciousness':

What ails me is the absolute frustration of my primeval societal instinct. The hero illusion starts with the individualist illusion, and all resistances ensue.[1] I think societal instinct much deeper than sex instinct—and societal repression much more devastating. There is no repression of the sexual individual comparable to the repression of the societal man in me, by the individual ego, my own and everybody else's. I am weary of my own individuality, and simply nauseated by other people's. (CL 989)

Myself, I suffer badly from being so cut off. But what is one to do? One can't link up with the social unconscious. At times, one is *forced* to be essentially a hermit.[2] . . . And then there will *never* be a millenium. There will *never* be a "true societal flow"—all things are relative. Men were never, in the past, fully societal—and they never will be in the future. But more so, more than now. Now is the time between Good Friday and Easter. We're absolutely in the tomb. If only one saw a chink of light in the tomb door. . . . I do think that man is related to the universe in some "religious" way, even prior to his relation to his fellow man . . . (CL 993)

The longing for the 'impersonal' activity of male communion has become subordinated in the sense of ease in a larger inclusive body. Much of the writing of this last phase shows a glamorising of a pastoral past, a simplistic yearning for a resurrection in a fantasied community of 'togetherness', umbilically connected with the cosmos.

In 'Nottingham and the Mining Country' (P 133–40), Lawrence revisits the country of his childhood. He insists that the miners were not brutalised by the industry, but in their dark underworld knew 'a sort of intimate community' developing their intuitive consciousness, 'physical awareness and intimate togetherness', while the individualist women were materialistic and possessive. He sees the ugliness of the mining towns as revelatory of the inhuman spirit of industrial capitalism, and imagines how the towns might have been if the mining companies had built them like Italian hill towns, and encouraged song and dancing and folk art, instead of 'forcing . . . all human energy into a competition of mere acquisition'. Modern civilisation frustrates 'that instinct of community which would make us unite in pride and dignity in the bigger gesture of the citizen'.

With this essay should be set the extraordinary so-called 'Autobiographical Fragment' (P 817–36), which begins like a development of that essay before turning into a modern Rip Van Winkle story, with the narrator finding himself reawakened and reborn in another world. The piece begins with a lament for the loss of 'sense of latent wildness and unbrokenness . . . in the pitch-dark Midland nights', and for the taming or emasculating of the men by domineering idealistic women. 'This countryside is dead: or so inert, it is as good as dead.' The narrator then recounts how he went to a former childhood haunt, a quarry (that first appeared in *The White Peacock*) and entered 'a little slantingly upright slit or orifice in the rock . . . living rock like hard, bright flesh, faintly perfumed', curled up in it, and went to sleep. He awakens, or is reborn, naked, a thousand years later, to find a new-old world where people wear little or no clothing, the mines have disappeared, and the old mining town has been replaced by a new Jerusalem with 'yellow, curved walls . . . and round faintly conical towers rearing up . . . golden like the golden flesh of a city'. The Congregational chapel has even been replaced by a phallic tower, with

a ball of light at the top! The people have an Egyptian calm and stillness, and engage in primitive religious ritual at sun-set. After he has
been ritually bathed and fed, he is told by the chief that he had slept
like a chrysalis, and woken like a butterfly:[3]

"Why are you afraid to be a butterfly that wakes up out of the dark for
a little while, beautiful?"
    "It is true. I am like a butterfly, and I shall only live a little while. That
is why I don't want to eat."

Lawrence accepts his personal transience, and dreams of the larger
communion, which however is always expressed regressively.

Let us prepare now for the death of our present "little" life, and the re-
emergence in a bigger life, in touch with the moving cosmos.
    It is a question, practically of relationship . . . we are perishing for lack
of fulfilment of our greater needs, we are cut off from the great sources of
our inward nourishment and renewal, sources which flow eternally in the
universe. . . . It means a return to the ancient forms . . .
    The sense of isolation, followed by the sense of menace and of fear, is
bound to arise as the feeling of oneness and community with our fellow-men
declines, and the feeling of individualism and personality, which is existence
in isolation, increases.
            ('A Propos of *Lady Chatterley's Lover*' 1930; P2 487–515)

    Lawrence's criticisms of modern industrial 'bourgeois' society are
penetrating, often just, and remarkable for his time, but behind them
is often a regressive desire for a return to the earlier tribal or child
condition, a never-never land, such as in his conceptions of medieval
Europe in 'A Propos . . .' or ancient Etruria in *Etruscan Places*, or
submergence in the womb-tomb.
    Much of the writing of the time has a thinness about it, either an
evasion of the complexity of reality, or a tone of bitter, brilliant
sterility, or even of irritated exhaustion. Such stories as 'The Rocking-
Horse Winner' and 'The Lovely Lady' are very good ghost-story
satires, but close to being mere psychological parables, with little root
in the solid physical and social world; in the former a little boy
unsuccessfully attempts in masturbatory fantasy to satisfy a materialistic greedy mother, and dies in the attempt, and in the latter, an old
mother who denies her son independent life is herself destroyed.
The verses of *Pansies* (1929) and *More Pansies* (1932)—thought-
flowers—mingle witty aphorism, jeering impatience and slapdash
writing with beautiful fragments; the verse is mostly in his late
Whitmanesque style, sometimes little more than rhythmical or merely
cut-up prose, but sometimes very sensitive and effective. There is a
great deal of criticism, of varying quality, of materialist, competitive

society ('Wages', 'Red Herring', 'How Beastly the Bourgeois is' are among the better) where feelings are rapidly perverted ('Latter-day Sinners' and 'What Matters' are 'about' his friend Aldous Huxley, 'Energetic Women' about the monstrous regiment created by feeble men, 'In a Spanish Tram Car' rejects indulgence in illicit sexuality). There are many references to, and parallels with, the contemporary prose, especially *Lady Chatterley's Lover*: two, 'Poor Bit of a Wench!' and 'What Ails Thee?', provide amusing dialogues between Mellors–Lawrence and Connie–Frieda. Some poems celebrate a future of the 'democracy of touch' and tender relatedness ('Future Religion'), seeing the wholeness and divinity in man ('For a Moment' looks back to the story 'Tickets, Please'). The conclusion of 'Climb down, O lordly mind',

> Non cogito, ergo sum.
> I am, I do not think I am. (CP 473)

may be misinterpreted, but should be set against 'Thought':

> Thought, I love thought . . .
> Thought is not a trick, or an exercise, or a set of dodges,
> Thought is a man in his wholeness wholly attending. (CP 673)

Other poems show, implicitly or explicitly, a retreat from 'frictional' sexuality to something profounder and less 'sensational' (such as 'Touch Comes' and the light, nicely judged 'Elephants are slow to Mate') and even from active sexuality altogether ('Chastity' and the comic 'The little wowser') to the delight of withdrawal into isolation. 'Delight of Being Alone' collects several favourite images:

> I know no greater delight than the sheer delight of being alone.
> It makes me realise the delicious pleasure of the moon
> that she has in travelling by herself throughout time,
> or the splendid growing of an ash-tree
> alone, on a hill-side in the north, humming in the wind. (CP 610)

There is a sequence of poems on withdrawal into isolation and the annihilating union with primary nature, such as 'Desire Goes Down into the Sea':

> I have no desire any more
> towards woman or man, beast or creature or thing.
>
> All day long I feel the tide rocking, rocking
> though it strikes no shore
> in me.
>
> Only mid-ocean. (CP 454)

Such withdrawal is the theme of the story *The Man Who Loved Islands*. Here there is a clear movement in three stages, from society, to private life, to isolated confrontation with, and submergence in, nature. In disgust with contemporary society, the unnamed protagonist (derived partly from Compton Mackenzie, but chiefly Lawrence himself) retreats to his own island utopia, where he is 'the Master', in a society of benevolent idealism that attempts 'to regain Paradise by spending money' and by 'a general goodwill'. These principles being only half man's nature, the other half appears in visions of the island as 'a jumping-off place into nothingness' and in the islanders becoming possessed by impulses towards passionate savagery, 'the blood and the passion and the lust which the island had known'.[4] The forces of 'civilisation' cannot conquer nature, and the islander retreats from his utopian island to a smaller life on a smaller island; this is private, domestic life, cut off from relationship with any larger community. Here the protagonist passively submits to 'automatic' sexual desire, seduced by his servant; after impregnating and marrying her, he flees from the tender trap.

The third island presents him cut off from all life: the barren rock has no people or trees, he has the sheep removed, the seabirds stop coming; 'he loathed with a profound repulsion the whole of the animal creation'. Soon he is sealed up in snow, awaiting death with 'a cruel satisfaction'. The impulse towards inhuman self-assertion and introversion is self-destructive, and destructive of all life: this is the essence of the individualistic dream. 'How can the bourgeois still pretend to be free, to find salvation individually? Only by sinking himself in still cruder illusions, by denying art, science, emotion, even ultimately life itself.'[5]

Crude illusion and the destruction of bourgeois 'order' are the concerns of the first substantial fiction of this last phase, *The Virgin and the Gipsy* (1930), that combines caricatures of reality with fabulous romance. Some of its inadequacy is suggested in its use of material from earlier works. The contrasting daughters, nasty-genteel clergyman, and oppressive family loyalty of 'Daughters of the Vicar' reappear, as does the desire-and-drowning theme from 'The Horse-Dealer's Daughter'; from *Women in Love* comes the blond athletic major, associated with snow and 'unconnected with life', as well as the sisters' discussions on men, love and marriage; from *The Lost Girl* comes the outsider jerking his head in mute sexual signal to the woman upstairs. Here, as there, the demon lover is outside the social order, beyond the 'pale', dispossessed and malevolent: 'His race was very old, in its peculiar battle with established society, and had no conception of winning. Only now and then it could score' (VI).

The story's return to the past is partly due to its having been occasioned by a visit by Frieda's grown-up daughters. Professor Weekley is translated into the allegorically named Reverend Saywell, blandly hateful of real feeling. The runaway wife is remembered by the daughters as glowing with life, whereas he sees her as degenerate and vicious, whom he had first regarded as a pure snow-flower. Such whiteness is a denial of life: when he insults his daughter Yvette she becomes 'white . . . and still as a snowdrop, the white snow-flower of his conceit' (IV), but in her genuinely virginal innocence she may also be imaged elsewhere as a white snow-drop growing naturally out of winter into spring.

The domestic scenes are on two levels: vividly realised scenes of domestic strife and squalid comedy, possibly deriving from incidents related to Lawrence, and splendid caricature, as in the grotesque presentations of Aunt Cissie and particularly the grandmother, gross in body and will-to-power, and toadlike in her bulk, ugliness and propensity for devouring other life. Once one has read *Cold Comfort Farm* by Stella Gibbons, however, one cannot accept such a presentation. Aunt Cissie's frustrated sexuality poisons her, Granny is a devouring monster, the Rector thinks 'unspeakable depravities' of his daughter as of his wife, one daughter, Lucille, is a mere social being, the young men just house-dogs. Yvette's frustration makes her slightly perverse. 'She seemed so virginal. At the same time, there was a touch of the tall young virgin *witch* about her, that made the house-dog men shy off. . . . Where among them was the subtle, lonely, insinuating challenge that could reach her ?' (V).

She wants to submit to the 'pariah' gipsy, the perverse demon-god of night and vengeful male potency, who casts his spell over her, almost literally, as when he nearly seduces her at his camp one day:

The waking sleep of her full-opened virginity, entranced like a snowdrop in the sunshine, was upon her.

The gipsy, supremely aware of her, waited for her like the substance of a shadow, as shadow waits and is there. . . . She was only aware of the dark strange effluence of him bathing her limbs, washing her at last purely will-less. She was aware of *him*, as a dark, complete power. (VI)

This seduction is prevented by the arrival of another couple, Major Eastwood and his Jewess; their function in the tale is to contrast with the gipsy's values their own sophisticated bohemianism, that is a mere reaction from conventionality, bolstered by a private income and without real depth of questioning. The Major is useful for two points that he makes. One is a distinction (that some critics neglected to bear in mind in discussing *Lady Chatterley's Lover*) between

sexual appetite and real desire, of which the Major, in unwitting
self-betrayal, says, "desire is the most wonderful thing in life. Anybody
who can really feel it is a king, and I envy nobody else!" The other,
is to say of the gipsy's escape from pneumonia, "He's a resurrected
man to me". His own resurrection is only a parody.

The gipsy is an anticipation of 'The Man Who Died': his quasi-
divine power is revealed by association with the gipsy-woman's
prophetic powers, his own hypnotic power, and in Yvette's reflections
on her denial of him:

She felt rather like Peter when the cock crew, as she denied him. Or rather,
she did not deny the gipsy; she didn't care about his part in the show,
anyhow. It was some hidden part of herself which she denied: that part
which mysteriously and unconfessedly responded to him. And it was a
strange, lustrous black cock which crew in mockery of her. (VII)

The phallicism of the divinity is blatant.

Yvette has to develop in self-realisation before she is ready for the
gipsy, at the end. The flood caused by the collapse of the Roman
foundations of her world, which destroys the Rector's house, drowns
Granny, and brings the gipsy and Yvette together, embodies the
overwhelming, inhuman power of nature. The mother's sexual
self-liberation was regarded by 'the family' as a 'peculiarly *dangerous*
sort of selfishness, like lions and tigers', and this flood is seen by
Yvette as 'a shaggy tawny wave-front of water advancing like a wall
of lions. The roaring sound wiped out everything' (IX). The inhuman
flood is also death, occasioning rebirth; after their icy drenching,
Yvette and the wounded gipsy have literally to warm each other to
life in her bed. The flood and the night together are apocalyptic,
remembered by Yvette as 'the world's-end night'. She is reborn, in
the words of the gipsy, 'braver in the body' (able to climb down a
ladder!), but the gipsy, having doubly saved her, has vanished.
Reconciliation between the demonic, sensual being and the world of
civilisation can only be momentary; no permanent union seems
possible to Lawrence—not, at least, in this world.

Lawrence has lost any real belief in his power to change society,
or really to relate his vision with reality. Something of this loss and its
consequences becomes apparent in comparing the first and final versions of *Lady Chatterley's Lover* (1928). This novel is full of social
criticism, but is basically evasive and escapist, with unreal, idealised
lovers hiding from a caricatured mechanical world in a genital wood,
where the penis is a bud, Connie's body a forest or jungle, and flowers
are tangled in pubic hair; sex is an escape from consciousness, and then
there is a release from sexuality into peaceful chastity.

The book was written three times between October 1926 and January 1928; in some ways the first version, the so-called *The First Lady Chatterley* (Dial Press, N.Y., 1944) is, while technically inferior, superior to the final version in its realism and humanity. The three main characters are much more probable and human, and less simply schematic. Lawrence asserts there,

Man need not sacrifice the intellect to the penis, nor the penis to the intellect . . . man has a new aim in life, to maintain a truce between the two and some sort of fluctuating harmony. Instead of deliberately . . . setting out to murder the one in order to exalt the other. (p. 192)

This balance does not exist in the final version, where Clifford Chatterley is not only 'unmanned' but reduced to a monstrous infant, while Mellors is complete man—potent, worker, gentleman-looking, educated—and 'devil' as well. His predecessor, Parkin, is by contrast less 'attractive' and more probable. Uncouth and bristling as his large moustache, his front teeth knocked out, and lacking middle-class education or accent (he is in fact a Communist) he makes an unlikely lover for Lady Chatterley. He is even subjected to some satire, as when Connie observes him going to prosecute some poachers:

. . . the whole mining population resented the summoning of poachers intensely. But it seemed to give him satisfaction. He strode with a grand sort of stride, baggy coat-tails flapping. The son of man goes forth to war! She smiled to herself grimly. (p. 80)

Again, when Parkin sends her an awkward little note, inviting her to visit him in Sheffield where he has gone to work (as Mellors could not have done), he signs it with his initials, O.P., which leads her friend Duncan Forbes to nickname him, cripplingly, 'Op.

Connie's visit to the Sheffield workmen is important, as it initiates a lengthy consideration of the alternative of Communism. Duncan Forbes even concludes,

"Perhaps if the communists *did* smash the famous 'system' there might emerge a new relationship between men: *really* not caring about money, *really* caring for life, and the life-flow with one another. . . . I've hated democracy since the war. But now I see I'm wrong calling for an aristocracy. What we want is a flow of life from one to another—to release some natural flow in us that urges to be released." (p. 306)

Lawrence did not long dally with anything that might really change the 'system', as it would merely replace one system with another, and in *Lady Chatterley's Lover* Mellors merely advocates symbolic red trousers and folk art for the humanisation of emasculating industrialism.

Parkin remains a real, awkward individual and no hero, whereas Lawrence needed a hero—not necessarily a Cipriano, but still someone who believed that

there is a principle in the universe, towards which man turns religiously —a *life* of the universe itself. And the hero is he who touches and transmits the life of the universe. (CL 994)

Mellors, being less human than Parkin, can be more heroic. To turn now to the heroine—in two senses of that word, as *Apocalypse* suggests:

Accept . . ., recognise the natural power in the man, as men did in the past, and give it homage, then there is a great joy, an uplifting, and a potency passes from the powerful to the less powerful. . . . Give homage and allegiance to a hero, and you become yourself heroic. (pp. 26–7)

In the first version Connie is much more ordinary, is less sexually experienced, more attached to her social position and even to Clifford, more critical of her gamekeeper lover. She regards emigration as evasion, and cannot see herself as a workman's wife—symbolised for her as the cooking of bloaters. At the end, when she has committed herself to Parkin, she still will not consider living in

a workman's dwelling! But some farm-house, or some suburban villa with nine or ten rooms—she didn't care! Anything, to be in contact with life. And if she could possibly be in *contact* with the working people, well and good. It would be nonsense to pretend to be one of them. (p. 319)

Connie's resistance to social subjection is paralleled in her sexual relationship with Parkin: she finds sexual satisfaction with him very quickly, but is never in sexual subjection, and it is her upper-class feminine mockery that concludes the book, when she reflects how she had accepted her 'tomb' existence at Wragby

till she had loved Parkin—her Op. Yes, she loved him. He was a man, if he wasn't a gentleman. Anyhow there came a breath of fresh air with him, and a breath of fresh life. My lady's f—er, as he called himself so savagely! How he had hated her for not taking him fully seriously in his manly f—ing! Ah well! The future was still to hand. (p. 320)

Parkin's efforts are effectively cut down to size by the publisher's castratory dash, which in turn mutely supports Lawrence's eloquence in 'A Propos of *Lady Chatterley's Lover*' about the importance of the words.[6] It is doubtful if, for most readers, Lawrence has succeeded in 'cleansing' the four-letter words from obscene associations; in fact, they soon become little more than another *motif* in the book, little better than Mellors's switching of speech-styles. Mellors, of course, uses conventional educated speech for anything complex, and Lawrence does much of his work through imagery, as usual.

Lady Chatterley's Lover is concerned partly with Lawrence's attempt to 'purify the language of the tribe' (to borrow Eliot's borrowing from Mallarmé), not by further refinement but by a regeneration of language and feeling, uniting words and physical reality, thought and feeling.

Probably, to the Crusaders, mere words were potent and evocative to a degree we can't realise. . . . In fact, thought and action, word and deed, are two separate forms of consciousness. . . . Yet they should be related in harmony. (P2 489)

All the great words, it seemed to Connie, were cancelled for her generation love, joy, happiness, home, mother, father, husband, all these great dynamic words were half dead now, and dying from day to day. (VI)

Language may be abstract and devitalising, separating man's consciousness from physical reality around and within himself, and even effectually destroying that reality for him. The relevance of this to Clifford, with his radio and wheel-chair, is obvious:

Now we have to educate ourselves, not by laying down laws and inscribing tables of stone, but by listening. Not listening-in to noises from Chicago or Timbuktu. But listening-in to the voices of the honourable beasts that call in the dark paths of the veins of our body, from the God in the heart . . . (P 759)

When Clifford pontificates to Connie,

all the brilliant words seemed like dead leaves. . . . They were not the leafy words of an effective life, young with energy and belonging to the tree. (V)

When he applies the phrase "still unravished bride of quietness" to the woodland flowers, Connie thinks,

How she hated words, always coming between her and life: they did the ravishing, if anything did: ready-made words and phrases, sucking all the life-sap out of living things. (VIII)

On the evening after her first sexual encounter with her lover, Clifford reads Racine to her. The first version makes the point more powerfully, that formalisation and verbalisation are less effective as communication than reverent touch:

Not for one second did she really hear what he said. But it sounded to her like the uncouth cries and howls of barbarous, disconnected savages dancing round a fire somewhere outside of the wood. Clifford was a smeared and painted savage howling in an utterly unintelligible gibberish somewhere on the outskirts of her consciousness. She, deep within the sacred and sensitive wood, was filled with the pure communication of the other man, a communication delicate as the inspiration of the gods. (p. 53)

The phrase 'the sacred wood' almost explicitly remembers Frazer, suggesting how the novel may be seen as a 'renewal-of-the-Waste Land' romance, with a 'priest-king' supplanting his exhausted predecessor. Clifford lives solely in the world of mental excitation, divorced from real feeling, whereas

The body feels . . . real anger, real sorrow, real love, real tenderness, real warmth, real passion, real hate, real grief. All the emotions belong to the body, and are only recognised by the mind. (P2 493)

Even Connie's sexual encounters in her student days were only the winning of intellectual arguments, 'like the last word'. Her affair with Michaelis, the perverse and dispossessed male, and forerunner of the truly potent Mellors, is only a reaction to her husband's 'mental-lifer' cronies, who believe that the courage to say "Shit!" in front of women will restore a drooping heart and penis.

The novel continually, and crudely, contrasts brutal mechanical civilisation, and organic nature. Connie's drive through the Midlands initiates a powerful diatribe against industrial England, less subtle and penetrating than the insights of *The Rainbow* and *Women in Love*: here the miners are merely degenerate and exhausted.

Something that men *should* have was bred and killed out of them. Yet they were men. They begot children. Terrible, terrible thought! . . . They belonged to the coal, the iron, the clay, as fish belong to the sea and worms to dead wood. The anima of mineral disintegration! (XI)

Connie has no Gudrun-like ambiguous feelings; the link with Lawrence's miner father is severed; now that Lawrence and his father are met in Mellors (whose name almost anagrammatises Morel) the perverse appeal of the male underworld is diminished. With this drive may be put the conversation between Connie and Clifford; there Clifford's ruthless capitalistic exploitation mirrors his denial of responsibility for the workmen.

'They built their own Teutershall, that's part of their display of freedom.'
'. . . I can't live their lives for them. Every beetle must live its own life.'
(XIII)

Clifford is as much beetle as them, for all—as Gerald Crich would agree—are part of the machine:

"Aristocracy is a function, a part of fate. And the masses are a functioning of another part of fate . . . there is a gulf, and an absolute one, between the ruling and the serving classes. The two functions are opposed. And the function determines the individual." (XIII)

So almost any man, he thinks, will do as father for the next Chatterley. After this, Connie and the mechanical centaur move on into the wood where, in clumsy allegory, the wheel-chair crushes the flowers. Comparison of the first and final versions reveals how the tone has changed to an unremitting hostility towards Clifford. The first version:

And the chair began slowly to advance down the gentle slope till it came to the great sheets of bluebells and rode through them. A strange ship! A strange vessel surging through scented blue seas! The last pinnace left in the unknown oceans, steering to the last discoveries! Quiet and content, like the captain at the immortal wheel, Clifford sat in an old black hat and slowly, cautiously steered. And Constance, one of the mere boats, came slowly in his wake in a gray knitted dress, down the long gentle slope. (p. 126)

The later passage is much more one-sided and jeering in tone, and slightly forced:

And the chair began to advance slowly, jolting down the beautiful broad riding washed over with blue encroaching hyacinths. O last of all ships, through the hyacinthian shallows! O pinnace on the last wild waters, sailing in the last voyage of our civilisation! Whither, O weird wheeled ship, your slow course steering. Quiet and complacent, Clifford sat at the wheel of adventure: in his old black hat and tweed jacket, motionless and cautious. O Captain, my Captain, our splendid trip is done! Not yet though! Down hill, in the wake, came Constance in her grey dress, watching the chair jolt downwards. (XIII)

After this, when the chair breaks down and the gamekeeper is called to assist, the earlier version displays an easier relationship than the later; Clifford is less hectoring and enraged, the gamekeeper less pathetically exhausted, and Connie does not kiss his hand behind Clifford's back. In the final version, Clifford is the target of almost pure hatred; in the first, while he degenerates, he remains pathetic —and *human*—as well.

The wood provides one of the major symbols of the novel. Partly it is, as Clifford says, the heart of England, but the heart of England was cut out during the war, and Clifford can only preserve the corpse. It is the sexual awakening of the Sleeping Beauty that enlivens it. Connie had earlier sensed the vital power of the trees:

Perhaps they were only waiting for the end. . . . But perhaps their strong and aristocratic silence, the silence of strong trees, meant something else. (VI)

Immediately after this she has her first vision of Mellors's body as he washes himself. In the earlier works this ritual was performed by maternal woman; now the man ministers to himself—but it still brings him into relation with the woman. Later when Connie goes to keeper's cottage again the wind in the trees seems to her 'the breath of Persephone . . . out of hell on a cold morning'; she sits down (like Lawrence in *Fantasia*) under a phallic tree, 'that swayed against her with curious life, elastic, and powerful, rising up. The erect, alive thing, with its top in the sun!' (V).

It is after this that Connie enters upon the sexual relationship with Mellors. The first sexual encounter arises from his tender compassion for her (when she weeps over a little chick, both as childless woman, and as lacking its insouciant self-confidence), and is simply a comfort, like sleep; on the second occasion, when she is more conscious, she feels 'left out' from what seems rather ridiculous. It is not until the third time that she achieves orgasmic release, brought about by self-submission; that evening she feels 'like a forest soughing with the dim, glad moan of spring, moving into bud' (X). With this satisfaction, she is briefly tempted by Lawrence's old fear, to become the Bacchanal woman, using and destroying the phallus-bearer; the first version emphasises this more (p. 307) but the final version cannot face this, and has Connie quickly choose the 'voiceless song of adoration'.

In the fourth encounter (to continue the catalogue!) Mellors displays impressive potency for his age, achieving orgasm three times in rapid succession. The first time, Connie again feels left out and derisive, but then subdues her own resistance to primary creative power (cf. 'Blessed are the Powerful', P2 440, 442):

it came with a strange thrust of peace, the dark thrust of peace and a ponderous, primordial tenderness, such as made the world in the beginning. . . . She was gone, she was not, and she was born: a woman. (XII)

The man is the creator and gives birth to the woman; sexuality, power and tenderness are reconciled for the first time. Afterwards, 'As she ran home in the twilight the world seemed a dream; the trees in the park bulging and surging at anchor on a tide, and the heave of the slope to the house was alive'. Physical reality has become alive, she has entered the cosmic womb, regained a childlike

state of innocence, of naïveté. . . . [T]he individual is only truly himself when he is unconscious of his own individuality, when he is unaware of his own isolation, when he is not split into subjective and objective . . . but . . . as if all were connected by a living membrane. (P 761)

However, cold reality soon intrudes upon the womb-world; first there is the incident of the wheel-chair, and then Mellors's memories of the women in his life, drawn from the women in Lawrence's own life. The first girl is a version of Miriam (Jessie Chambers), the the second is like Helena in *The Trespasser*, and the third, Bertha Coutts, seems to be Frieda, at least at the beginning of the marriage. In her is the sexual self-assertion that Lawrence feared, that Connie had enforced upon Michaelis, and Ursula upon Skrebensky (where the imagery of rending beaks also appears).

Retreating from these unhappy memories, the lovers are briefly reduced to their genitals, John Thomas and Lady Jane, while Mellors achieves orgasm three times and contemplates the end of humanity. However humanity intrudes again, when Connie's sister comes to take her away to Venice. Her aggressiveness provokes Mellors into rudeness and sexual innuendo. ' "Women like you needs proper graftin'." He was looking at her with an odd, flickering smile, faintly sensual and appreciative.' The phrasing echoes the description of Birkin before his anal intercourse with Ursula: which is what Connie is subjected to by Mellors, to restore his male supremacy. This is their seventh sexual encounter, which, it has been pointed out,[7] must be related to Lawrence's discussion of the opening of the seventh seal in 'Revelation', in *Apocalypse*. There he interprets the book with seven seals as 'the seven centres or gates of [man's] dynamic consciousness. We are witnessing the opening, and conquest of the great psychic centres of the human body' (*Apocalypse*, p. 18).

Thus Parkin had complained that the upper class have

"always got a door shut in your face an' they're always behind the door, laughing at you. . . . You folks [like Connie] is all doors . . . niver open 'em all, not to God nor man nor the devil. You've always got yourselves shut up somewhere where nothing can get at you . . ."
"But one must have *some* place private to oneself," she said. (pp. 247–8)

Parkin's words reveal insecurity, the fear of mockery, as well as the theme of sterile self-containment. *Apocalypse* is relevant:

Petty little personal salvation, petty morality instead of cosmic splendour· . . . Poor, paltry, creeping little world we live in, even the keys of death and Hades are lost. How shut in we are! (Ibid., pp. 44–5)

Mellors, however, has the key to this private place, where death, Hades, the anus and ultimate reality are one in the underworld.

The worship of the underworld powers, the chthonioi was perhaps the very basis of the most ancient Greek religion. When man has neither the strength to subdue his underworld powers—which are really the ancient powers of his old, superseded self—nor the wit to placate them with sacrifice and the burnt holocaust, then they come back at him, and destroy him again. Hence every new conquest of life means a "harrowing of hell". (Ibid., p. 129)

G

The seventh stage is a death and birth at once. Then the final flame-point of the eternal self of a man emerges from hell, and at the very instant of extinction becomes a new whole cloven flame of a new-bodied man with golden thighs and a face of glory. (Ibid., pp. 119–20)

In Connie's reflections after the event, we are told how

the deep organic shame, the old, old physical fear which crouches in the bodily roots of us, and can only be chased away by the sensual fire at last . . . was roused up and routed by the phallic hunt of the man, and she came to the very heart of the jungle of herself . . . the real bed-rock of her nature, and was essentially shameless. . . . That was how oneself really was! . . . At the bottom of her soul, fundamentally, she had needed this phallic hunting out, she had secretly wanted it . . . what one supremely wanted was this piercing, consuming, rather awful sensuality. (XVI)

This is not tenderness (here dismissed as 'sentiment'), as Connie admits, but the sensuality that Birkin had demanded, in the possession and acceptance of mankind's ultimate physical reality. The brief return of confidence in phallic sexuality, female tenderness and acceptance has given way to the old denial of female satisfaction, and assertion of male supremacy. Apocalyptic schemes notwithstanding, this does not seem like simple liberation from physical inhibition; one senses special pleading, and the lovers' new liberty is not convincing.

After this, Connie goes to Venice where she sees a decadence even less human than did the hero of Thomas Mann's *Death in Venice* (reviewed superciliously by Lawrence back in 1913), while Mellors is pestered by the return of Bertha Coutts, whose spirit he had overcome in Connie. Mrs Bolton, Clifford's nurse (a very well-drawn character), gradually becomes his Magna Mater, pushing him on to greater mechanical effort, and bathing and caressing him in the ultimate degradation of Lawrence's great ritual, while he kisses her breasts almost incestuously.

On Connie's return, she and Mellors meet, in allegorical fashion, at 'The Golden Cock in Adam Street at seven'; he still fears subjection to her—"I can't be just your male concubine"—and needs reassurance about the value of his principle of physical sympathy. He proclaims,

"Especially the English have got to get into touch with one another, a bit delicate and a bit tender. It's our crying need."
"Then why are you afraid of me?" she said. (XIII)

No enemy could have exposed him more effectively. Again she warms him into trust in her and self-confidence; but again the 'real' world threatens, and in his concluding letter to Connie from his farmhouse retreat, he is filled with forebodings of "a bad time coming! If things go on as they are, there's nothing lies in the future but death and destruction, for these industrial masses." (XIII)

For themselves, there is the "Pentecost, the forked flame" created by his untender domination and her tender submission. The letter concludes with a celebration of the peace of chastity (cf. 'Chastity', CP 469); further sexual activity is postponed to next year (the life to come) and in the meantime, having usurped the rival husband, and dominated the woman, Mellors–Lawrence is content with sexual quiescence, and silence.

> Words, after speech, reach
> Into the silence . . .
>
> Desire itself is movement
> Not in itself desirable;
> Love is itself unmoving . . .
> . . . Quick now, here, now, always—
> Ridiculous the waste sad time
> Stretching before and after.
> (T. S. Eliot, 'Burnt Norton', *Four Quartets*)

II

'*AN EXIT FROM THE FALLEN SELF*'

The last substantial fiction, 'The Man Who Died' (published 1929, as *The Escaped Cock*), follows the pattern of sexual regeneration followed by withdrawal into quiescence, and presents an equally narcissistic and compensatory fantasy. In the essay 'The Risen Lord' (P2 571–7), which should be related to this story, Lawrence asserts that 'the great religious images are only images of our own experiences, or of our own state of mind and soul'. The essay provides an allegory of Lawrence's life. In the image of Madonna and Child, man sees himself as 'the innocent saviour-child enthroned on the lap of the all-pitying Virgin Mother', as the young Lawrence saw himself and his mother (as described in *Fantasia*). Then came the Fall, the Great War, the onset of sexuality, which are all the same, and

we have the men of middle age, who were all tortured and virtually put to death by the war. They accept Christ Crucified as their image, are essentially womanless, and take the great cry: *Consummatum est!—it is finished!*

Lawrence now looks to the young (the future) and the doctrine of Christ Risen from a tomb world, that the Catholic Church might yet teach. He insists that the resurrection of Christ, of the body, demands the full body (the phallic body), full physical life. The new Jews, standing up for human sympathy and community, will fight against money, and machines, and prostitution, and all that tangled mass of self-importance and greediness and self-conscious conceit which adds up to Mammon . . .

However for 'The Man Who Died', involvement with reality, and even such windy rhetoric of social change, are impossible, and are displaced by private salvation and escape. After the story of the restraint upon the allegorical cock comes the account of the painful rebirth in the womb-tomb of 'the man'. After the pain of life and death, his sole desire is for non-involvement with humanity. The peasants who succour him think he may be 'a dead king from the region of terrors . . . still cold and remote in the region of death', while he sees them as merely 'slow inevitable parts of the natural world'. By contrast, the nonhuman natural world is presented throughout the story with great vividness, but with considerable abstractness. In a typically expressionist synaesthetic passage, the cock-crows and self-assertion of the living merge into wave-crests,

crests of foam, out of the blue flood of the invisible desire, out of the vast invisible sea of strength, and they came coloured and tangible, evanescent, yet deathless in their coming.

(Here is Lawrence's familiar blue non-living source of life, and evanescent foam of individuality.) The man looks and feels middle-aged, not thirty-three; he denies the philosophy of selfless love, as being as much a compulsion upon freedom as the peasant women's desire of him. He moves away, taking with him the cock, that is eventually released to a fuller sexual life, having usurped a predecessor; there seems little prospect of the same happening to the man, who moves into silence, beyond the reach of words, responding only in a general way to the 'phenomenal world, which is raging, and yet apart . . . which leaves [him] alone'.

The second part deals with his arrival at the temple of Isis-in-search, set in Lawrence's dream-pastoral Mediterranean world (evoked very similarly in *Movements in European History*). The virginal young priestess of the temple is dedicated to the cult of piecing together the dismembered fertility god Osiris, in a reversal of Lawrence's old nightmare of the rending, devouring Bacchantes. She has been told by 'a philosopher' to reject the normal virile men, and wait for 'the reborn man', and to offer 'her soft, gold depths such as no other flower possesses, to the penetration of the flooding, violet-dark sun that has died and risen and makes no show'.

When she sees the frailty of this man, she feels a maternal pity, and is for the first time 'touched on the quick at the sight of a man, as if the tip of a fine flame of living had touched her'. Believing that he is her Osiris, she invites him into her temple. Though he fears the onset of desire, he responds to her submission, her 'making herself completely penetrable'; in the temple, she ritually strips and anoints him in 'the bath of life', soothing the (sexual) scars on his body where 'his blood had left him, and his essential seed'. Her body, crouching before him (like Connie's) becomes for him the cleft rock of life. "On this rock I build my life," he says, before announcing with ludicrous literalism the resurrection of the phallic body: "I am risen!" No demands have been made on him, their real identities remain unknown, simply the woman has completely prostrated herself and worshipped him.

When she becomes pregnant and starts to envisage their life together, he foresees the difficulties of entering 'the little day', and following Lawrence's usual fearfully evasive pattern, moves on.

"I have sowed the seed of my life and my resurrection, and put my touch for ever upon the choice woman of this day. . . . But the gold and flowing serpent is coiling up again, to sleep at the root of my tree.

"So let the boat carry me. Tomorrow is another day."

The parallel with the conclusion of *Lady Chatterley's Lover* is clear in the attainment of sexual confidence with a completely submissive woman, the leaving of a child, the return of sexual quiescence, and the slipping away on a dark current. For all its beauty, this fable has the false simplicity of wish-fulfilment; there is no attempt to grapple with reality, and the language is extremely 'rhetorical', filled with repetition and poeticism; perhaps the best writing of the last phase is found in fact in the *Last Poems* and *Etruscan Places*.

Before discussing these, some consideration should also be given to *Apocalypse*, published posthumously, in 1932. In this, his commentary upon 'Revelation', he again outlines his theory of man and his history, looking back first to his own childhood, then to the early Jews, and then to the beginnings of man's society. In such a return he sees a vague hope for the future; but the book is essentially regressive.

Describing how he was, as a child, steeped in Biblical symbolism, Lawrence evokes the evangelistic chapels of his youth:

Strange marvellous black nights of the north Midlands, with the gaslight hissing in the chapel, and the roaring of the strong-voiced colliers. Popular religion: a religion of self-glorification and power, forever! and of darkness. No wailing "Lead kindly Light" about it. (p. 16)

This male, demonically passionate faith, like the Hymns of Quetzal-coatl, he explains as a late, debased version of the old religion that asserted the powerful vitality of the cosmos, transmitted through ritual and the hierarchy of spiritually powerful god-men king-fathers:

The primal need, the old-Adamic need in a man's soul, is to be, in his own sphere and as far as he can attain it, master, lord, and splendid one . . . (pp. 33–4)

. . . every great king makes every man a little lord in his own tiny sphere, fills the imagination with lordship and splendour, satisfies the soul. The most dangerous thing in the world is to show man his own paltriness as hedged-in male. (pp. 34–5)

Lawrence suggests that his mother would have respected his father as a Chapel Elder—failing to fulfil his god-king-father qualities, he prevented the transmission of such power to his son.

The late medieval Catholic Church reappears as the last embodiment of such a religion, but even better, apparently, was the understanding of the early Christians. For them, Jesus was not just a meek-and-mild sacrificial victim but

a vast cosmic lord . . . the lord of all motion . . . his face like the sun in full strength, the source of life itself, the dazzler, before whom we fall as dead. (p. 41)

He is the god of life and death in one, who

holds the keys that unlock death and Hades. He is Lord of the Underworld. . . . The dead and the lords of death, who are always hovering in the background of religion away down among the people, these Chthonioi of the primitive Greeks, these too must acknowledge Jesus as a supreme lord. (pp. 43–4)

So, in this sun-god of death at the heart of the pagan cosmos, Lawrence evokes the male power that is both source and destroyer of individual being, the power that he must assume, and that annihilates him.

Since then, however, there has been a series of Falls, to modern democracy, self-denying altruism and egalitarianism, the rule of the weak, and a rationalism and self-assertive individualism that have severed the sense of connection with a living cosmic body:

We may see what we call the sun, but we have lost Helios for ever, and the great orb of the Chaldeans still more. We have lost the cosmos, by coming out of responsive connexion with it, and this is our great tragedy . . . (p. 47)

For two thousand years man has been living in a dead or dying cosmos, hoping for a heaven hereafter. And all the religions have been religions of the dead body and the postponed reward. (p. 95)

The recovery and possession of male potency would return him into such a cosmic womb—a sort of male womb, as in the essay 'David'.

The resurrection of the body should come from the recovery of primitive understanding, which works through intuition and symbol. Lawrence's account of this, and of how to interpret the method of 'Revelation' by appreciating

the mental working of the pagan thinker or poet . . . who starts with an image, sets the image in motion, allows it to achieve a certain course of circuit of its own, and then takes up another image. (p. 96)

sounds much like standard late Symbolist poetic theory,[8] which suggests again the close relation between Symbolism and the religious impulse.

He then provides an elaborate and not very lucid analysis of 'Revelation' (*Apocalypse* is really only an early draft), distinguishing between what he sees as distortions by later writers of 'the religion of the weak', and the original expression of the old cosmic religion. Close discussion of the interpretation, that is based on the philosophy of the *Fantasia* days, is not practicable here, but some of the nature of the analysis may be suggested. The four horsemen of the apocalypse are interpreted as various psychological states, as the 'humours' of ancient science, and as planets and gods (the colour symbolism probably illuminates the lanterns in *Women in Love*). The seven seals are 'the seven centres or gates of [man's] dynamic consciousness', and their opening in sequence is a progress through the psychic and bodily underworld, culminating with the seventh seal, the death of the old being and the birth of the new. The woman clothed with the sun is the great creative mother, but in maleficent aspect becomes the devouring Magna Mater and Whore of Babylon. The dragon is the libido, 'the symbol of the fluid, rapid, startling movement of life within us', but the colour symbolism is somewhat confusing. He prays to the first dragon of all to return, to the

lovely green dragon of the new day, the undawned day, [to] come in touch and release us from the horrid grip of the evil-smelling old Logos! Come in silence, and say nothing. Come in touch, in soft new touch like a springtime, and say nothing. (p. 171)

For Lawrence, as for many Symbolists, language moves towards silence, and rationality and self-consciousness towards the primary being, as when

the tribe lived . . . in naked contact with the cosmos, the whole cosmos was alive and in contact with the flesh of men, there was no room for the intrusion of the God idea. (p. 179)

This is a return from independent living to primary being in a condition of womb-like security, what Freud calls the 'oceanic' state. The

eloquent conclusion expresses awe at 'the vast marvel' of being alive
and part of the larger body,

> part of the living, incarnate cosmos. I am part of the sun as my eye is part
> of me. That I am part of the earth my feet know perfectly, and my blood
> is part of the sea. My soul knows that I am part of the human race, my soul
> is an organic part of the great human soul, as my spirit is part of my nation.
> In my own very self, I am part of my family [his parents]. There is nothing
> of me that is alone and absolute except my mind, and we shall find that the
> mind has no existence by itself, it is only the glitter of the sun on the surface
> of the waters.
> So that my individualism is really an illusion. I am part of the great whole
> and I can never escape . . . what we want is to . . . re-establish the living
> organic connections, with the cosmos, the sun and the earth, with mankind
> and nation and family. Start with the sun, and the rest will slowly, slowly
> happen. (p. 223)

Like Gethin Day, Lawrence is 'coming into his own'. This appears
in *Etruscan Places* (written in 1927, published in 1932), one of his
most satisfying works, remarkable for its beauty, vividness, and
freshness of writing. In this account of a visit to some Etruscan
tombs is summed up Lawrence's dream culture, the community that
he longed for, that he is free to create because he knows little of the
reality (a humourless German is introduced to indicate the futility of
the 'scientific' approach). The civilisation is apprehended through its
art, and there is an inevitability in the circumstance of it being an
'underworld' art, set underground in tombs, the product of a dead
culture, celebrating the unity of life and death.

Lawrence skilfully juxtaposes past and present to reveal contrasting
values and quality of life: on the one hand, the modern and the Roman
civilisations, of materialism, force, civic authority and ethics, on the
other, the Etruscans and Lawrence himself, whose amoral morality
has been described as 'vicious', but whose vivid response to the
fullness of life and death transcends the fixities of conventional art
and morality. The best symbol of their life and art is the briefly
passionate phallic flower, the striped, cat-smelling asphodel, a 'sparky,
assertive flower with just a touch of the onion about it' to suggest
the rank 'unaesthetic' body scent.

A left-over of the Etruscan male, the dispossessed Pan, appears
in a shepherd who is also Lawrence himself:

> But now you will hardly see one of these men left, with the unconscious,
> ungrimacing faun-face. They were all, apparently, killed in the war: they
> would be sure not to survive such a war. Anyway the last one I know, a
> handsome fellow of my own age—forty and a bit—is going queer and
> morose, crushed between war memories, that have revived, and remorseless

go-ahead womenfolk. Probably when I go South again he will have disappeared. They can't survive, the faun-faced men, with their pure outlines and their strange non-moral calm. Only the deflowered faces survive. (I)

He serves to introduce the Etruscans, the epitome of natural male transience, whose buildings, being of wood, left no trace, 'So that the Etruscan cities vanished as completely as flowers. Only the tombs, the bulbs, were underground.' The bulb-tomb serve as growth-points for the Etruscans and, by implication, for us; death should be seen not as mere negation, but as positive. Those who attempt to deny and conquer the natural order of being, with all its implications, come to fear it.

Curiously enough, with the idea of the triumph over nature arose the idea of a gloomy Hades, a hell and purgatory. To the peoples of the great natural religions the after-life was a continuing of the wonder-journey of life. (IV)

Such a Hell is found in the body that civilised consciousness rejects, 'the living body of darkness' and the underworld that is the anus whence comes the fertilising flow; when that is accepted, physicality and decay are accepted, and man is free to live naturally. By accepting life and death as one, the Etruscans re-entered the living cosmos, and could live and breathe freely (an early motif in Lawrence's work, that now figures more largely, as his tuberculosis increased):

The things they did, in their easy centuries, are as natural and as easy as breathing. They leave the breast breathing freely and pleasantly, with a certain fullness of life. Even the tombs. (I)

Outside the tombs are symbols of the phallus[9] and the womb, the symbols of the physical world rejected by the Romans:

They hated the phallus and the ark, because they wanted empire and dominion and, above all, riches: social gain. You cannot dance gaily to the double flute and at the same time conquer nations or rake in large sums of money. (I)

Such possessiveness and accretion of materiality, and prevention of the natural flow, are opposed to 'delicate sensitiveness'; the stone is opposed to the nightingale (flown in from Keats and still in love with death); the Etruscans embody the principles of spontaneity and transience.

Why this lust after imposing creeds, imposing deeds, imposing buildings, imposing language, imposing works of art? The thing becomes an imposition and a weariness at last. Give us things that are alive and flexible, which won't last too long and become an obstruction and a weariness. Even Michelangelo becomes at last a lump and a burden and a bore. (II)

Etruscan vases in the museum are contrasted with classical Greek urns,
those elegant "still-unravished brides of quietness". But get over the strange
desire we have for elegant convention, and the vases and dishes of the
Etruscans, especially many of the black bucchero ware, begin to open out
like strange flowers, black flowers with all the softness and the rebellion
of life against convention, or red-and-black flowers painted with amusing
free, bold designs. It is there nearly always in Etruscan things, the naturalness
verging on the commonplace, but usually missing it, and often achieving an
originality so free and bold, and so fresh, that we, who love convention and
things "reduced to a norm", call it a bastard art, and a commonplace. (II)

These dark flowers of the dark flow are now not responded to
perversely, as *fleurs du mal*, but as natural organic products. The
relevance of this passage to Lawrence's own art, *Last Poems* in particular, has been pointed out.[10] This book provides the aesthetic
behind many of the verses in *Pansies*, also, which are brief spurts of
feeling, 'the quick ripple of life'. The two chapters on 'The Painted
Tombs of Tarquinia' display some of Lawrence's finest prose—easy,
colloquial and unpretentious, yet fresh and lively and of great beauty.
What he says of Etruscan art applies to his own art here.

It is not impressive or grand. But if you are content with just a sense of the
quick ripple of life, then here it is . . .

You cannot think of art, but only of life itself, as if this were the very life
of the Etruscans, dancing in their coloured wraps with massive yet exuberant
naked limbs, ruddy from the air and the sea-light . . .

There is a mystery and a portentousness in the simple scenes which go
deeper than commonplace life. It seems all so gay and light. Yet there is a
certain weight, or depth of significance that goes beyond aesthetic beauty.
(III)

The aesthetic is not one of superficial casualness but derives from a
Symbolist aesthetic of *correspondance*, and intuition: 'all things corre-
sponded in the ancient world, and man's bosom mirrored itself in the
bosom of the sky, or *vice versa* . . .'; the science of augury is analogous
to the process of artistic comprehension:

. . . if you live by the cosmos, you look in the cosmos for your clue. . . . All
it depends on is the amount of *true*, sincere, religious concentration you
can bring to bear on your object. An act of pure attention, if you are capable
of it, will bring its own answer. And you choose that object to concentrate
upon which will best focus your consciousness.
. . . The soul stirs, and makes an act of pure attention, and that is a discovery.
(III)

The organisation of the entrails is then analogous to the organisation of the psyche of the individual, man as a whole, and the cosmos. The discipline is of truth to feeling, rather than the discipline of imposed consciousness.

Lawrence picks out the animals in the wall-paintings, such as his favourite dolphins leaping in the water,

in and out of [the sea, 'that vast primordial creature that has a soul also, whose inwardness is womb of all things, out of which all things emerged, and into which they are devoured back'] suddenly, as a creature that suddenly exists, out of nowhere. He was not: and lo! there he is! . . . He is so much alive, he is like the phallus carrying the fiery spark of procreation down into the wet darkness of the womb. . . . And the sea will give up her dead like dolphins that leap out and have the rainbow within them. (III)

Likewise, he comments upon the duck (a less sensationalist version of Birkin's Chinese goose amidst the flux), that is

to man, the symbol of that part of himself which delights in the waters, and dives in, and rises up and shakes its wings. It is the symbol of man's own phallus and phallic life . . . that awareness of alertness in him, that other consciousness, that wakes in the night and rouses the city. (III)

The individual dies and is reborn from the source, for death and life are one: such vivid life comes from a religious sense, of immanent deity, as in the description of the woman dancing, that shows how Lawrence warmed and surpassed the formalism of the Symbolist cult of the dancer:[11]

They are dancing in the open, past little trees, and birds are running, and a little fox-tailed dog is watching something with the naïve intensity of the young. Wildly and delightedly dances the next woman, every bit of her, in her soft boots and her bordered mantle, with jewels on her arms; till one remembers the old dictum, that every part of the body and of the *anima* shall know religion, and be in touch with the gods. (III)

Here is Lawrence's version of Symbolist unity of being, of man in accord with all nature.

To the Etruscan all was alive; the whole universe lived; and the business of man was himself to live amid it all. He had to draw life into himself, out of the wandering huge vitalities of the world. The cosmos was alive like a vast creature. . . . Out of the fissures of the earth came breaths of other breathing vapours direct from the living physical underearth, exhalations carrying inspiration. (II)

—a potent pun for poor tubercular Lawrence, who drew breath and reassurance from this underworld. Drawing in such power, man fulfilled himself, became 'god's body, visibly, red and utterly vivid. So he was a prince, a king, a god, an Etruscan Lucomo [priest-king].'

Only a few—like Lawrence—were fully capable of being such priest-kings, possessed of the 'vital potency of the universe', and only they could

bring out life and show the way into the dark of death, which is the blue burning of the one fire . . . the life-bringers and the death-guides, leading ahead in the dark, and coming out in the day with more than sunlight in their bodies. (III)

The original of the guide in the dark, with the blue light, must have been a coal-miner with his lamp, who also illuminates 'Bavarian Gentians'.

The essential understanding, the 'one radical thing', was the understanding of 'the mystery of the journey out of life, and into death' (Lawrence's obsession, here as always). Lawrence even—absurdly— appears in such a Lucomo, 'seated silent within another world of power, disciplined to his own responsibility of knowledge for the people', solving their problems with 'a few words' before departing in his chariot, leaving the awe-struck populace to have 'as far as possible . . . a gay time'. The life of these child-people derives from their security in a palpable cosmos, as expressed in their art.

The subtlety of Etruscan painting, as of Chinese and Hindu, lies in the wonderfully suggestive *edge* of the figures. It is not outlined. It is not what we call "drawing". It is the flowing contour where the body suddenly leaves off, upon the atmosphere. The Etruscan artist seems to have seen living things surging from their own centre to their own surface. And the curving and contour of the silhouette-edge suggests the whole movement of the modelling within . . . (IV)

The passage relates directly to the account of Cézanne, in 'Introduction to the Paintings'. All are in harmony, for all derive from the common source. Multiplicity, duality, are only how life appears to the consciousness, whereas the non-living reality behind life is One:

The soul itself, the conscious spark of every creature, is not dual; and being the immortal, it is also the altar on which our mortality and our duality is at last sacrificed. (III)

The last part of the book shows Lawrence rooting around in bat-filled holes with bat-like, malaria-ridden men, in an image of the degeneration of male power into diseased futility; the cities seem dead, indifferent to the apocalyptic light he perceives; the museum's funerary urns depict the rending of Adonis, the hunting-down of the boar, 'the wild, fierce fatherly life hunted down by dogs and adversaries'.

The book ends in some melancholy, but Lawrence has had his vision: of integrated, harmonious being; of momentariness in poise with, and revealing, the dark, still source beneath life; of the transvaluation of life and death—upon which he had been engaged, from almost the beginning of his career—so that tomb and womb fuse together.

Throes of wonder and vivid feeling throbbing over death. Man moves naked and glowing through the universe. Then comes death: he dives into the sea, he departs into the under world. (III)

Or, as T. S. Eliot put it:[12]

> Home is where one starts from. As we grow older
> The world becomes stranger, the pattern more complicated
> Of dead and living. Not the intense moment
> Isolated, with no before and after,
> But a lifetime burning in every moment
> And not the lifetime of one man only . . .
> We must be still and still moving
> Into another intensity
> For a further union, a deeper communion . . .
> . . . In my end is my beginning.

With this volume, as the most successful writing of the last phase, may be ranked the *Last Poems* (1932). These gather up themes and images from 'The Flying Fish,' *Apocalypse* and *Etruscan Places,* and indeed, some of them can only be interpreted in the light of those works. Lawrence dreams of a return to the pre-idealist male world, where the phallic being is unhindered, as in 'For the Heroes are Dipped in Scarlet':

> Oh, and their faces scarlet, like the dolphin's blood!
> Lo! the loveliest is red all over, rippling vermilion
> as he ripples upwards!
> laughing in his black beard! (CP 689)

Divinity does not precede physical existence, but is its essence, and only finds fulfilment in it, as in the delightful 'Red Geraniums and Godly Mignonette'. In 'Whales Weep Not!', that remembers the whale-families in *Moby Dick*, human life is transformed to animal life, which is in touch with superhuman deities. The copulation of whales is superhuman, a true phallic marriage, where the phallus in an umbilicus with the cosmic power, like Jacob's Ladder:

> And over the bridge of the whale's strong phallus, linking the
> wonder of whales
> the burning archangels under the sea keep passing, back and
> forth. . . (CP 694)

In the last poems, Lawrence prepared himself for the consummation with death, that would be a rest from 'the striving and the horrid strife'

of living, from consciousness and from individuality; in poem after
poem he seeks 'lovely oblivion', to be 'completely lapsed and gone/
and healed from all this ache of being'.

In 'The Ship of Death' (CP 716–20) he used the Etruscan's little
tomb-boat for the dead as his central metaphor. The poem begins
with impersonal statement, only implying his own condition, and
including the reader.

I

Now it is autumn and the falling fruit
and the long journey towards oblivion.

The apples falling like great drops of dew
to bruise themselves an exit from themselves

And it is time to go, to bid farewell
to one's own self, and find an exit
from the fallen self.

II

Have you built your ship of death, O have you?
O build your ship of death, for you will need it.

The grim frost is at hand, when the apples will fall
thick, almost thundrous, on the hardened earth.

And death is on the air like a smell of ashes!
Ah! can't you smell it? . . .

The rhythm is an easy, supple variation on a five-stress norm, the
language simple, even colloquial, employing repetition of words and
phrases to build up a pattern of images. At the beginning the dropping
of fruit is a variation of his old image of the creative dropping of seeds
or nuts or dung in the naturalness of decay as a preparation for new
life. The soul is fearful of the cold exposure to death; Lawrence briefly
considers suicide as an evasion, but accepts whatever will come; by
accepting 'not to be' alive, he will truly 'be' his real self. The soul
prepares its little boat humbly, even domestically, for the flood of
the Absolute that sweeps it into utter oblivion. Then, in the utter
blackness, dawn returns,

the cruel dawn of coming back to life out of oblivion

The flood subsides, and the body, like a worn sea-shell
emerges strange and lovely.
And the little ship wings home, faltering and lapsing
on the pink flood,
and the frail soul steps out, into her house again
filling the heart with peace.

Perhaps just one night of oblivion is over; perhaps after death there is a rebirth, in another world. The 'life' of the underworld beneath life appears most magnificently in 'Bavarian Gentians' (CP 697), where familiar motifs of blueness, living darkness, the flower, the underworld and the myth of Dis and Persephone fuse together. Again, there is quiet self-effacement in the opening lines; then the ordinary world and the conventional associations of words are effaced by the repetition and variation of key words, and the break-down of normal syntax:

. . . Bavarian gentians, big and dark, only dark
darkening the day-time, torch-like with the smoking blueness of Pluto's
   gloom,
ribbed and torch-like, with their blaze of darkness spread blue
down flattening into points, flattened under the sweep of white day
torch-flower of the blue-smoking darkness, Pluto's dark-blue daze,
black lamps from the halls of Dis, burning dark blue,
giving off darkness, blue darkness, as Demeter's pale lamps give off light,
lead me then, lead me the way . . .
[Down to where Persephone is]
. . . a darkness invisible enfolded in the deeper dark
of the arms Plutonic, and pierced with the passion of dense gloom.
among the splendour of torches of darkness, shedding darkness on the lost
   bride and her groom.

The light of consciousness is almost obliterated in the 'darkness visible' of the under, inner world. As he said in *Apocalypse*, he is at one with his family, lost with his mother in the embrace of the lord of the underworld, wrapped in the living body of darkness, the life that is not life.

'This place no good.' This postscript to one of Lawrence's last letters (CL 1245) seems to epitomise the impulse behind much of his career and writing. An exile since birth, he sought always an impossible home:

We travel, perhaps, with a secret and absurd hope of setting foot on the Hesperides, of running our boat up a little creek and landing in the Garden of Eden. This hope is always defeated. There is no Garden of Eden, and the Hesperides never were. Yet in our very search for them, we touch upon the coasts of illusion, and come into contact with other worlds . . . (P 333)

In this review he also says that 'one gradually gets a new vision of the world if one goes through the disillusion absolutely', as he did; disillusion presented him with a vision of the world as threatening or lifeless, a mask or hollow shell or swarm of insects, while he escaped to mythical enclosures, of dark potency. Lawrence craved union with the Other, but feared loss of identity in the devouring woman and

earth-body; seeking self-creation he feared inversion, whether a
masturbatory self-consciousness or absorption in the same sex. To
steer between such perils was his Odyssey. He bitterly resented his
mother forcing him into consciousness and individuality, and imaginatively transformed the phallus into an umbilicus connecting him with
a cosmic womb, finding unconsciousness and ease within the male body
in the living body of darkness, where creation and decay, life and
death are one.

> The breath of life is in the sharp winds of change
> mingled with the breath of destruction.
> But if you want to breathe deep, sumptuous life
> breathe all alone, in silence, in the dark,
> and see nothing. (PC 698)

Gasping for breath, the dying Lawrence found his beginning in his
end.

In his symbolic, personal art, Lawrence considered the plight of the
isolated individual in a multiple world of competing individualities.
He strove for an acceptance of the totality of man's being, as the only
liberation from the dehumanising inhibitions of modern civilisation.
His effort was to produce a spirit not of exploitation but of respect
for the free play of living energy, whether within oneself or others
or the natural world, to create a greater sympathy and sense of wholeness. Where his art sometimes fails is when he disregards the adjust-
ment of the symbolic with the realistic levels of writing, or when he
has committed some 'passionate exclusion', where personal fantasy
or compensation have distorted or narrowed the complexity of life.
Like all artists, especially perhaps Romantic artists, he projected his
own agonies and crises on to the world he saw; but like all great
artists, his courageous exploration of his own nature enabled him to
become a profound—and indeed, on occasion, apparently prophetic
—analyst and interpreter of the crisis in the culture of his own times,
a crisis that seems in many ways to have become more extreme since
then. As he wrote of Dana (SCAM 209):

He has lived this great experience for us, we owe him homage.

1. cf. the letter to Witter Bynner, in 1928, rejecting the 'heroism' of *The
Plumed Serpent* in favour of 'tenderness' (CL 1045).
2. See 'The Man Who Was Through with the World', J. R. Elliott Jr., (Ed.),
Essays in Criticism IX, July 1959, pp. 213–21, which is a more optimistic version
—though incomplete—of 'The Man Who Loved Islands'.
3. cf. 'Butterfly' (CP 696).

4. 'In bourgeois society social relations are denied in the forms of relations between men, and take the form of . . . a property relation, which, because it is a dominating relation, is believed to make man free. But this is an illusion. The property is only a disguise for relations which now become unconscious and therefore anarchic but are still between man and man and in particular between exploiter and exploited.' C. Caudwell, op. cit., p. 45.

5. C. Caudwell, op. cit., p. 72.

6. '. . . a proper reverence for sex, and a proper awe of the body's strange experience . . . means being able to use the so-called obscene words, because these are a natural part of the mind's consciousness of the body. Obscenity only comes in when the mind despises and fears the body, and the body hates and fears the mind. . . . We shall never free the phallic reality from the "uplift" taint till we give it its own phallic language, and use the obscene words' (P2 490, 514).

7. J. F. Kermode, 'Spenser and the Allegorists', *Proceedings of the British Academy*, vol. XLVIII (London, 1962), pp. 275–7 particularly.

8. cf. Dylan Thomas: 'A poem by myself . . . is a host of images. I make one image . . . let it breed another, let that image contradict the first, make of the third image bred out of the other two together, a fourth contradictory image . . .' W. Y. Tindall, *A Reader's Guide to Dylan Thomas* (London, 1962), p. 26.

9. Which must have pleased Lawrence. In a letter to Brewster before the visit to the tombs, he wrote how he put a phallus in every picture that he painted, 'out of positive belief, that the phallus is a great sacred image: it represents a deep, deep life which has been denied in us, and still is denied' (CL 967).

10. C. Hassall, 'Black Flowers: A New Light on the Poetics of D. H. Lawrence', in Moore, *Miscellany*, op. cit., pp. 369–76.

11. See J. F. Kermode, *The Romantic Image* (London, 1957).

12. T. S. Eliot, 'East Coker', *Four Quartets* (London, 1945).

CHRONOLOGY

Chronology of dates of composition of works discussed. (A complete chronology will be found in K. M. Sagar, *The Art of D. H. Lawrence*, Cambridge, 1966, from which this is derived.)

Prose works and titles of volumes are capitalised, poems italicised, LWHCT = *Look! We Have Come Through!*

1885	Born in Eastwood, Nottinghamshire.
1901	Met Jessie Chambers. Joined surgical goods firm.
1902	Started as student teacher.
1906	Began two-year teacher's course at Nottingham University College.
	Began first version of THE WHITE PEACOCK. *The Piano*. A COLLIER'S FRIDAY NIGHT.
1908	Second version of THE WHITE PEACOCK. First versions of several stories in THE PRUSSIAN OFFICER.
Oct.	Teaching post in Croydon.
1909	Third version of THE WHITE PEACOCK.
1910	Final revision of THE WHITE PEACOCK. THE WIDOWING OF MRS HOLROYD.
March	Began THE TRESPASSER (as THE SAGA OF SIEGMUND).

Oct.	Began SONS AND LOVERS (as PAUL MOREL).
Nov.	Broke 'betrothal' with Jessie Chambers.
9 Dec.	Mother died.
1911	More stories, later revised for THE PRUSSIAN OFFICER.
1912	LWHCT: *Moonrise* to *Hymn to Priapus*.
Jan.	Left Croydon and teaching, because of tuberculosis.
Jan.–Feb.	Rewrote THE TRESPASSER.
March	Met Frieda Weekley.
3 May	Eloped to Germany.
May–July	LWHCT: *Ballad of a Wilful Woman* to *A Doe at Evening*.
Aug.–Nov.	Completed SONS AND LOVERS.
Aug.–Dec.	LWHCT: *Song of a Man Who is Not Loved* to *December Night*.
1913	
Jan.–March	LWHCT: *New Year's Eve* to *Coming Awake*.
	Began and discontinued THE LOST GIRL (as THE INSURRECTION OF MISS HOUGHTON).
Jan.–April	Middle section of TWILIGHT IN ITALY (first version).
March–June	First version of THE RAINBOW and WOMEN IN LOVE (as THE SISTERS).
April–Dec.	LWHCT: *Spring Morning* to *Song of a Man Who Has Come Through*.
	THE PRUSSIAN OFFICER.
Sept.–Oct.	Last two essays of TWILIGHT IN ITALY.
Sept.–Jan. 1914	Second version of THE RAINBOW.
1914	
Feb.–May	Third version of THE RAINBOW.
June	Returned to England.
June–July	LWHCT: *One Woman to All Women* to *Elysium*.
Sept.–Nov.	STUDY OF THOMAS HARDY.
Dec.–March 1915	Final version of THE RAINBOW.

1915
March–Sept.   THE CROWN.
Sept.   ENGLAND MY ENGLAND (first version).
                     Revised TWILIGHT IN ITALY

1916
March–Oct.   LWHCT: *Manifesto* to *Craving for Spring*.
April–Nov.   WOMEN IN LOVE.
Nov.   THE HORSE DEALER'S DAUGHTER (as THE
                     MIRACLE), SAMSON AND DELILAH.

1917   Planned to leave for America, but passports refused.
Feb.   THE REALITY OF PEACE.
Aug.–June 1918   Essays on American literature, as THE TRANSCEN-
                     DENTAL ELEMENT IN AMERICAN LITERATURE.
                     LOVE.
Oct.   Expelled from Cornwall, suspected of spying.
Dec.   Began AARON'S ROD.

1918
July–Jan. 1919   MOVEMENTS IN EUROPEAN HISTORY.
Nov.   THE BLIND MAN. First version of THE FOX.
Nov.–Dec.   EDUCATION OF THE PEOPLE.
Winter   FANNIE AND ANNIE, YOU TOUCHED ME, WINTRY
                     PEACOCK, MONKEY NUTS, TICKETS PLEASE.

1919
March   ADOLF.
Summer   Rewrote THE FOX.
Aug.   PREFACE to American edition of NEW POEMS.
Sept.   FOREWORD to WOMEN IN LOVE. Discontinued
                     AARON'S ROD.
Nov.   Left England for Italy (Florence).
Dec.–Jan. 1920   PSYCHOANALYSIS AND THE UNCONSCIOUS.
                     DAVID. Visited Monte Cassino.

1920
Feb.   Went to Sicily.

Feb.–May	Final version of THE LOST GIRL.
May	REX.
Summer	Early poems from BIRDS BEASTS AND FLOWERS.
July	Recommenced AARON'S ROD.
Sept.–Oct.	AMERICA LISTEN TO YOUR OWN.
Autumn–Sept. 1921	Bulk of BIRDS BEASTS AND FLOWERS (to *Man and Bat*).

1921

Jan.	Visited Sardinia.
Feb.–March	Wrote SEA AND SARDINIA.
May	Completed AARON'S ROD.
May–July	FANTASIA OF THE UNCONSCIOUS.
Oct.–Dec.	THE CAPTAIN'S DOLL, THE LADYBIRD, new ending to THE FOX.

1922

Jan.	INTRODUCTION TO 'MEMOIRS OF THE FOREIGN LEGION BY M[AURICE] M[AGNUS].
March	Arrived in Ceylon.
April	Arrived in Australia.
June–July	KANGAROO (except last chapter).
Aug.	Left for New Mexico.
Sept.	INDIANS AND AN ENGLISHMAN, TAOS, last chapter of KANGAROO.
Winter	Final version of STUDIES IN CLASSIC AMERICAN LITERATURE.

1923

May–June	First draft of THE PLUMED SERPENT (as QUETZAL-COATL).
Dec.–Jan. 1924	Visit to England and Germany

1924

Jan.–Feb.	LETTER FROM GERMANY, THE LAST LAUGH, JIMMY AND THE DESPERATE WOMAN, THE BORDER LINE.
	Return to New Mexico.

May	DANCE OF THE SPROUTING CORN, INDIANS AND ENTERTAINMENT, PAN IN AMERICA.
June	THE WOMAN WHO RODE AWAY.
July–Sept.	ST MAWR.
Summer?	REFLECTIONS ON THE DEATH OF A PORCUPINE.
Aug.	THE HOPI SNAKE DANCE.
Sept.	Father died.
Sept.–Oct.	THE PRINCESS.
Nov.	Recommenced THE PLUMED SERPENT.
Dec.	CORASMIN, MARKET DAY, WALK TO HUAYAPA, THE MOZO.

1925

Feb.	Completed second draft of THE PLUMED SERPENT. Collapsed with near-fatal illness.
March–April	THE FLYING FISH.
May–June	Final revisions of THE PLUMED SERPENT.
Summer	Essays on THE NOVEL.
Sept.	Returned to Europe.
Nov.	A LITTLE MOONSHINE WITH LEMON.

1926

Jan.	THE VIRGIN AND THE GIPSY.
March	THE ROCKING-HORSE WINNER.
Aug.	Last visit to England.
Autumn	? THE MAN WHO LOVED ISLANDS. Review of H. M. Tomlinson 'Gifts of Fortune'.
Oct.–Nov.	First version of LADY CHATTERLEY'S LOVER.
Dec.–Feb. 1927	Second version of LADY CHATTERLEY'S LOVER.

1927

Feb.	JOHN GALSWORTHY.
Feb.–March	THE MAN WHO WAS THROUGH WITH THE WORLD.
April	THE ESCAPED COCK, PART ONE (= THE MAN WHO DIED, PART ONE), THE LOVELY LADY.
April–Oct.	ETRUSCAN PLACES.
July	Review of W. Wilkinson 'The Peep Show',

Oct.	AUTOBIOGRAPHICAL FRAGMENT.
Nov.–Dec.	Prepared COLLECTED POEMS.
Dec.–Jan. 1928	Final version of LADY CHATTERLEY'S LOVER.

1928

June	Left Italy for France.
June–Aug.	THE ESCAPED COCK, PART TWO (= THE MAN WHO DIED, PART TWO).
June–Nov.	Poems for PANSIES.
Dec.–Jan. 1929	INTRODUCTION TO THESE PAINTINGS.

1929

Jan.–Aug.	MORE PANSIES (to *Dearly Beloved Mr Squire*).
Summer	NOTTINGHAM AND THE MINING COUNTRY, THE RISEN LORD.
Sept.	MORE PANSIES.
Autumn	? A PROPOS OF LADY CHATTERLEY'S LOVER.
Sept.–Dec.	LAST POEMS.
Oct.–Dec.	APOCALYPSE.

1930

Feb.	Entered the Ad Astra Sanatorium at Vence.
2 March	Died, at Vence.

SELECT BIBLIOGRAPHY

BIOGRAPHIES

H. T. Moore, *The Life and Works of D.H.L.*, London, 1951 (rev. ed. 1964).
H. T. Moore, *The Intelligent Heart*, London, 1955.
Edward Nehls, *D.H.L., A Composite Biography*, Wisconsin, 1957–9.

BOOKS ON LAWRENCE

J. M. Murry, *Son of Woman*, London, 1931.
C. Carswell, *The Savage Pilgrimage*, London, 1932.
F. Carter, *D.H.L. and the Body Mystical*, London, 1932.
H. Gregory, *Pilgrim of the Apocalypse*, London, 1934.
Frieda Lawrence, *Not I, But the Wind*, London, 1935.
Anthony West, *D.H.L.*, London, 1950.
E. J. Hoffman and H. T. Moore (Eds.) *The Achievement of D.H.L.*, Oklahoma, 1953.
F. R. Leavis, *D.H.L.: Novelist*, London, 1955.
Mark Spilka, *The Love Ethic of D.H.L.*, Indiana, 1955.
Graham Hough, *The Dark Sun*, London, 1956.
H. T. Moore (Ed.), *A D.H.L. Miscellany*, Illinois, 1959.
Eliseo Vivas, *D.H.L., The Failure and the Triumph of Art*, Northwestern U.P., 1960.
Kingsley Widmer, *The Art of Perversity*, Washington, 1962.
Daniel A. Weiss, *Oedipus in Nottingham*, Seattle, 1962.
Julian Moynahan, *The Deed of Life*, Oxford, 1963.

Mark Spilka (Ed.), *D.H.L., A Collection of Critical Essays*, New Jersey, 1963.

George H. Ford, *Double Measure*, N.Y., 1965.

H. M. Daleski, *The Forked Flame*, London, 1965.

K. M. Sagar, *The Art of D.H.L.*, Cambridge, 1966.

C. Clarke, *River of Dissolution*, London, 1969.

G. Salgado, (Ed.), *A Casebook on Sons and Lovers*, London, 1969.

C. Clarke, (Ed.), *A Casebook on The Rainbow and Women in Love*, London, 1969.

D. Cavitch, *D.H.L. and the New World*, N.Y., 1969.

For a full bibliography of Lawrence criticism see the checklist by M. Beebe and A. Tommasi, *Modern Fiction Studies*, V (spring 1959) i, and the extensive bibliography in K. M. Sagar, *The Art of D. H. Lawrence*.

INDEX

Titles of poems are in italic